CANDIDATE

FOR

C
A
E

**FIONA
JOSEPH**

✦

**PETER
TRAVIS**

**PHOENIX
ELT**

incorporating
PRENTICE HALL MACMILLAN

New York   London   Toronto   Sydney   Tokyo   Singapore

Contents

	Reading	Writing	Speaking	Listening	
1 **Starting off** *page* 6	Problem page: •skimming Overview of CAE exam •scanning	Reply to a problem page	Getting to know each other	Conversation between 3 learners of English: •global understanding •specific information	
2 **Education** *page* 17	Article on the British university system: •predicting •skimming •specific information	Letter to a newspaper Report for a competition entry	**Exam Focus:** **discussing and reaching agreement**	Interview with an educationalist: •global understanding •specific information Education in East and West: •global understanding •specific information	
3 **Citizens of the World** *page* 28	Extract from 'The Happy Isles of Oceania': •predicting •scanning and information transfer •inference and speculation **Exam Focus:** **multiple matching**	**Exam Focus:** **a travel guide** Formal letter and informal note	Making and dealing with interruptions	3 foreigners discuss life in England: •global understanding •specific information **Exam focus:** **multiple choice**	
4 **Health Issues** *page* 40	**Exam Focus:** **sentence and paragraph cloze** Magazine feature on giving up smoking: •predicting •summary skills •comprehension	Magazine article Advice leaflet	Stress quiz Discussion and reaching agreement	Interview with an acupuncturist: •global understanding •specific information Account of trying to give up smoking: •specific information Advice on dealing with anxiety: •note taking	
5 **The World of Language** *page* 51	Extract from 'Talk, Talk, Talk': •skimming •finding the main ideas Advertisement on body language: •scanning	Text summary	Giving instructions Giving a talk	Lecture on working with the deaf: •comprehension and inference •following instructions 2 learners practise for Paper 5: •specific information	
6 **Food and Drink** *page* 63	Article on European drinking habits: •skimming •information transfer Article on McDonalds: •summary skills •understanding the purpose of a text	Describing a process (formal) **Exam Focus:** **a letter to an international magazine**	Sharing information Taking part in a debate	**Exam Focus:** **identifying speakers** How to grow garlic: •specific information	

Vocabulary development	Pronunciation	Exploring language	Language Awareness
Phrases for giving advice Terminology	Helping yourself to improve	Common grammatical errors	Improving grammar
Common expressions using 'as … as' Language of discussing		**Exam Focus: discourse cloze**	Dependent prepositions Questions (1)
Ways of getting around			Language of obligation Reported speech
Common expressions connected with health	Word stress	**Exam Focus: proofreading**	Defining and non-defining relative clauses Passive or active?
Words for talking about language Guessing unknown words	Pronunciation of marker words	**Exam Focus: informal to formal writing**	Formal and informal language Expressing time
Food collocations Using synonyms in writing Recording vocabulary	Vowel sounds		Participles (1) Expressing possibility

	Reading	Writing	Speaking	Listening	
7 **The Human Condition** *page* 76	Article on memorising: •skimming •specific information	Article for a newsletter	Giving descriptions	3 adults who were gifted children: •global understanding •specific information and inference **Exam Focus:** **gap fill**	
8 **Leisure** *page* 87	Book and film reviews: •skimming •scanning and inferring A visit to Alton Towers: •appreciating the writer's tone	Language of reviews **Exam Focus:** **letter of complaint**	Viewing and reading habits **Exam Focus:** **describing photographs**	**Exam Focus:** **identifying topics and opinions** 2 learners practise for paper 5: •specific information	
9 **Human Relationships** *page* 98	Couples in crisis: •skimming Article on types of love: •predicting •comprehension	Magazine article Reply to a problem page	Parenting **Exam Focus:** **information gap**	Extract from a love letter: •global understanding •specific information	
10 **Work** *page* 109	**Exam Focus:** **multiple matching**	**Exam Focus:** **a letter to a friend**	Choosing a career Trade unions	Interview with a dancer: •specific information Account of psychometric testing: •specific information	
11 **Power Relationships** *page* 121	Article on assassination: •identifying paragraph topics **Exam Focus:** **multiple choice** Description of life in Trikeri: •scanning •inference Newspaper extracts: •scanning	Account for an encyclopaedia Formal report	Male and female roles Role play	Extracts from a radio show: •global understanding **Exam Focus:** **gap-fill**	
12 **Crime and Punishment** *page* 134	Articles on smacking children: •global understanding •appreciating the style of a text **Exam Focus:** **paragraph cloze**	**Exam Focus:** **a letter to a newspaper**	Types of crime Fear of crime	**Exam Focus:** **identifying topics and speakers** Advice from a Crime Prevention Officer: •specific information	

Key	146
Record Sheet	147
Writing Skills Development	148
Tapescripts	153
Grammar Reference	166

Vocabulary development	Pronunciation	Exploring language	Language Awareness
Collocations Word-building (roots and affixes)		**Exam focus:** **proofreading**	Verb forms (1) 'Will', 'would' and 'used to'
Vocabulary to describe books, films and TV	Ways of improving fluency	Punctuation marks	Questions (2) Future forms
Describing personal characteristics Emotions		**Exam Focus:** **discourse cloze**	Conditionals Past forms
Common colloquial expressions Common abbreviations	Pronunciation of connected speech	**Exam Focus:** **lexical cloze** **and open cloze** **Exam Focus:** **expanding from notes**	Verb forms (2) Participles (2)
Guessing unknown words Opposites Homophones		**Exam focus: open cloze**	Emphatic structures Multi-word verbs
Types of crime Synonyms	Pronunciation in word families		Perfect tenses Articles

UNIT 1

Starting Off

PART ONE
Getting to know each other

Lead-in

1 Think about the following questions by yourself for a few minutes and then share your ideas with a group of colleagues.

- Which famous person (past or present) would you most like to be stuck in a lift with? What questions would you ask him or her?
- If you were stranded on a desert island (with food, water and shelter) what personal object would you most like to have with you?
- Which year of your life would you re-live if you had the chance? Why?

2 Which aspect of studying English do you find most frustrating? Can you express it in one sentence? Write it down on a piece of paper and give it to your teacher, who will then give you further instructions.

Roading (rĕd'ing) n. perusal ; interpretation of a passage ; public lecture or recital.

Writing (rīt'ing) n. act of writing ; that which is written ; a book ; a manuscript ; —pl. official papers ; deeds.

Reading technique: skimming

1 Quickly skim read the following extracts from the problem page of an English language magazine. Put a tick next to those problems which are similar to the ones which you discussed in the previous activity.

I study English for 6 hours per week in secondary school. For 1 hour each week we have conversation classes with a native speaker of English where we talk about topics such as drugs, politics and culture. I know it's a really good opportunity to practise my spoken English, but I never make a contribution to the discussion. It's not that I don't have an opinion, or that I'm shy, but more that I don't have the vocabulary to express my views. I feel really frustrated at the end of the lesson. Nobody else in the group seems to have the same problem.
Katalin

I'm a 24-year-old business student from Malaysia and I've been attending English classes at night school for the past 5 years. Up to now I've considered myself to be a good student. Last month I went to Britain to visit my relatives over there and it was awful. Nobody could understand me (was my pronunciation really that bad?) and I couldn't understand them. What went wrong? My English teacher is very good and I always score the highest in grammar tests.
Fazlinda

I'm writing to ask your opinion on a matter which is really annoying me. Well, actually, there are two problems. The first is that my English teacher never corrects my mistakes when I am speaking. Isn't that her job? How am I going to improve otherwise? Also, she's always telling me that now I am an advanced student, I should forget all the rules of grammar that I learnt when I was younger.
Günther

Can you help me? I really want to speak English perfectly, with the correct English accent. Do you have any good ideas? I have a particular problem with sounds like 's'.
José

I am working as an au pair in London looking after 2 small children. I love my job but the way that English people speak is a little puzzling. For example, I often hear them say things like 'more friendlier' whereas I thought it should be 'more friendly'. It also seems to be common for them to say 'we was' instead of 'we were'. Can you explain this? Would it be impolite of me to correct them?
Lana

I am an intermediate student of English (I have been studying it for 3 years). I'm quite good at reading and writing but listening is very difficult for me. My teacher suggested that I listen to the World Service every day in order to improve my listening. The problem is that it's hard for me to understand every word. Do you have any ideas about how to make listening to the radio easier? I like to keep up with the current news in particular.
Yuki

2 Working in the same groups, discuss the reply you would give to each of the letter writers. When you have finished, report your ideas to the whole class.

3 Which of your (or your colleagues') problems were not mentioned? What advice would you give?

Vocabulary development: phrases for giving advice

Look at the following phrases and decide with a partner which form of the verb should follow.

a –ing
b bare infinitive
c to + infinitive

what about ...?   I'd advise you ...
you ought ...   you could always ...
you'd better ...   it might be a good idea ...
have you considered ...?   I suggest you ...
why don't you ...?   if I were you, I'd ...

Writing skill: a reply to a problem page

1 Imagine your group are the editors of the English language magazine. Choose one of the letters from page 7 as the 'star letter' and together draft a short reply to the writer, incorporating some of the phrases for giving advice.

2 When you've finished, pass the letter to another group who should comment on your advice and your group's writing skills (including grammatical accuracy).

Exploring language: common grammatical errors

1 From the letters you've seen and your own experience, what are the most common grammatical errors that students make at this level? Discuss with a partner.

2 Look at the other letters that the class have written and see if your predictions were correct.

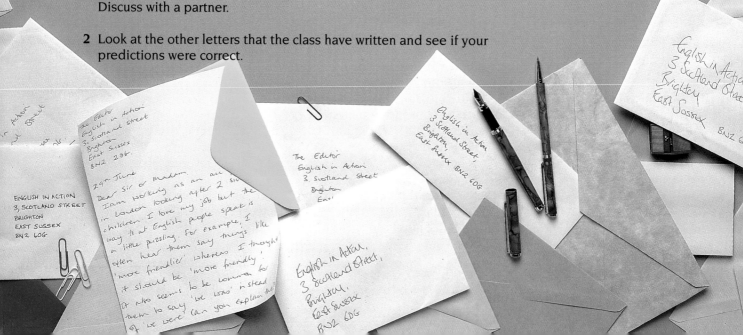

PART TWO
You the language learner

Lead-in

In Part One you looked at some of the common problems for language learners. Having studied English to advanced level you have almost certainly developed your own methods of learning a language and have some strong opinions on the subject. Work with a partner and discuss the following points.

a The best way to learn vocabulary is to write it down. ☐

b Reading more in English can improve your writing. ☐

c It's sometimes hard to see your improvements in a foreign language. ☐

d You have less need for a dictionary as your English improves. ☐

e One advantage of studying English in an English speaking country is that native speakers can correct you. ☐

f You can be a fluent speaker without being good at grammar. ☐

📼 Listening technique: global understanding

You are about to hear a conversation between three learners of English who have spent one year studying in England. They are discussing the points listed above and their improvements (or otherwise!) in English. Order the points as you hear them mentioned by putting the appropriate number in the box.

📼 Listening technique: specific information

1 Listen to the discussion a second time. Look at the list of points below and make notes about what the speakers say about each of them:

● Speaking/Pronunciation
● Listening
● Grammar
● Reading
● Writing
● Vocabulary

2 How would you rate yourself in each of these areas (good, average, weak)? Which areas do you hope to improve?

Exploring pronunciation: helping yourself to improve

How important is good pronunciation to you? If you are serious about improving your pronunciation, then it's a good idea to learn the sounds of English.

Vowels and dipthongs	Consonants
1 i: as in *see* /si:/	1 p as in *pen* /pen/
2 ɪ as in *sit* /sɪt/	2 b as in *bad* /bæd
3 e as in *ten* /ten/	3 t as in *tea* /ti:/
4 æ as in *hat* /hæt/	4 d as in *did* /dɪd/
5 ɑ: as in *arm* /ɑ:m/	5 k as in *cat* /kæt/
6 ɒ as in *got* /gɒt/	6 g as in *got* /gɒt/
7 ɔ: as in *saw* /sɔ:/	7 tʃ as in *chin* /tʃɪn/
8 ʊ as in *put* /pʊt/	8 dʒ as in *June* /dʒu:n/
9 u: as in *too* /tu:/	9 f as in *fall* /fɔ:l/
10 ʌ as in *cup* /kʌp/	10 v as in *voice* /vɔɪs/
11 ɜ: as in *fur* /fɜ:(r)/	11 θ as in *thin* /θɪn/
12 ə as in *ago* /əgəʊ/	12 ð as in *then* /ðen/
13 eɪ as in *page* /peɪdʒ/	13 s as in *so* /səʊ/
14 əʊ as in *home* /həʊm/	14 z as in *zoo* /zu:/
15 aɪ as in *five* /faɪv/	15 ʃ as in *she* /ʃi:/
16 aʊ as in *now* /naʊ/	16 ʒ as in *vision* /vɪʒ(ə)n/
17 ɔɪ as in *join* /dʒɔɪn/	17 h as in *how* /haʊ/
18 ɪə as in *near* /nɪə(r)/	18 m as in *man* /mæn/
19 eə as in *hair* /heə(r)/	19 n as in *no* /nəʊ/
20 ʊə as in *pure* /pjʊə(r)/	20 ŋ as in *sing* /sɪŋ/
	21 l as in *leg* /leg/
	22 r as in *red* /red/
	23 j as in *yes* /jes/
	24 w as in *wet* /wet/

1 Look at the underlined vowel sounds in the following pairs of words. For each pair, say if you think the sounds are pronounced in the same way (S) or differently (D). Then use the phonemic chart to write in the appropriate vowel sound(s) as in the first example. These words are commonly mispronounced by learners of English!

a	identif<u>y</u>	(D)	/ aɪ /	e	r<u>e</u>present	( )	/	/
	happ<u>y</u>		/ i: /		b<u>e</u>tter		/	/
b	<u>i</u>ll	( )	/	/	f	tow<u>ar</u>ds	( )	/	/
	<u>I</u>		/	/		c<u>ar</u>		/	/
c	t<u>o</u>pic	( )	/	/	g	b<u>ou</u>ght	( )	/	/
	t<u>o</u>tal		/	/		c<u>ou</u>gh		/	/
d	disc<u>u</u>ss	( )	/	/	h	mon<u>ey</u>	( )	/	/
	b<u>u</u>s		/	/		th<u>ey</u>		/	/

2 Do the same for these consonant sounds.

a	<u>ch</u>urch	( )	/	/	e	li<u>s</u>ten	( )	/	/
	ar<u>ch</u>itecture		/	/		li<u>s</u>t		/	/
b	wea<u>th</u>er	( )	/	/	f	controver<u>s</u>ial	( )	/	/
	clo<u>th</u>es		/	/		mea<u>s</u>ure		/	/
c	cli<u>mb</u>	( )	/	/	g	in<u>j</u>ured	( )	/	/
	bo<u>mb</u>		/	/		<u>j</u>ail		/	/
d	re<u>f</u>rigerate	( )	/	/	h	<u>kn</u>ee	( )	/	/
	tar<u>g</u>et		/	/		<u>k</u>ettle		/	/

3 Correct word stress is also a very important element of pronunciation. You may pronounce the sounds correctly, but if the stress is on the wrong syllable people may find it hard to understand you when you speak. Work in two groups, A and B, and identify which syllable has the main stress in your group of words.

Example: c̄apital

Group A	Group B
1 identify	1 forty
2 advertisement	2 preposition
3 fashionable	3 information
4 photography	4 consequence
5 university	5 unhappy
6 problem	6 develop
7 logical	7 experiment
8 fourteen	8 wonderful

4 When you have finished, pair up with someone from the other group and ask your partner to help you check your answers. Don't be afraid to say the words aloud!

PART THREE
A candidate for CAE

Lead-in

These are some of the questions that language students frequently ask about CAE:

- How similar is the format to the First Certificate in English (FCE)?
- Is it easier than the Certificate of Proficiency in English (CPE)?
- How many papers are there? How long does each paper last?
- Do I have to pass all papers to pass the exam?
- What type of people do the exam? Would I be suitable?
- What can I do with my qualification? Do employers recognise it?
- Do I have to know a lot about grammar?
- Where and when can I take the exam?
- How can I prepare for the exam?

1 Work in pairs. How many of these questions do you know the answer to?

2 Write down any other questions you may have about CAE.

Reading technique: scanning

Now scan the following explanation of the CAE to confirm your ideas or to find the answers to the questions you didn't know.

The Certificate in Advanced English (CAE) is an internationally-recognised advanced level examination, designed for adolescents/young adults or professional people, and is useful for those who use (or intend to use) English for study or professional purposes. Thus the exam has an emphasis on language tasks that are related to the real world. The level of CAE is approximately two thirds above that of FCE and a third below that of CPE. The exam is held twice a year in examination centres all over the world.

There are five papers in total and they carry equal weighting.

PAPER 1: READING
(Time allowed: 1 hour + 15 minutes)

You will read four different texts (totalling approximately 3000 words) which come from a variety of everyday sources, e.g. newspapers and general interest magazines, leaflets, guides or advertisements. There are around 50 questions in total which are presented in a variety of formats, such as multiple choice, multiple-matching and sentence or paragraph clozes.

Skills needed: skimming, scanning, understanding of text organisation, appreciating style, reading between the lines.

PAPER 2: WRITING
(Time allowed: 2 hours)

Section A is compulsory and this task requires you to read two or three short texts and apply the information to write one piece of 250 words, or two pieces totalling 250 words.

Section B offers a choice of four questions of which you must complete one. You are required to perform tasks such as writing formal or informal letters, giving directions or instructions, writing leaflets, guides, reports and reviews. The writing tasks are similar to those you might perform in the real world.

Skills needed: ability to write clear, accurate and fluent prose with a specified audience and purpose in mind, ability to select relevant information from a text (Section A only) and to understand and fully complete the task.

PAPER 3: ENGLISH IN USE
(Time allowed: 1 hour 30 minutes)

This paper aims to test your knowledge of how the language works. You must answer all questions here.

Section A contains two cloze passages, each with 15 items. The first is a multiple-choice format and aims to test knowledge of general vocabulary and collocation. The second passage has gaps which you must fill in and aims to test knowledge of grammatical structure.

Section B consists of two questions. The first is a short text (around 200 words) which contains a number of spelling, punctuation or grammatical errors which you have to find and correct. The second question gives you a text in a particular register, e.g. informal, and asks you to transform the information into another register, e.g. formal, by filling in a gapped text.

Section C contains two questions. The first of these is sometimes called a 'discourse cloze'. In this question you have to read a text (around 300 words) which has phrases or whole sentences missing and choose the correct item from a list of options. In the final question you are given a set of notes, often in abbreviated form, which you must expand into full, grammatically accurate sentences.

Skills needed: knowledge of how the language works (vocabulary, grammar, formal and informal registers, how texts are organised), and the ability to apply this knowledge to the proofreading of texts or the expansion of notes into full sentences.

PAPER 4: LISTENING
(Time allowed: 45 minutes)

You will answer four compulsory sets of questions after listening to four different texts. Section A is a monologue, Section B is usually a monologue (although it may contain prompts from other speakers), Section C is a conversation, and Section D is a series of short extracts. All texts are heard twice with the exception of Section B. The question formats are varied, including multiple choice, ticking boxes and writing brief notes.

Skills needed: Listening for global and detailed understanding, appreciating or inferring attitude, identifying topics, speakers, viewpoints, etc.

PAPER 5: SPEAKING
(Time allowed: 15 minutes)

You will conduct the speaking paper with another candidate and two examiners. This paper has four phases.

In Phase A you will introduce yourself (or if you know your partner well you may be asked to introduce him or her) to one of the examiners, and you will be asked questions about yourself, your interests, career ambitions, etc.

In Phase B you and your partner will each be given a different visual prompt and you will take turns to describe your picture while your partner performs a task. (This phase is sometimes called an 'information gap'.)

In Phase C you are both given some 'problem-solving' task in which you must collaborate to reach some form of agreement with your partner.

In Phase D you are asked to report or summarise your discussion in Phase C to the examiners, and to clarify or expand any of the points raised.

Skills needed: Interacting and taking turns to speak with your partner, describing a picture clearly and accurately, giving and justifying a point of view.

Reading technique: scanning

Using this book will help you to prepare for the exam. Flick through Units 2 to 12 of this book and look out for the pages which are marked with the 'Exam Focus' sign. (This sign tells you that the activity is designed to replicate the type of question that will appear in the CAE exam.) Write the relevant page number from the book in the chart below for future reference.

Example: **Speaking**

                 Phase B

                 ....p91....

Reading

multiple choice	multiple-matching	sentence/paragraph cloze
....	....	....

Writing

Section A	Section B
....	....

English in Use

Section A		Section B		Section C	
Q1	Q2	Q3	Q4	Q5	Q6
....		....		....	

Listening

Section A	Section B	Section C	Section D
....	....	....	....

Speaking

Phase A	Phase B	Phase C	Phase D
	....	....	....

Vocabulary development: terminology

1 How many of the following vocabulary terms do you know the meaning of? Can you give examples to illustrate each of them?

word family*	compound*	specialist	affix*
root*	synonym*	collocation*	idiom/expression*
multi-word verb*	abbreviation*	homophone*	colloquialism*
antonym			

2 Match the underlined words in the following sentences with the correct terms from the above list.

a I've been feeling really <u>tired</u> lately
   Yes, you have been looking a little <u>worn-out</u>.   (**synonym**)

b At a <u>rough</u> calculation you owe me four pounds.
   Well, to be <u>precise</u>, it's three pounds seventy-five.   (   )

c Yesterday was something of a <u>red letter day</u>. I won $10,000 on the
   National Lottery.   (   )

d To operate this particular computer <u>program</u> you need to use a <u>mouse</u>. (   )

e I can't <u>put up with</u> this behaviour any longer.   (   )

f Unemployment causes a great deal of <u>un</u> <u>happi</u> <u>ness</u> in the world today. (   )
                                                                          (   )

g Do you think he's <u>suited</u> to this project?
   Yes, I'd say he was eminently <u>suitable</u>.   (   )

h Would you like a room with a view?
   Yes, I want to be able to <u>see</u> the <u>sea</u> from my window.   (   )

i This <u>coffee's</u> a bit <u>strong</u>, isn't it? Do you want more milk in it? (   )

j Do you like reading <u>science-fiction</u> stories?   (   )

k Did you know the government is planning to put up <u>VAT</u> again?   (   )

l Can you get me a packet of <u>fags</u> from the newsagents?   (   )

3 In which unit can you find further practice for those areas of vocabulary marked with *?

1 Read the following authentic newspaper article. Who do you feel most support for: the boss or the workers?

£100,000 for boss £5 each for staff

Health bosses have sparked outrage by doubling a top manager's pay to nearly £100,000 and giving nurses a £5 Boots voucher.

More than 5,000 staff were handed the gift voucher as a reward by Southampton University Hospitals Trust after it had a record-breaking first year.

But the chief executive, David Moss, was given a more substantial reward for the trust's success – a bumper 100% pay rise. He has rocketed to the fourth-highest-paid health chief after his salary was doubled to nearly £100,000.

By comparison, nursing staff in the NHS were given a pay rise of 1.5%.

Mr Moss, 46, a father of three, defended his rise, saying it was justified because he has a very stressful job. 'I have a wide range of responsibilities, I have a very demanding job for which, I admit, I am quite well paid.'

Mr Moss was also given one of the £5 vouchers to spend in the High Street chemists.

A hospital spokesman said: 'Of course David Moss earns more money because he is the chief executive, and that is the nature of organisations. It is the difference between working for a company and then becoming a director of it.'

A spokesman for the staff union, Unison, said the gift voucher was 'insulting'. 'All the staff are shocked,' he said.

(Independent)

2 Authentic texts can be an invaluable source for self-study. Imagine you wanted to exploit this text for particular grammatical structures. Can you find a structure that appears frequently in the text?

3 Work in pairs. Student A should underline all the indefinite articles, student B all the definite articles. See if their use in the text confirms the explanations set out in the Grammar Reference section, p 174.

4 See if you can find examples of the following:

  a the definite article: with a noun that has already been referred to; when making reference to a unique noun
  b the indefinite article: with a countable singular noun referred to for the first time

5 You might find it useful to make a collection of short authentic texts which offer good examples of particular structures.

Keeping a record of your learning

1 At the end of every unit of this book you have the opportunity to think about what you have learned. Use this review page to do the following:

a record what you have done
b make a note of useful vocabulary
c assess your strong and weak areas and plan your future learning accordingly.

2 Look at this sample review of Unit 1.

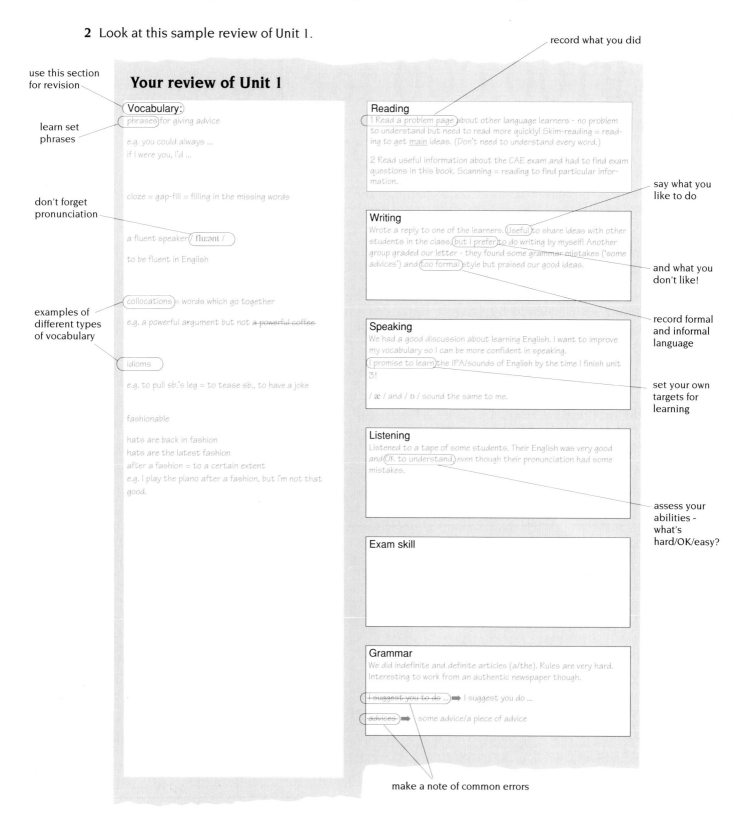

record what you did

use this section for revision

Your review of Unit 1

Vocabulary:

learn set phrases

phrases for giving advice

e.g. you could always ...
if I were you, I'd ...

cloze = gap-fill = filling in the missing words

don't forget pronunciation

a fluent speaker / ˈfluːənt /

to be fluent in English

examples of different types of vocabulary

collocations = words which go together

e.g. a powerful argument but not a powerful coffee

idioms

e.g. to pull sb.'s leg = to tease sb., to have a joke

fashionable

hats are back in fashion
hats are the latest fashion
after a fashion = to a certain extent
e.g. I play the piano after a fashion, but I'm not that good.

Reading
1 Read a problem page about other language learners - no problem to understand but need to read more quickly! Skim-reading = reading to get main ideas. (Don't need to understand every word.)

2 Read useful information about the CAE exam and had to find exam questions in this book. Scanning = reading to find particular information.

say what you like to do

Writing
Wrote a reply to one of the learners. Useful to share ideas with other students in the class, but I prefer to do writing by myself! Another group graded our letter - they found some grammar mistakes ('some advices') and too formal style but praised our good ideas.

and what you don't like!

record formal and informal language

Speaking
We had a good discussion about learning English. I want to improve my vocabulary so I can be more confident in speaking. I promise to learn the IPA/sounds of English by the time I finish unit 3!

/ æ / and / ɒ / sound the same to me.

set your own targets for learning

Listening
Listened to a tape of some students. Their English was very good and OK to understand even though their pronunciation had some mistakes.

assess your abilities - what's hard/OK/easy?

Exam skill

Grammar
We did indefinite and definite articles (a/the). Rules are very hard. Interesting to work from an authentic newspaper though.

I suggest you to do ... ➡ I suggest you do ...

advices ➡ some advice/a piece of advice

make a note of common errors

Education

PART ONE
Gender in education

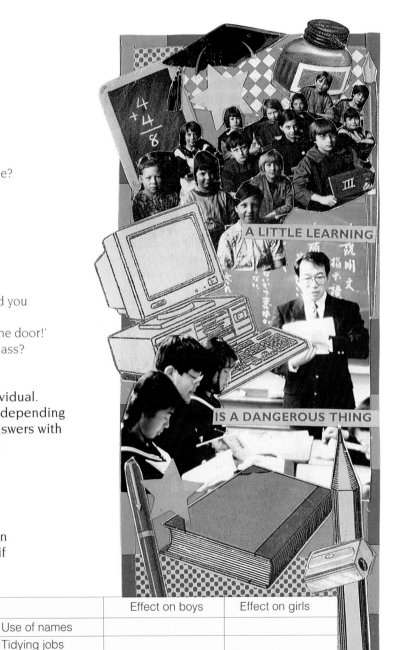

Lead-in

British adults were asked the following questions about their experiences at school:

a Did your teachers address you by your family name?
b Were you regularly asked to tidy away materials after lessons?
c Were you often praised for being neat and tidy?
d Were you ever asked to move heavy objects like tables or equipment?
e Were you often given responsible jobs like running errands?
f Were you asked to do things? For example: 'Would you close the door please?'
g Were you told to do things? For example: 'Close the door!'
h Did you receive your fair amount of attention in class?
i Did you contribute as much as everybody else?

The answers varied according to the sex of the individual. Write M (male) or F (female) next to each question depending on who you think would answer 'yes'. Share your answers with the group and try to work out the reasoning behind each question.

Listening technique

1 Global understanding: listen to an extract from an interview with a leading educationalist to check if your answers were correct.

2 Specific information: draw a table like the one opposite. Listen a second time and fill in as much information as you can.

3 Do you agree, or is this a case of experts exaggerating a point? Are girls and boys treated differently at school? Do boys talk too much? In the early stages of this course, who's been doing most of the talking, the men or the women?

	Effect on boys	Effect on girls
Use of names		
Tidying jobs		
Heavy duty jobs		
Responsible jobs		
Contributions		
Attention time		

Reading technique: predicting

Read this introduction to an article criticising the British university system.

Why might men be more successful than women at gaining Firsts?

Are female students naturally less intelligent than their male counterparts? Or is their failure to gain anywhere near as many Firsts at university a reflection of the education system itself?

Reading technique: skimming

 Give yourself two minutes to skim read the text. Try to gain an overall impression by reading the first sentence in each paragraph. Are any of your ideas mentioned?

IN THE FINAL ANALYSIS

I have just taken Finals. I did the best I could but, statistically, I know I am only half as likely to get a First as the man sitting at the desk in front. This is not because he is a genius; it's because he is a man. While 10.3 per cent of men get Firsts, only 6.2 per cent of women do. It's time we sorted out why.

'Well, it's because women are just more stupid, aren't they?' was one male tutor's answer. However, the (thankfully small) 'Women are dim' posse receive a kick in their false teeth when they are told that in places where the class of degree is mainly dependent on continuous assessment rather than exams, women and men get equal proportions of Firsts. Emma Westcott, women's officer of Oxford University Student Union, calls the issue of gender imbalance in examinations 'the issue of the moment' and believes 'it is evident that the current results indicate the dysfunction of the system, not the failure of the individual.'

So what is wrong with this system? And why should it be women who suffer most from it?

The examination system is found stressful by many, not just by women, and the absurdity of classifying the degree of a three-year course by a week-long stamina test has often been pointed out. A woman may also have the added stress that if she should suffer from PMT during that week, she may perform less well, so the spreading-out of exams would be a benefit. Many academic institutions now realise this and continuous assessments and split Finals are playing an increasingly large role.

However, according to English tutor Dr Julia Briggs, 'Exams are designed and set by a male-structured course and a male structured concept of education'. Tutorials are often confrontational, demanding an aggressive style of scholarship alien to many women. Seminars require the ability to voice opinions to a group, which can be similarly problematic.

Is it being stereotypical, though, to say that men can argue better and speak better in academic situations? I don't think so because patterns such as these appear to emerge from an early age. Dale Spender, in her book Invisible Women, showed how in schools, girls were praised for being tidy, neat and conscientious, while boys were expected to be more diverse, creative and flashy, and were thus encouraged to take more risks.

This would explain why men get more Firsts and more Thirds; their risk taking is either brilliant or terrible, never average. Women students were found to be less keen on taking risks and this is supported by anecdotal evidence. English tutor Dr Lynda Mugglestone says, 'Men are more willing to venture views that can be totally ridiculous, while women often lose confidence in their own opinions.'

Conversational analysis by linguists Zimmerman and West has shown that generally women are not given the space to speak. In mixed-sex conversations, the number of interruptions made by men is huge compared with those by women. This is mirrored by many women's aversion to speaking up in academic situations. A good example of this was seen at a seminar on women's art, which was attended by thirty women and three men; each man made a verbal contribution, while not one of the women did. Men, it seems, are more likely to vocalise their opinions, even on a topic concerning women.

Back in the schoolroom, girls are often used as a negative reference group, their participation not encouraged and their opinions undermined by the boys. Women can be assumed to be less intelligent before they even start. Psychologist P. Goldberg carried out a study in which students were separately given identical articles with separate names at the top. Essays headed by a male name were more often than not judged to be better.

These findings are worryingly supported by exam statistics. Take the School of English at Birmingham University, for example, where 80 per cent of the English students are women. In 1991, one women and four men were awarded Firsts; in 1992, five women and one man. What made such a difference? In 1992, for the first time, scripts were numbered and anonymous.

(Guardian)

Reading technique: specific information

1 Here are the answers to several questions based on information in the text. Can you work out what the questions are?

    a 4.1 per cent.
    b Thankfully, not very many.
    c On courses that offer continuous assessment instead of exams.
    d If she's suffering from PMT.
    e They often find them confrontational.
    f When they show 'feminine' abilities like being tidy.
    g It's a reflection of the fact that they take more risks, even when they're completely wrong.
    h Because they lack confidence in their own opinions.
    i 33.
    j Yes, even with issues that concern women.

2 The education system in England seems to prejudice females. How does your country's educational system compare? Are girls treated differently from boys at school? Do aspects of the system favour male students? Or do you think it's all a fuss over nothing?

See **Language awareness: questions (1)**

Vocabulary development: common expressions

1 Many English expressions contain the construction 'as ... as'. Look at this extract from 'In the Final Analysis'. Can you rewrite it using an 'as ... as' construction?

    'Well, it's because women are just more stupid.'

Now find five more examples in the text where males and females are compared and rewrite them using 'as ... as'.

2 Here are some common idiomatic expressions using 'as ... as', some more logical than others! Begin by completing the expressions that have an obvious link.

    Example: a As quiet as a mouse.

3 Of those that remain, connect any that have the same first letter.

    Example: d As cool as a cucumber.

4 Use a dictionary to check your answers and to find out which of these idioms are used to describe animate objects (A) or inanimate objects (I) or both (B).

a	As quiet as	a bone
b	As cold as	a feather
c	As smooth as	a pancake
d	As cool as	a door-nail
e	As dry as	gold
f	As fit as	a picture
g	As light as	ice
h	As pretty as	life
i	As flat as	the hills
j	As regular as	new
k	As dead as	a baby's bottom
l	As good as	a cucumber
m	As good as	clockwork
n	As old as	a fiddle
o	As large as	a mouse

PART TWO
Education East and West

Lead-in

1 Experts are fond of telling people what's best for them and educationalists are no exception. However, having spent many years of your life at school, you no doubt have opinions of your own on the subject! Which of the statements opposite comes closest to your own views on the school system?

2 Share your ideas with the group. Are your colleagues generally happy with the system of education in their country or does it require fundamental change?

▶ Children should be:
  a) categorised as academic or not at an early age and then sent to an appropriate school.
  b) allowed to develop at their own pace.

▶ Schools should be primarily concerned with:
  a) achieving academic success in the major subjects.
  b) avoiding 'failure' by offering a wide range of subjects.

▶ Progress and success should be measured by:
  a) examinations.
  b) coursework.

▶ Children learn best when:
  a) they are competing against each other.
  b) they are co-operating with each other.

▶ Discipline at school should be:
  a) very strict.
  b) easy going.

▶ Teachers should:
  a) know their subject inside out.
  b) know *how to teach* their subject.

▣ Listening technique

1 Global understanding: you are going to hear a teacher comparing the Japanese education system with the American and British model. Are her views similar to your own?

2 Specific information: Listen again and decide if the statements opposite are true (T) or false (F).

3 Susan clearly favours the Japanese education system. What's your opinion?

a Susan thinks the Japanese education system is too strict.
b Exams at the end of primary school determine a Japanese child's future education.
c The system in Britain and America avoids categorising pupils at an early age.
d Susan believes that competitive exams encourage students to work hard.
e There are fewer subjects to choose from in Japan.
f Pupils in Britain and America are encouraged to compete rather than cooperate.
g Western teaching methods can waste a lot of time.
h Pupils in America are under little pressure because there is no discipline.

EXAM FOCUS
(English in Use,
Section C)
discourse cloze

Choose the best phrase or sentence below to fill each of the blanks in the following text. Write one letter (A–J) in each of the numbered spaces. Three of the suggested answers do not fit at all. The first one has been done for you.

Easy living at Japan's colleges

Undergraduate life in Japan is blissful, largely because school life is not. The Ministry of Education recently revealed that entrance exams for private high schools still include questions on subjects not covered by the state primary school curriculum:

(0) __I__, you have to be ahead of the pack by age 11. Good schools offer a direct route to the universities. Consequently, the students who will be sailing blithely through their final university term this winter spent most of their youth doing hours and hours of homework and endless exams. (1) _____, they have all of the basic education that a Japanese corporation needs.

(2) _____ except recover from the rigours of school and prepare for the rigours of corporate life. One 1987 poll found that the average Japanese university student spends 30 minutes every day reading comics, 26 minutes reading newspapers and just 49 minutes reading books. (3)_____ spent less than half an hour every day reading books, and a full 17% came out with the astonishing admission that they hardly ever read at all. Japanese undergraduates watch television or videos for an average of 105 minutes every day – exactly the same amount of time they spend on comics, newspapers and books combined.

(4) _____ to an academic regime that even students admit errs on the side of indulgence – it takes up too much time. Companies are trying to persuade the Ministry of Education to shorten four-year degree courses by a year. (5)_____ for up to six years and operate on the assumption that anyone bright enough to get into a university is bright enough for on-the-job training. (6) _____ is less important than the fact that you went to a university in the first place.

(Guardian)

A Around half of those polled

B Students recommended by professors

C Japanese companies routinely train graduate recruits

D By the time they gain admission to a university

E Hiring by Japanese companies

F Corporate Japan apparently has just one objection

G No one is expected to do very much in college

H At the very minimum

I To get into a good school

J How well you did at university

1 Read through the text first to get a general understanding and then read the extracts A–J.

2 When you've finished check your answers carefully. For example, a comma in the text might indicate you need a full clause. What word is likely to follow 'objection'(F)? What kind of word would you expect to find after 'university'(D): a noun, a pronoun, a verb, etc.?

See Language awareness: dependent prepositions

Writing skill: a letter to a newspaper

1 You are reading an English newspaper and you see the letter opposite.

2 You decide to write a reply to the newspaper giving your views on the subject.

Use some of the following phrases in your letter to help you get started.

Dear Editor,

We hear so much lately about the declining standards in our schools in Britain ... Isn't it time we admitted that we've simply got it wrong? I feel we should look more closely at the Japanese model of education. Maybe we could all learn a useful lesson.

Yours faithfully,

Sarah Patel (Ms)

Starting	Sarah Patel (Letters, October 1) is right to argue that ... I read with great interest the views of Sarah Patel (Letters, October 1) ... The misguided remarks by Sarah Patel (Letters, October 1) prompted me to write ...
Stating viewpoint	I agree/disagree wholeheartedly/completely/in part with the point that ... I share/don't share her view that ... Does the writer not think/realise/appreciate that ...?
Main body of letter	In my country ... My feeling is that ... Perhaps we should ...
Concluding	Let us hope that ... To sum up ...

PART THREE
Teacher, you're the tops!

Lead-in

The comments opposite were made by some young adults who were asked to recall some of the special qualities of their favourite schoolteachers. Match them with the correct word or phrase from the box below.

What makes a good teacher?
a good counsellor
b enthusiastic/stimulating
c patient
d a strict disciplinarian
e fair-minded
f well-informed/up-to-date
g a good sense of humour
h attractive looks/personality
i demanding

He used to treat us all in the same way and never had his 'favourites'.

Our teacher was always telling funny stories, anecdotes or jokes in order to make us laugh.

I used to have a crush on one of my teachers, so of course I worked really hard in his classes.

She was really tough on us. Heaven help us if we forgot our homework or were late for class.

She never minded explaining things over and over again if we didn't understand.

My teacher was a real expert in her field – we were lucky to have her.

He really loved his subject and so he brought it to life for us.

If ever we had any personal problems our teacher was always there to give good advice.

We had to work hard in class *and* do loads of homework.

Vocabulary development: the language of discussing

1 What phrases do you normally use for agreeing and disagreeing when you're discussing in English? List them with a partner.

2 The phrases opposite are commonly used by native speakers in an informal discussion. Look at the list below and match each phrase with the appropriate category.

  A Introducing or adding points
  B Agreeing
  C Partly agreeing
  D Politely disagreeing
  E Asking for repetition or explanation

Well, yes but ...(D)
Another thing is ...
I suppose that's true ...
Sure
Pardon?
What did you say?
My feeling is that ...

I'm not sure I agree with you on that
From my point of view ...
Sorry?
Personally speaking ...
What do you mean by that exactly?
Exactly!
That's true to a certain extent/degree

'A parent has two duties to his child, says an old Jewish proverb: to find them a partner, and a good teacher. Anyone who's ever had a good teacher knows just what a difference it makes, not just to your education but to your life.'

How far do you agree with the above quotation? What are some of the qualities of a good teacher? Discuss with your partner and try to decide on the top three qualities of a good teacher.

1 Work on your own and look at the list of qualities of a good teacher on the previous page. Put them in order of importance (1 = most important, 9 = least important). You should draw on your own personal experience.

Can you think of any other qualities?

2 Work with your partner for five minutes. Try to decide on the top three qualities of a good teacher and be prepared to report your conclusions to your class teacher.

3 When you have finished, look at the Vocabulary Development list and tick those phrases which you feel most comfortable with and would probably use in the future.

Writing skill: a report for a competition entry

1 Read the details of the competition which recently appeared in a magazine.

2 You have decided to enter this competition. Choose a teacher you respect and admire very much. Now list the particular qualities of your chosen teacher, and think of a particular instance where this quality is demonstrated.

Example: Patient
'One particular example of her patience and understanding was when ...'

3 Write a first draft of your report in class. Swap drafts with your partner and read each other's report as though you were one of the competition judges. Grade your partner's work out of 20 in the following way:

Language: accuracy of grammar/vocabulary/spelling (10 pts)
Content: interest/persuasiveness/final impression on the reader (10 pts)

Is the report a competition winner? Can you suggest any improvements that your partner could make?

4 When you have exchanged ideas write a final draft.

TEACHER – YOU'RE THE TOPS!

DO YOU KNOW A TEACHER WHO DESERVES TOP MARKS? YOUR REPORT COULD WIN THEM A PRIZE.

We're looking for the very best teacher – what she or he *must* have is a special quality: perhaps an ability to enthuse pupils, to make lessons fun, imaginative and exciting; perhaps they have helped someone with problems at home or guided a particular talent. Just tell us in under 300 words what makes your nominated teacher so special and you could both win a prize.

(*SHE magazine*)

LANGUAGE AWARENESS
dependent prepositions

1 Some extracts from the text 'In the Final Analysis' appear opposite, this time with several prepositions omitted. Can you work out which ones they are? When you've finished, refer back to the article on page 18 to check your answers.

a ... where the class of degree is mainly dependent _____ continuous assessment ...

b ... women and men get equal proportions _____ Firsts.

c ... if she should suffer _____ PMT ...

d ... girls were praised _____ being neat and tidy ...

e Women students were found to be less keen _____ taking risks ...

f ... while women often lose confidence _____ their own opinions ...

g ... interruptions made by men is huge compared _____ those by women ...

h This is mirrored _____ many women's aversion _____ speaking up in ...

i ... the inequalities inherent _____ the educational system ...

2 There are many expressions in English that contain a dependent preposition + noun. There are no rules to help you choose the correct one, you simply need to learn the expression as a whole. Can you supply the correct preposition for the phrases opposite?

Choose from the list provided:

on	by	at	in	for	with	from

a ...... a start
b ...... balance
c ...... any chance
d ...... long last
e ...... any case
f ...... other words
g ...... time to time
h ...... the whole
i ...... purpose
j ...... mistake
k ...... least

l ...... addition to
m ...... average
n ...... respect to
o ...... now on
p ...... a change
q ...... all costs
r ...... all means
s ...... confidence
t ...... no account
u ...... a hurry
v ...... the surface

3 Choose from the phrases above to complete these sentences.

a It wasn't a mistake at all. You did it ....

b I'm fed up with going to the cinema. Shall we go to the theatre .... ?

c Sorry, I can't tell you. It's a secret. She told me ....

d Sorry, I can't stop. I'm ....

e You haven't seen Sarah .... , have you?

f I am writing .... your letter of 21st August.

g Can I borrow your pen for a moment? Yes, ...

h Well, he can be a bit selfish, but .... I quite like him.

i This supermarket's expensive. I'm going to shop in the market ....

j We see them .... , but not very often.

EXAM TIP: Prepositions can be very important in Paper 3 (English in Use) Section A (open cloze) and Section C (expanded notes).

LANGUAGE AWARENESS
questions (1)

1 ▭ Listen to the following explanation and example of how not to participate in a conversation.

2 ▭ Listen again. What kinds of words or phrases could the husband have used to 'help' the conversation along?
Example: 'Really?'

3 Now listen to a second example. Make notes of the 'helpers' and 'reply questions' that show interest, surprise, agreement, etc.

Helpers	Reply questions
Really?	Did you?

4 How do reply questions that mean 'I agree' differ in form from the others?

5 Supply the correct reply question for each of the statements in A.

6 ▭ Listen to the recording of a popular television game in England, the 'Yes–No' game. In particular, note how the host uses 'helpers' and reply questions.

7 Now play the game yourself. Does anyone in the group think they can last one minute without saying 'yes' or 'no'? Use the helping phrases and reply questions to try and catch them out.

8 Look at the mini-dialogues in B. Explain the (sometimes deliberate!) misunderstandings in each case.

> **EXAM TIP: Reply questions and 'helpers' are extremely useful in making a conversation interactive. Paper 5 gives you the chance to show your interactive or turn-taking skills, so try to get in the habit of being an active listener.**

A

a   I've just seen a great film.
    ....?

b   I had to go to the doctor's yesterday.
    ....?

c   Julia's really grown.
    Yes, ...?

d   I'd love to be rich.
    ....?

e   I'd never been abroad before my last holiday.
    ....?

f   He has his hair cut every week.
    ....?

g   They had a beautiful house in the country.
    ....?

h   What a terrible film that was!
    Yes, ...?

i   I'd prefer to leave early.
    ....?

j   Nothing scares me.
    ....?

k   I'll be on holiday this time next week.
    ....?

B

a   Excuse me?
b   Why? What have you done?

a   How do you do?
b   Fine, thanks.

a   What do you do?
b   When?

a   How are you?
b   How are you?

a   Can you open the window?
b   Yeah ... easily!

a   What's she like?
b   Painting, tennis ... going to the cinema.

a   Have you got the time?
b   Yes, thanks.

a   How long will the car be in the garage?
b   Er ... about three meters.

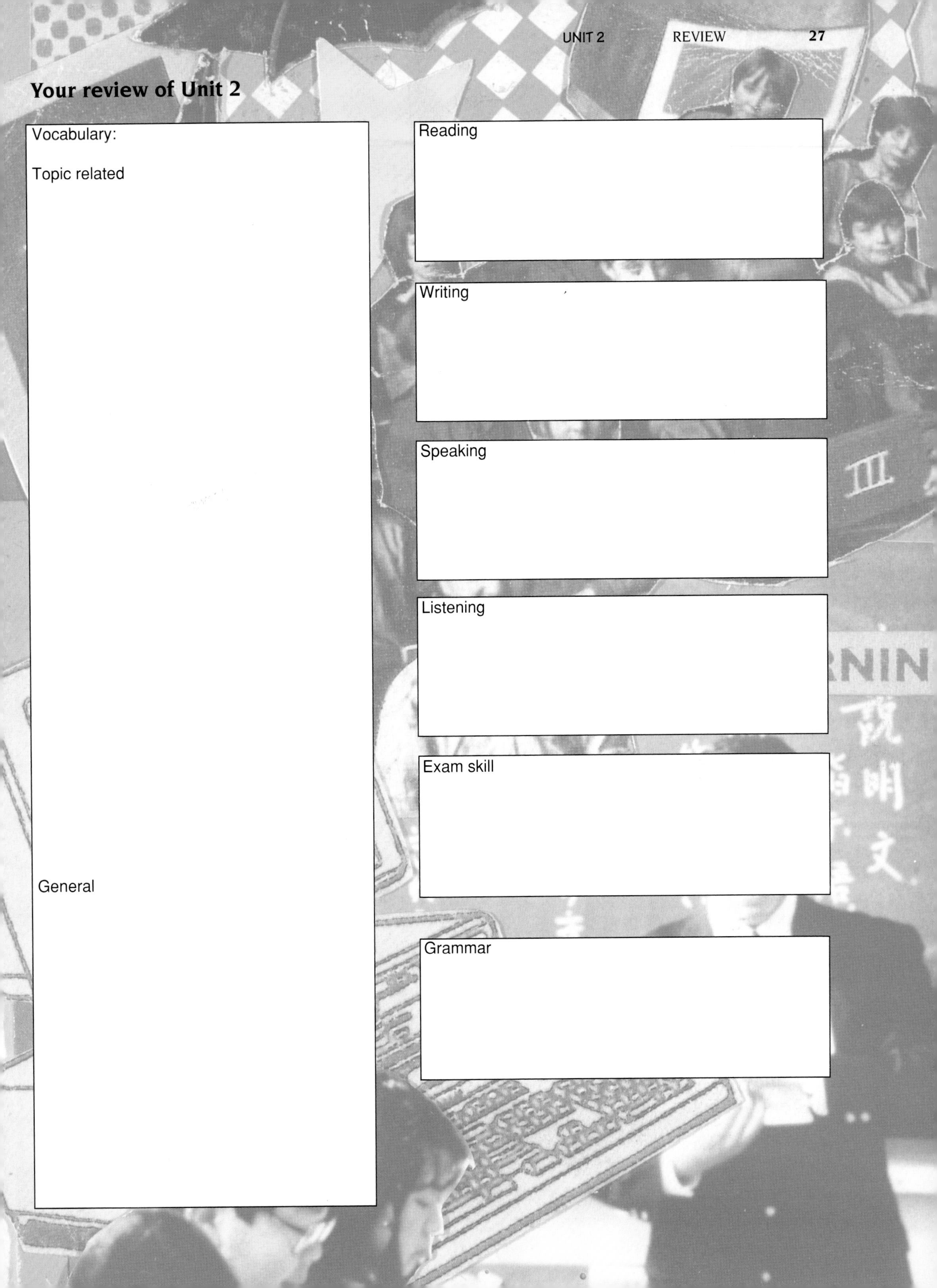

Your review of Unit 2

Vocabulary:

Topic related

General

Reading

Writing

Speaking

Listening

Exam skill

Grammar

UNIT 3

Citizens of the World

IT TAKES ALL SORTS

TO MAKE A WORLD

OUTWARD JOURNEY
FLIGHT No. | DA
BY081A Y 07OCT9

PART ONE
Missing home?

Lead-in

How much do you know about life in Britain today? Is what you know based on experience (e.g. visits to Britain), general knowledge or popular stereotypes? In small groups, consider the following points:

making friends/	attitudes to foreigners
socialising	transport
politics	shopping
food	studying in Britain
family life	living standards
the weather	

Listening technique: global understanding

1 Would the prospect of living in Britain for a considerable period of time excite you or leave you feeling apprehensive?

2 Gusta (from Holland), Petros (from Greece) and Andrea (from Germany) are all currently studying in Britain, in an inner-city university. Listen as they compare some aspects of British life with those of their own country. Which of the points from the lead-in are mentioned by each speaker? Put a tick next to the relevant topic.

Listening technique: specific information

1 Below are three statements relating to each speaker. Listen again and decide if the statements are true or false.

Gusta   a She likes the meat in England.
            b She still eats 'dead animals'.
            c Dutch meat is of far better quality than English meat.

Petros   a Tutors sometimes don't understand the student's point of view.
            b Tutors always behave in a logical way.
            c He approves of the tutors' behaviour towards foreign students.

Andrea a English children's parents don't buy them very much.
            b Differences are more to do with living standards than culture.
            c She feels the English children don't realise how lucky they are.

Speaking skill: making and dealing with interruptions

If you were offered the chance to spend one year in any country of your choice, where would you go? What's so appealing about this country:

- the climate?
- the people?
- the food?
- the scenery?
- the lifestyle?

Spend a few moments considering your opinions and then tell your partner. Your partner should listen for a few seconds and then take every opportunity to interrupt you, perhaps with a question or a statement. Respond to the interruption and continue with your explanation. You can use some of the expressions opposite to regain control. Those marked * are for use if you start to get annoyed!

Expressions to interrupt:	Expressions to regain control:
'Sorry but ...'	Yes, well anyway ...'
'Excuse me but ...'	'Anyway ...'
'Just a minute.'	'As I was saying ...'
'Hold on a minute.'	'Where was I? Oh yes ...'
'Hang on.'	'Is that all?' *
	May I continue?' *

Vocabulary development: getting around

1 Look at the following expressions that describe various ways of travelling. Tick the appropriate sections of the chart to show the meaning of each expression.

	Long Distance	Short Distance	Departing	Budget Travel	Regular Travel
to go globetrotting	☐	☐	☐	☐	☐
to live out of a suitcase	☐	☐	☐	☐	☐
to nip round	☐	☐	☐	☐	☐
to go for a spin	☐	☐	☐	☐	☐
to see the world	☐	☐	☐	☐	☐
to go back-packing	☐	☐	☐	☐	☐
to make a move	☐	☐	☐	☐	☐
to go on an outing	☐	☐	☐	☐	☐
to bum around	☐	☐	☐	☐	☐
to get under way	☐	☐	☐	☐	☐
to be always on the move	☐	☐	☐	☐	☐
to set off	☐	☐	☐	☐	☐
to pop round	☐	☐	☐	☐	☐

2 Choose expressions from the chart to complete these sentences.

a Is that the time? I think we'd better .... Thanks for a lovely evening.
b I'll be .... early Saturday morning to avoid the traffic.
c I'm just going to .... the corner to see John. I won't be a minute.
d Shall we .... in the new car?
e The school took the children .... yesterday. They visited a local farm.
f He .... during his year abroad. He never stayed in one place for more than a night.

You have been asked to contribute to one of a series of travel guides about your country. Each guide has a specific audience in mind:

- young people studying
- working travellers
- independent travellers (with an emphasis on females travelling alone)

- holiday makers
- business people

Choose one of these audiences and write a 250 word guide to staying in your home town.

1 What information would you look for in a good travel guide?

- first-hand accounts of experiences
- recommended hotels
- shopping
- entertainment
- restaurant recommendations
- advice on local customs

- health precautions
- maps of the whole country
- town plans
- colour photographs
- historical information

Is there anything else that you would add to the list?

2 Select three or four areas to write about and try to make your advice relevant to your audience.

3 Organise your information into note form.

Example:
Guide for young people studying

SHOPPING
– opening hours

– staying long-term:
  avoid tourist shops

– not much money:
  cheap supermarkets

LOCAL CUSTOMS
– dress
– addressing people
– tipping

ENTERTAINMENT
– how to get a student card
  for discounts in cinema/theatre

– cheap places to eat out

– clubs/discos/bars

See Language awareness: the language of obligation

PART TWO
Getting away

Lead-in

1 How good is your general knowledge? Look at the names of seven explorers and their nationality. Can you match their names with the appropriate places and dates?

2 Why do people like these set out on such journeys? Is it simply to find fame and fortune?

Willem Barents (Dutch)	China	1597
James Cook (English)	Quebec	1492
Jacques Cartier (French)	America	1770
Marco Polo (Italian)	North Pole	1603
Christopher Columbus (Italian)	Greenland	1534
Robert Peary (American)	Australia	1809
Samuel De Champlain (French)	Newfoundland	1271

EXAM FOCUS
(Listening, Section C)
multiple choice

📼 **You are going to hear a woman talking about her own reasons for travelling. Can you guess her reasons? Listen and choose the correct statement A, B, C or D. You will hear the tape twice.**

1
A Two-week holidays were too short for Holly's needs.
B She was simply interested in having a break from work.
C Holly thinks two-week holidays are never long enough.
D The two-week holidays she went on never seemed long enough.

2
A Holly's friends were going through an emotional crisis.
B Her friends weren't brave enough to give up their jobs.
C Holly was in a similiar situation to her friends.
D Holly's friends thought she was brave to give up her job.

3
A Holly couldn't persuade her friends to travel with her.
B Holly preferred to travel on her own.
C Holly was worried about not getting another job when she got back.
D Her friends were really jealous.

4
A Holly is surprised that other people don't travel in the same way.
B There's more chance of something unusual happening if you travel.
C People spend too much time thinking about travelling.
D Holly is surprised that travelling changed her life.

5
A Having stereotypes of people can be healthy.
B Holly still thinks she's narrow-minded.
C Holly has questioned her earlier stereotypes.
D People abroad see things from a different perspective.

1 Read the multiple choice options before you listen.

2 Generally speaking, multi-choice questions contain an obviously incorrect answer, two answers that, until closer inspection, appear correct and one correct answer. Listen and try to narrow down your choices by rejecting what you think is the obviously incorrect answer in each section.

3 Now listen for a second time. Of the three answers that remain, try to reach agreement with your colleagues on which of them is the only totally correct answer.

See **Language awareness: reported speech**

Reading technique: prediction

Read the first paragraph of an extract from Paul Theroux's travel book *The Happy Isles of Oceania*. What do you think his reasons were for travelling?

There was no good word in English for this hopeless farewell. My wife and I separated on a winter day in London and we were both miserable, because it seemed as though our marriage was over. We both thought: What now? It was the most sorrowful of goodbyes. I could not imagine life without her. I tried to console myself by saying, *This is like going on a journey, because a journey can be either your death or your transformation,* though on this one I imagined that I would just keep living a half-life.

Reading technique: scanning and information transfer

1 Scan the rest of the extract as quickly as you can. There are twenty different place names mentioned. How many can you find in one minute?

2 Now read it more carefully and then study the map. Circle those places that you know for certain the writer has lived in or visited.

3 Put these places in chronological order by writing the appropriate number next to the circle. For example, if you think he lived in Melbourne first, write '1' next to Melbourne.

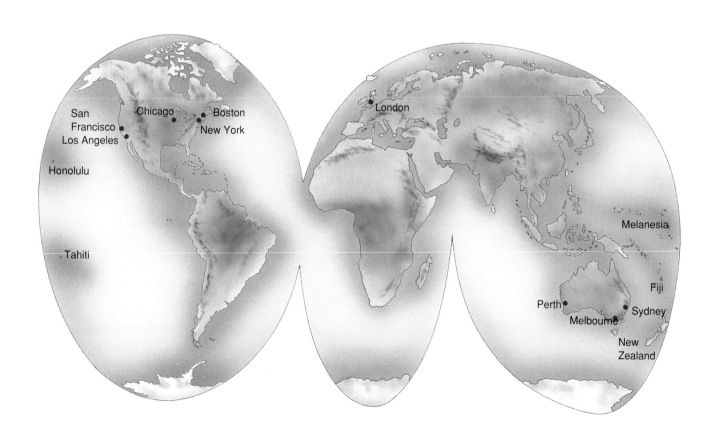

From habit, when I was alone, I slept only on the left side of the bed, and so I felt lonelier when I woke up with a big space beside me. At last I felt so woeful that I went to my doctor.

'Your blood pressure is fine,' she said, 'but I don't like the look of that.'

She touched a discoloration on my arm. She used the misleadingly sonorous name 'melanoma' to describe it. I heard melanoma and I thought of Melanesia. The Black Islands. Eventually she gouged out the black spot and put in four stitches and said she would let me know if this piece of my arm, this biopsy the size of an hors-d'oeuvre, was serious. 'I mean, if it's a carcinoma.'

Why did all those horrors have pretty names?

Needing to be reassured by the familiar sights and sounds of the place where I was born, I went to Boston, but I felt too defeated to stay. And home is sometimes so sad. One day a message came from Melbourne. *Are you free for a book promotional tour in New Zealand and Australia?* I thought, *Any excuse.* So I continued on my journey, carrying a tent, a sleeping bag and collapsible kayak. I headed west, by plane, to Chicago, San Francisco and Honolulu where, to cheer myself up, I took the big bandage off my stitched arm and put on yellow Garfield the Cat bandaids.

I went farther away, deeper into the Pacific, thinking: Planes are like seven-league boots. I could be in New Zealand or Easter Island tomorrow. And yet the Pacific was vast. It had half the world's free water; it was one third of the earth's surface.

More than an ocean, the Pacific was like a universe, and a chart of it looked like a portrait of the night sky. This enormous ocean was like the whole of heaven, an inversion of earth and air, so that the Pacific seemed like outer-space, an immensity of emptiness, dotted with misshapen islands that twinkled like stars, archipelagos like star clusters, and wasn't Polynesia a sort of galaxy?

'I've been all over the Pacific,' the man next to me said. He was from California. His name was Hap. 'Bora-Bora. Moora-Moora. Tora-Tora. Fuji.'

'Fiji,' his wife said.

'And Haiti,' he told me.

'Tahiti,' his wife said, correcting him again.

'Oh, God,' he said. 'Johnston Island.'

This sinister little island, with the Stars and Stripes flying over it, is 800 miles west of Honolulu, and was formerly a launching site for H-bombs. More recently, nuclear waste was stored there, along with neve gas and stacks of hydrogen bombs. A recent accident had left one end of Johnston Island radioactive. Few Americans have heard of it. The anti-nuclear New Zealanders can tell you where it is and why it terrifies them.

'What was that like?'

'Who said I got off the plane?' Hap said.

'We're members of the Century Club,' his wife said. 'You can only join if you've been to a hundred countries.'

'What does "been to" mean? Pass through the airport? Spend a night? Get diarrhoea there?'

'Guess he's not a member!' Hap said, joyously.

Tourists don't know where they've been, I thought. Travellers don't know where they're going.

(Paul Theroux: *The Happy Isles of Oceania*)

Reading technique: inference and speculation

Read the text more closely and discuss the following questions with your partner.

a Why do you think his marriage is over? Is there anything in the text that tells us?

b 'Why did all these horrors have pretty names?' What does 'horror' mean in this context?

c Why do you think he feels that 'home is sometimes so sad'?

d What generalisations does he make about Americans compared to New Zealanders?

e How does Hap's first comment, 'I've been all over the Pacific', contrast with the writer's description of the Pacific in the previous paragraph?

f What is Paul Theroux's view of his travelling companions? What kind of people do you think would belong to the Century Club?

g How do you think the writer would define having 'been to' a country?

h 'Tourists don't know where they've been, travellers don't know where they're going.' Are you a traveller or a tourist? How would you distinguish between the two?

PART THREE
Activity holidays

Lead-in

Here's a chance to discover how well you know the other people in your group. Look at the holidays shown in these pictures. Which do you think would best suit each individual? Think of reasons to justify your choices.

Reading technique: predicting

Below is the introduction to an article describing 'activity holidays'. Read the introduction and try to guess what type of activities are available.

If you don't mind getting your hands dirty, putting your back into physical work and sharing fairly basic accommodation with about a dozen strangers, working holidays could be just the thing for you. No special skills or qualifications are usually needed except a sense of humour and a willingness to muck in, although a few breaks do require skilled volunteers who can operate power tools such as chain saws, or who have a higher degree of fitness and stamina.

EXAM FOCUS
(Reading) multiple matching

Now read the article and try to match the facts about different holidays (1–10) with the correct section (A–E). Write the appropriate letter in the boxes.

On which holiday(s) might you:

1 sleep on the floor ☐
2 swim with dolphins ☐
3 meet lots of students ☐
4 work in a shop ☐
5 work with elderly people ☐ ☐
6 get free accommodation ☐ ☐
7 taste home-made beer or wine ☐
8 be a guide ☐
9 help with scientific research ☐
10 eat vegetarian meals ☐ ☐

Choose the most suitable title for each of the five sections from the list A–G.

11 Section A ☐
12 Section B ☐
13 Section C ☐
14 Section D ☐
15 Section E ☐

A Working the land
B No modern conveniences
C The cost of caring
D A breath of fresh air
E In the wings
F All at sea
G Find your feet

A

The British Trust for Conservation Volunteers (BTCV) organises holidays in the UK for groups of a dozen, including a leader trained in the skills of the task undertaken. Members of the group take turns to cook for the whole gang, but it's simple, filling fodder of the meat-and-two-veg variety (with a vegetarian option).

The BTCV keeps the cost of its holidays down by using simple accommodation. There are some twin-bedded rooms, but people often have to share. In some cases, beds are no more than a mat on the floor of the village hall, so sleeping bags may be necessary, as will patience when queuing for the showers.

B

If your holiday budget is limited and bird-watching is a keen hobby, why not become a volunteer warden with the Royal Society for the Protection of Birds (RSPB) at any one of 30 reserves throughout Britain? In return for labour, volunteers get free accommodation with cooking facilities (single people may be asked to share). Some reserves are happy to accept families.

Although serving in the souvenir shop is one possibility, much of the work is quite physical, such as clearing bracken, repairing fences and cleaning out ditches. The best bit is showing visitors around and identifying the birds.

C

Nearly 2,000 people have discovered the merits of Working Weekends on Organic Farms (WWOOFs). Members receive a list of farms, smallholdings or country homes where help is needed. Not all tasks are of the heavy digging variety: they may include helping with the lambing or grape harvest. In return for labour, volunteers get free bed and board, which usually means good home-cooked vegetarian food washed down with home-brew or organic wine.

Many WWOOFs hosts are in remote rural areas, but a pick-up from the nearest station can be arranged if needed. The scheme attracts mainly students, though there are regular WWOOFers in their 60's and some farms accept families with young children.

D

If you want to travel further afield and you've got cash to back up your conscience, an Earthwatch project could be for you. This ingenious institution, founded in America over 20 years ago, provides funding and volunteers for scientific research projects world-wide.

Projects include rain forest research in the Upper Amazon, exploring the Barrier Reef, investigating dolphin intelligence in Hawaii and excavating prehistoric remains on Majorca.

What's more, you don't have to be young and bursting with health to join in. Earthwatch has many volunteers in their 80's, and some expeditions, like the popular mammoth graveyard excavations in Hot Springs, South Dakota, will even suit people with walking difficulties. But, like BTCV breaks, you have to be prepared to muck in, stay in simple accommodation and possibly share the cooking.

The aim of the organisation is to provide scientists with willing volunteers to help in their research. What volunteers pay not only covers bed and board, but also goes towards the cost of their chosen project.

The cost of the project does not include your travelling expenses, however, and once the airfare is included most breaks top one thousand pounds.

E

Tour operators have not been slow to mount the green bandwagon. Some are genuinely caring and make regular donations to wildlife or conservation charities, but few, so far, offer you the chance actually to do something constructive while you're away.

Discover the World, a company which works exclusively with well-known organisations like the World Wildlife Fund for Nature, is offering a few holidays with the Whale and Dolphin Conservation Society.

Holiday-makers can choose to observe whales along the north shore of the Gulf of St Lawrence, Canada, or swim with dolphins off the Bahamas while studying their behaviour. Both holidays cost around one thousand five hundred pounds.

---

1 Read the whole text first as quickly as possible. Try to keep a mental note of the content of each section.

2 Working through numbers 1–10 systematically, go to the section where you think each answer is located. (You need to work extremely quickly so don't start reading the text again from the start!) Don't forget that some numbers require two answers.

3 For questions 11–15 quickly read each section again and try to work out what the main focus of the section is before you match it to one of the titles.

Writing skill: a formal letter and an informal note

1 Imagine you work for a travel agency that acts on behalf of the organisations in the article on page 35. You have received the following
note and an extract from a 'Working Holidays Organisations' brochure
from your secretary.

> We had a few calls today about working holidays. John Williams is the most urgent.
> Can you send him a letter giving him some advice on which holiday(s) would be
> most suitable? Avoid giving him any contact numbers or addresses - we don't want
> to lose any business! I said I'd give Sally Cartwright a ring this afternoon. Could you
> leave a note on my desk with any advice?
>
>   Thanks, Jan

> **John Williams: 33, works in the fire service, can't afford anything too
> expensive. Travelling with wife and a fourteen-year-old son.**
>
> **Sally Cartwright: 64, retired psychologist, interested in wildlife.
> Travelling alone. Wants to get away from Britain.**

2 Look at the 'Working Holidays Organisations' brochure. As quickly as
you can, decide which holidays are suitable for John Williams.

3 Now read the corresponding sections of the article and underline
useful information.

4 Decide on the organisation of your letter and the level of formality
required.

5 Write the letter (about 150 words) and then follow a similar procedure for the note (100 words). You may add your own ideas but do
not alter the given facts.

Working Holidays Organisations

- Discover the World: Tel. 016977 48361. Offers over 20 projects world-wide (4 in the UK)
  Age restrictions vary. Projects range from £295 to £1,000 per person.
- Earthwatch: Tel. 01865 311600. Offers 156 projects world-wide (9 in the UK). Members
  must be over 17. Membership fee: £22. The average cost of a project is £800 per person,
  excluding flights.
- The British Trust for Conservation Volunteers (BTCV): Tel. 01491 39766. Runs 600 breaks
  in England, Northern Ireland and Wales. Volunteers must be over 16. Membership fee:
  £12 (£17 for two or a family). Prices from £28.50 per person for a week full board.
- Working Weekends on Organic Farms (WWOOFs): More than 150 participating
  establishments in the UK. Children under 16 must be accompanied by an adult.
  Membership fee £8. For details write to: 19 Bradford Road, Lewes, Sussex.
- The Royal Society for the Protection of Birds (RSPB): Around 30 participating reserves in
  England, Scotland and Wales. Volunteers must be over 16 or over 13 if accompanied by
  parents. For details write to Sandra Manners, Reserves Management Department, RSPB,
  The Lodge, Sandy, Bedfordshire.

(BBC Holidays)

LANGUAGE AWARENESS
the language of obligation

1 Below is a list of words and phrases that can be used to express varying degrees of obligation. Are they generally used in formal (F) or informal (I) situations or both (B)?

must ( )   you are obliged to ( )   it is advisable ( )
it's best if ( )   to be permitted to ( )   mustn't ( )
ought to ( )   you are required to ( )   have to ( )
needn't ( )   you are recommended to ( )   should ( )
don't need to ( )   it is not necessary to ( )
it is the responsibility of ( )   you should avoid ( )
to be allowed to ( )

2 🔲 You would expect to find examples of informal language in conversational English. Listen to the following dialogue and refer to the tapescript on page 156. Underline all the words and phrases expressing obligation. Do they correspond with your choices above?

3 Use the following information to write advice for people wishing to travel abroad. Write out the sentences in full, and replace the underlined words or phrases with more formal equivalents from the list above. You may need to change the word order.

Example:
CURRENCY Tourists/<u>can't</u>/leave/country/local currency
Tourists are not permitted to leave the country with local currency

VISA <u>Don't need</u>/visas/visits/less than one month
VACCINATIONS Cholera/typhoid/vaccinations/<u>good idea</u>/but/<u>don't have to</u>
DUTY FREE <u>It's up to</u>/individual/not to exceed/duty-free allowance
PHOTOGRAPHY Tourists/<u>not allowed to</u>/take/photographs/restricted/areas
NUDISM <u>It's best to</u> /seek/local information/nude sunbathing
HEALTH Tourists <u>have to</u>/adequate/insurance/obtain/health-care
CAR HIRE <u>It's a good idea</u>/hire/car/before arriving

4 What are the differences in meaning between the following sentences?

a We didn't need to reserve a seat. We knew the train would be empty.
b We needn't have reserved a seat, the train's empty!

a Passengers must confirm their flight 24 hours before departure.
b Don't forget you have to confirm your flight 24 hours before you leave.

a You should arrive at the airport two hours before departure time.
b You should have arrived at the airport two hours before departure time.

a He was allowed to enter the country on a tourist visa last year.
b You could enter the country on a tourist visa before they changed the rules.

Refer to the Grammar Reference (page 167) to check your ideas.

5 Complete the sentences below using the following verbs:

be allowed to   must   have to   need
should   can

a It's been sunny since we left the house. We .... (bring) this umbrella.
b We .... (telephone). We knew they were expecting us.
c You .... (order) the tickets sooner. We'll never get a seat now.
d Don't miss the next train or you .... (walk) home.
e You know the rules, son. You .... (tell) us if you're coming home late.
f My parents were quite easy going. But I .... (do) my fair share of housework.
g I'll always remember the first time I .... (smoke) at home. It was a really strange feeling.
h Excuse me. .... I (open) this window?

EXAM TIP: Identifying the need for formal and informal vocabulary is essential in Paper 2 (Writing) and Paper 3 (English in Use), Section B.

LANGUAGE AWARENESS
reported speech

1 Here is a list of sentences showing the major patterns in reported statements. Can you match them with their grammatical forms?

The book advised her not to drink the tap water.
The agent told him he should arrive at the airport two hours early.
The travel guide pointed out that travellers cheques were difficult to change.
The hotel manager agreed to offer him a different room.
The passenger admitted flying scared her to death.
Her friend congratulated her on choosing such a nice hotel.
He boasted about getting the highest marks.

a verb + gerund
b verb + object + (that) clause
c verb + (that) clause
d verb + object + preposition
e verb + preposition
f verb + infinitive
g verb + object + infinitive

2 In which category would you place the following reporting verbs? Some verbs can be placed in more than one category.

assure	explain	encourage	accuse	offer
threaten	apologise	suggest	deny	accept
remind	promise	invite	beg	agree

3 Fred is suspected of robbing the high street bank. These were some of his comments to the arresting officer:

I'll get my big brother if you keep bothering me.
I wasn't anywhere near the bank this morning.
You planted this money on me.
Look, why don't you let me buy you a drink.
Yes, I know I look suspicious with this mask on.
OK. I know I haven't got a leg to stand on.
Please don't arrest me ... my wife will kill me.
If you let me go, I'll be a good boy.
We could always split the money 50-50.

During the court case, the police officer informed the jury of Fred's comments. Report Fred's statements using the verbs in Exercise 2.

Example: He threatened to get his big brother.

4 🖾 Here are two answerphone messages. Read as you listen.

> Hello, it's M. Laurent here ... Michel Laurent. I'm phoning about my tickets to Paris. I still haven't received them and I'm leaving tomorrow (1). You obviously haven't bothered to take my earlier complaint seriously (2). Your agency gets a lot of business from my company (3), but if my tickets aren't in my office by this afternoon, I'll be taking my custom elsewhere (4). It might be a good idea if you phone me in my office as soon as possible (5).

> Hello, Mr Laurent, it's JJ Travel here. I got your message a few minutes ago. There really isn't anything to worry about. The tickets will be at the check-in desk for you to collect (6). If you'd prefer to have them today, I could get our messenger to deliver them to your office (7). I'm terribly sorry for causing you so much inconvenience (8). Our office was certainly slow in getting them to you (9). I do hope you'll continue to deal with us in future (10).

5 The manager of the travel agency has been told about this complaint. She has asked for a written report of what has happened. Work with a partner and match suitable reporting verbs listed in Exercise 2 to the numbers in the messages. Use the verbs to report the essence of the messages. Remember, it is not necessary to report every word.

(Look out for examples of reported speech in newspaper reports.)

Your review of Unit 3

Vocabulary:

Topic related

General

Reading

Writing

Speaking

Listening

Exam skill

Grammar

UNIT 4

Health Issues

PART ONE
Alternative medicine

Lead-in

What does the term 'alternative medicine' mean to you? Can you name the examples of alternative medicine shown in these pictures?

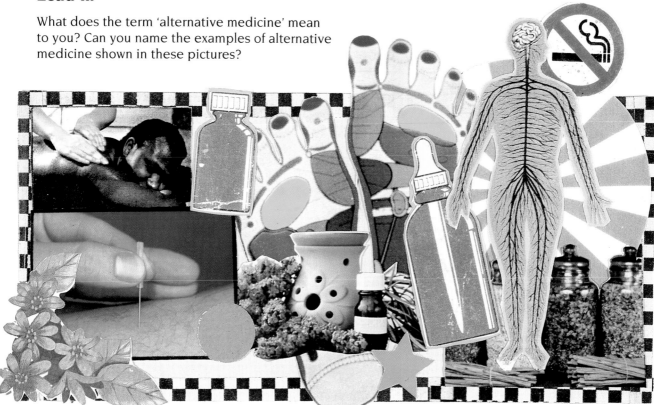

Reading technique: predicting

Imagine you're thinking about having acupuncture. How does this introduction make you feel about it? What information would you expect the rest of the article to contain?

Acupuncture gets to the point

Does the thought of all those long, shiny needles put you off the idea of acupuncture? Well, spare a thought for the earliest patients, who were treated with needles made of stone and later of bone and bamboo. Then came the earthenware needle, which was still used until recently in parts of China, though it has now given way to needles made of specially processed stainless steel, between half an inch and three inches long.

Read the text and then fill in the missing gaps (a–g) with one of the sentences (1–8). You will not need one of the sentences.

The first recorded use of acupuncture was in China 2,000 years ago, where it formed part of an ancient system of medicine.

a

By inserting needles into points just beneath the skin, acupuncture can relieve pain and is believed to help a host of other medical problems.

In major towns throughout China acupuncture still accounts for almost half of all medical treatments.

b

Like other forms of holistic medicine, the therapy aims to treat the whole person, not just the area where the symptoms occur, and is traditionally used in conjunction with herbal medicine, dietary therapy and massage.

The system is based on the belief that the body has two types of energy flowing through it, called yin and yang. Yin is the female force representing darkness, sedateness and coldness and is regarded as negative.

c

The Chinese think good health depends on the right balance of yang and yin, and that any imbalance in these energy flows can be corrected by inserting needles at certain points to unblock, lower or increase the flow.

d

Western practitioners are likely to apply more scientific terminology than yin and yang, but there is still much debate about exactly how acupuncture works. Many orthodox doctors believe it acts on the central nervous system, stimulating the body to heal itself.

e

'This modifies the patient's perception of pain,' says the British Medical Acupuncture Society.

In China acupuncture is used instead of modern anaesthetics, though in Britain it is more likely to be used in hospitals for extra pain relief during childbirth or to relieve chronic pain such as arthritis.

f

The endorphins theory doesn't explain why the treatment also affects the functions of the liver and gall bladder, or helps with depression, allergic reactions such as asthma and hay fever, and problems relating to the bowel.

The same stimulation that gets the endorphins working is believed to function as an anti-inflammatory mechanism and to revitalise the immune system.

g

1 But that figure could be as high as 80% in rural districts.

2 These points lie along the 12 invisible energy channels, or meridians, that are said to be connected to the body's various organs.

3 To balance this, yang is stimulating, warm, masculine and is regarded as positive.

4 But acupuncturists believe it goes further than pain relief.

5 One theory is that it does this by reaching the fine network of nerve pathways that run throughout the body.

6 Trials in China and the US have shown that it stimulates the brain to produce endorphins, or chemicals that act as natural painkillers.

7 The material used to make needles in China has become much more sophisticated.

8 But these days interest in it is worldwide.

1 When you have checked your answers, discuss what strategies you used to complete the activity. Record them at the end of the unit.

2 Were any of your questions or concerns answered?

🔲 Listening technique: global understanding

You are going to hear an interview with a trained acupuncturist. The main topics of the interview are listed opposite but are not in the correct order. As you listen, write a number in the relevant box to indicate the order in which you hear the topics mentioned.

a   patients she has treated ☐
b   future career options ☐
c   receiving treatment herself ☐
d   her training ☐
e   differences from Western medicine ☐
f   when her interest in acupuncture began ☐

🔲 Listening technique: specific information

Opposite are some extracts from a letter written by Margaret to an organisation which gives grants to people interested in setting up their own business. Unfortunately, Margaret's secretary, who typed the letter, has made several factual mistakes. Listen to the interview. How many can you find? Missing information does not count.

> ... acupuncture has helped me with several problems: stress, anxiety, confidence ...
> Alternative medicine can have side effects, but does help treat the person as a whole ...
> ... and basically makes you feel full of energy.
> ... and recent patients who I have cured include a woman who had Parkinson's Disease.
> I have received treatment myself in China ...
> It was during my stay in China that I started my training.
> I have completed a three-year course in acupuncture ...
> One aspect of the course examined whether acupuncture can treat people of different sizes and shapes.
> In the future I hope to train in homeopathy and aromatherapy ...
> ... and a rural clinic would allow me to be free from the stresses of modern life.

Vocabulary development: some common expressions

1 Fill in the missing words in the following sentences with 'sick', 'ill' or 'healthy', or one of the derivatives of these words.

2 For each of the expressions write your own explanation in English. Do you have similar expressions in your own language?

See Language awareness: defining and non-defining relative clauses

a   After he caught the flu he was off _____ for two weeks.
b   When I got married I promised to love my wife in _____ and in health.
c   I'm not keen on going to parties where I don't know anybody. I feel rather _____ at ease.
d   It's considered impolite to speak _____ of the dead.
e   My mother always used to say that 'Early to bed, early to rise, makes a man _____ , wealthy and wise'.
f   After drinking too much alcohol the previous night, she woke up feeling as _____ as a dog.
g   How are you these days?
    Not so bad. At my age you can't expect to be in rude _____ .
h   I hate the way he never does any work in the office. He makes me _____ .

PART TWO
Smoking

Lead-in

Which of the following statements do you most identify with?

- All smokers are selfish.
- Smokers should be congratulated for giving the government so much money in tax.

Reading technique: predicting

1 The following words and phrases all appear in the article below. Read through the list in order to predict the content of the text. Try to make a full sentence using each expression.

... intelligent people ...   ... devastating effects ...   ... continue to smoke ...
... bad habits ...   ... addiction ...   ... 65% ...
... poor success ...   ... nicotine replacement ...   ... good investment ...

2 Now skim read the text quickly (about one minute) to see if your predictions were correct. What strategy did you use in Unit 2 to skim read?

Quit while you're ahead

1 Question: which group of people can improve their health, fitness and longevity at a stroke? Answer: smokers who quit. Giving up tobacco leads to a dramatic and almost immediate improvement in their health – so why don't more smokers give up?

2 If you are a non-smoker you may be bewildered as to why intelligent people continue with a habit that they know has devastating effects on their health. If you are a smoker, you are probably about to turn the page. But this article is not another nag, it's an explanation of why three people in ten continue to smoke.

Don't mention addiction ...

3 The first study of smokers who quit was published in 1958. Not surprisingly, those who smoked fewer cigarettes found it easier to give up. It was ten years before the subject was researched again, but in the Seventies and Eighties interest intensified, and more than 200 studies into quitting have now been published.

4 In the late Seventies, expert opinions were sharply polarised. Psychologists believed smoking was a bad habit that would respond to therapy, while scientists insisted it was a simple addiction. In the Eighties, health educators started to mention the A word – but they were reluctant to emphasise it, because 'addict' conjures up an image of a helpless victim.

5 So they chose the message that you could quit smoking simply by stubbing out your last cigarette and throwing the packet away. They avoided a close examination of the relationship between the smoker and the cigarette and if the A word was mentioned, it carried the proviso that only a few smokers were addicted.

6 But moral fibre alone was not enough to inspire people to give up. It worked for some, but then every kind of technique from hypnotherapy to herbal teas, works for a few people. Unfortunately, 65% of those who quit will relapse within a year or two. This poor success rate has persuaded most – though not all – of those who want to help smokers that the A word is deeply relevant to the problem.

7 There was another good reason for underplaying addiction: apart from its negative connotations, little could be done about it. This has now changed with the introduction of nicotine replacement therapies. These provide the drug that the smokers crave, but in a clean form. It is not the nicotine but the tar and other harmful chemicals found in tobacco that kills 150,000 Britons every year. Smokers can now buy their therapy from their pharmacist in the form of nicotine chewing gums or skin patches that deliver decreasing doses of nicotine through the skin over a three month period. The 16-hour patches can be removed at bedtime, and other patches provide 24-hour cover. No one yet knows which is more effective.

8 Ironically, the gum and patches cost about the same as 20 cigarettes a day – although the three-month treatment is a very good investment if it works. In a few years smokers will also be able to buy nicotine sprays and inhalers, which will deliver their fix even faster.

... and don't forget pleasure

9 Health educators and clinic doctors are unlikely to prove unsuccessful if they treat smoking as just an addiction and try to forget the P factor – that smoking is also pleasurable. The addiction theory suggests that smokers light their first cigarette of the day to enjoy a buzz from the nicotine, and that every subsequent cigarette is smoked to avoid the effects of nicotine withdrawal.

10 But smokers enjoy their cigarettes and light up to augment other social pleasures such as having a coffee after a meal, relaxing after lovemaking, drinking with friends or simply to have a few quiet moments to themselves. They use cigarettes to break the ice when they meet someone new, or as a way of sharing a treat with a friend.

11 A cigarette smoker takes 10 drags from every cigarette, each one of which delivers a dose of nicotine to the brain within seven seconds. Smokers on 20 a day raise their hands to their mouths 200 times a day, 1,400 times a week and 73,000 times a year. Smoking is an addiction, a pleasure and a very strong habit.

(BBC Good Health)

Reading technique: summary skills

1 Read the text more closely and match the following headings with the appropriate paragraph (1–11).

   A Rapid results
   B Opposing views
   C An average smoker
   D Money well spent
   E Addiction more than a bad habit
   F Everyday pleasures

2 Write a heading of your own for each of the five remaining paragraphs. Compare your suggestions with those of a partner.

Reading technique: comprehension

1 Form two groups. Group A: look at paragraphs 1–6, Group B: look at paragraphs 7–11.

2 Look back at Unit 3 (page 31) and read again the explanation of how multiple choice questions are designed. You will need to refer to the tapescript as well. When you're ready design a set of multiple choice questions on your text.

3 Try out your questions on the other group.

See Language awareness: passive or active?

Listening technique: specific information

1 Listen to Nazir talking about his latest attempt at giving up smoking. Decide if the following statements are true or false:

   a He gave up for more than nine weeks.
   b He changed certain daily habits.
   c Using patches completely stopped him wanting a cigarette.
   d He couldn't find a chemist on the Monday morning.
   e He smoked eight cigarettes from a pack and then threw the rest away
   f He's now smoking two or three cigarettes a day.

2 Does Nazir's experience confirm the argument in 'Quit While You're Ahead' that smoking is more than simply a habit that needs to be broken?

3 Has the evidence in this unit made the non-smokers in the group any more sympathetic towards smokers?

Writing skill: a magazine article

You have been asked to write an article (of around 250 words) for a student magazine, giving advice on how to give up smoking.

1 Working with a partner, select what you feel is appropriate information from the article 'Quit While You're Ahead ' and the interview with Nazir. Add any other tips of your own.

2 Consider your audience and discuss the level of formality required. Then begin organising your ideas into paragraphs.

3 Your article needs to attract the readers' attention right from the start. You can do this by thinking of a catchy title and writing an interesting opening sentence. Which of the four opening sentences below do you find the most attention-grabbing?

   a These days smoking is a great problem for young people. They are putting their health at risk …

   b Does your partner turn away when you try to kiss him or her? Do you get short of breath whenever you take the stairs instead of the lift?

   c If you want to save your life, then continue reading …

   d Doctors have argued for years that smoking is bad for you …

4 Now you are ready to write your article. Ask your partner to read and comment on your first draft. Would it appeal to young people?

PART THREE
Stress and anxiety

Lead-in

1 Do you ever suffer from stress? Try the following quiz taken from a book on fitness called *The Y Plan* to test your current level of stress. Give yourself points for each answer:

Never = 0
Rarely = 1
Sometimes = 2
Often = 3

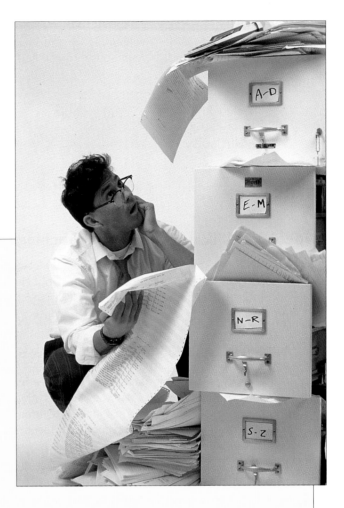

HEALTH

How often do you:

– feel run down or tired?

– have difficulty in sleeping?

– have stomach complaints?

– have back and body pains?

– have headaches/migraines?

– feel a tightness in the shoulders/jaw?

WORK

How often do you:

– have frustrated/bad relations with colleagues?

– feel vulnerable to criticism?

– have a sense of failure?

– feel indecisive/overwhelmed by job demands?

– feel a lack of enthusiasm for your job?

– feel you need more holidays?

PERSONAL

How often do you:

– feel a lack of enthusiasm and confidence?

– feel impatience with the family, flatmates and friends?

– become irritated by small things?

– feel pressure from people around you?

– feel guilt about work-time distracting from family and social life?

– have feelings of panic?

– grip a steering wheel hard?

– take alcohol or drugs?

Check your scores with the key on p 146

2 Compare your score with others in the group. Do those with high scores have a noticeably different lifestyle to those with low scores?

Exploring pronunciation: word stress

Look at the following list of words taken from the stress quiz. Working with a partner, sort them out according to where the main word stress occurs.

difficulty	frustrated	vulnerable	indecisive	overwhelmed	anxious
enthusiasm	confidence	impatience	irritated	pressure	distracting

Example:

1st syllable ▭ difficulty	2nd syllable	3rd syllable

Speaking skill: discussion and reaching agreement

1 The following extracts are from an article which appeared in the *Financial Times*. Do you agree with what the report says about the main causes of stress in the workplace? How sympathetic are employers to the issue of stress at work in your country?

Stress at work seen as a growing health risk

Stress at work is increasing sharply and should be recognised officially, a report urged yesterday ... Recent research from Manchester University showed that 90 million working days a year were being lost in the UK through stress ... The report by Professor Cox, an occupational psychologist, identified excessive periods of repetitive work, lack of management support and demanding work schedules as contributory causes of stress.

2 Are some professions significantly more stressful than others? Consider the following list of jobs and indicate the level of stress you think might be suffered by someone in each profession. Give them a stress rating of 1–10, giving reasons for your ratings.
(1 = little or no stress, 10 = dangerous amount of stress)

- secretary
- manager of a national sports team
- cleaner
- managing director of a company
- bus or train driver
- unskilled factory worker
- full-time housewife
- teacher
- politician
- surgeon
- other (add your own ideas)

3 Now share your opinions with a small group and see if you can reach agreement on which jobs are the most stressful and why.

EXAM FOCUS
(English in Use, Section B) proofreading skills

In most of the lines in the following text there is either a spelling or punctuation error. Write the correctly spelt word or show the correct punctuation. The first two lines have been completed as an example.

Coping with stress

0	Stress is often called a 20th century ilness but it has always been	_illness_
0	with us under different names. These days we regard stress as a	✓
1	neccessary evil of modern living, but stress is not negative – without	_____
2	it we would not enjoy some of the high points in life: The anticipation	_____
3	before a date, the tension before an important match, the organisation	_____
4	before a party – all these situations produce stress but, provided you	_____
5	can control it and not the other way round you will feel stimmulated,	_____
6	not worn down. Those situations have an obvious positive aspect.	_____
7	However sitting in a train that is late, being stuck in traffic, working	_____
8	to a tight deadline are much harder to manage or controll.	_____
9	Stress is now recognised as a medical problem and, as a significant	_____
10	factor in causing coronary heart desease, high blood pressure, high	_____
11	blood fats and high cholesterol count's. Patients are often unwilling	_____
12	to admit to stress problems, because they feel they are a form of	_____
13	social failure. Common signs of stress are increased tiredness,	_____
14	irritability and innability to cope.	_____

Listening technique: note taking

1 You are about to hear a doctor talking about the problem of anxiety. Before you listen, make a note on a piece of paper of the following headings:

Physical signs of anxiety

Dealing with anxiety

How anxiety can develop into a problem

The causes of anxiety

2 Now listen to the interview, taking notes under the appropriate headings. Be careful, as the headings are not in the correct order.

3 When you've finished the exercise compare your answers with a partner.

Writing skill: an advice leaflet

1 You have been asked to write a leaflet of around 250 words entitled 'Stress at work and how to cope with it'. You must include information on the following: causes, possible ill effects, ways of treating stress and anxiety.

2 Working with a partner, use the notes you made in the listening exercise, as well as your own ideas, and decide the content of your leaflet. Try to focus on specific audiences: e.g. business men and women – try a weekend in a health farm; computer operators – take regular breaks from the screen, do simple exercises.

3 Which tone(s) from the following list would be the most appropriate for your audience?

- light-hearted and humorous
- practical
- sympathetic and reassuring

LANGUAGE AWARENESS
defining and non-defining relative clauses

1 Working with a partner, see how quickly you can solve the problem below:

Four women decided to improve their health by taking up sporting pastimes, and within a month each found she had achieved something. Can you work out each woman's occupation, the sport she chose and what she gained from it?

Clues:

a The woman who pulled a muscle wasn't the cyclist.
b The cyclist, who broke her wrist, isn't a tax inspector.
c Mary Yates, who is a secretary, hates golf.
d The broken wrist wasn't sustained by Alma Nixon, who hates boats.
e The person who pulled a muscle was the golfer.
f The woman who dislocated her shoulder was rowing a boat.
g The woman who works as a tax inspector is Ivy Thorpe.
h Gail Scott, who isn't a lawyer, took up tennis and won a silver cup.

	Alma	Gail	Ivy	Mary
Tax inspector				
Secretary				✓
Lawyer				
Housewife				
Cyclist				
Golf				
Rowing				
Tennis				
Silver cup				
Pulled muscle				
Broken wrist				
Dislocated shoulder				

2 In which of the clues above could 'that' replace 'who'?
What does the use of commas in b, c, d and h suggest about the information in these clues?

3 Examine the sentences below. Then summarise the main differences between defining and non-defining relative clauses by completing the table below.

a He's the acupuncturist (that/who) you use, isn't he?
b A rapid rise in blood pressure, which can result from too much exercise, could be dangerous.
c I was told to stop smoking, which really depressed me.
d The gym (that/which) I belong to is in the centre of town.
e Teachers, who often work long hours, can show symptoms of stress.
f Teachers that/who often work long hours can show symptoms of stress.

	a	b	c	d	e	f
necessary information	✓					
extra information						
commas						
use of 'that'	✓					
omission of pronoun	✓					
defining or non-defining	*def.*					

4 Can you complete the sentence below? Refer to the Grammar Reference section on page 168, if necessary.

The relative pronoun can usually be omitted in defining relative clauses unless ...

5 Look again at the article on acupuncture on page 41. How many examples of defining and non-defining relative clauses can you find?

6 Using the information in the table above, fill in the gaps in the following text, supplying defining or non-defining pronouns and commas where required. If you think the relative pronoun can be missed out ... miss it out!

Mary .... is a secretary took up cycling. The injury .... Alma sustained was caused whilst playing golf. The woman .... wrist was broken was a secretary. Mary .... took up cycling was the woman .... broke her wrist. Gail has a silver cup .... she won playing tennis. Ivy's dislocated shoulder .... she got rowing a boat is very painful. The sport .... Mary hates most is golf. Gail won a trophy .... probably made the other three women rather jealous. She won the cup around the time .... Ivy was nursing her dislocated shoulder.

EXAM TIP: Useful for Paper 3 (English in Use), Section C (expanded notes).

LANGUAGE AWARENESS
passive or active?

1   Look at paragraphs 3 and 4 of 'Quit While You're Ahead'. Can you explain why the passive is used in one but the active in the other?

2   Decide whether the following statements are correct or could be improved by using either active or passive constructions.

   a   Baby given birth to by 58-year-old woman.
   b   Farm labourers pick the coffee beans and send them to the processing plant.
   c   Drinks will be served during the interval.
   d   If you don't pay your bill we will take further action against you.
   e   Unfortunately, the Government will have to raise interest rates next year.
   f   Unemployment has been reduced from 3 million to 1 million by the Government.
   g   I reckon the match will be won by Italy.
   h   Everyone involved in the case believes the thieves escaped in a stolen car. (careful!)
   i   People who buy this food should consume it within 24 hours of the date of purchase.
   j   You will be met at the airport by a representative of our company.
   k   Dad? Any chance of me being met at the station by you?
   l   Sorry son, I can't. A mechanic's repairing my car.

3   Where would you expect to find the following statements?

   a   You will be notified of our decision in due course.
   b   CAUTION! Building work being carried out
   c   This product should be refrigerated after opening.
   d   Finally, the end product is packaged and sent to retailers.
   e   Concorde Hijacked

4   Can you underline the passive forms in the statements above and match them to the following uses? Some can be used more than once.

   When the agent is unimportant such as when describing a process or experiment
   The agent is obvious or not known
   The agent is people in general
   To shift the emphasis in the statement
   Making the statement more formal

5   Look back at Exercise 2. Do you still agree with your original opinions?

6   Working in pairs, how many ideas can you come up with for the following situations? You must, of course, use passive structures – appropriately! One point for every suitable sentence. Your colleagues can act as judges.

   By the year 2050 ...
   Two hundred years ago ...
   At present, within a one-kilometre radius from where I'm sitting ...
   In a hundred years' time ...
   So far in my life ...

EXAM TIP: The ability to manipulate active and passive structures is a useful skill for producing formal and informal language in Paper 2 (Writing) and Paper 3 (English in Use), Section B.

Your review of Unit 4

Vocabulary:

Topic related

General

Reading

Writing

Speaking

Listening

Exam skill

Grammar

UNIT 5

The World of Language

PART ONE
Foreign accent syndrome

Lead-in

How can you tell when you are talking to someone who is not a native speaker of your language? Do you think that your language is difficult for foreigners to pronounce? Are there any typical mistakes that they make?

Reading technique: skimming

1 You are going to read an extract from a book called *Talk, Talk, Talk*. The extract has the title 'Foreign Accent Syndrome'. Read only the first sentence (i.e. the topic sentence) of each paragraph. Is the text about:

a the problems of speaking English with a foreign accent?
b how damage to the brain can affect the way you speak?
c people's attitudes to different regional accents within their own country?
d none of the above?
e not sure yet?

2 Read the text in full as quickly as you can. In which paragraph does the writer first tell you exactly what Foreign Accent Syndrome is?

1 In the world of language unusual individuals turn up all the time: sometimes they have surprising language abilities, like the young man in England who, although not capable of taking care of himself on a daily basis, is nonetheless conversant in sixteen different languages. Sadly, most of the individuals whom researchers think are worth noting have an impairment that by the deficit it creates tells us something about how language normally works in the brain. But occasionally there are cases in the medical literature so odd that it is difficult to see what can be made of them. That's the case with a condition called Foreign Accent Syndrome.

2 There have been a handful of people with FAS identified over the last ninety years. These are the people who, when they resume speaking after a slight stroke or some other injury to the brain, speak with a foreign accent! And these are not just English speakers who sound as though they are just learning the language as they recover. There were, early in the century, a Frenchman who, after a stroke, spoke with an Alsatian accent, and a Czech butcher who began to speak with a Polish accent. A 30-year-old Norwegian woman suffered a head injury during an air-raid in 1941, and picked up a German accent. There have been Chinese, New England and even English accents in native Spanish speakers, although the majority of accents seem to be German or Scandinavian. Some of the people affected lose their accent after a while, some don't.

3 A typical case was reported in 1990 by Dean Tippett, a doctor at the University of Maitland. A 33-year-old American man was admitted with an attack of slurred speech and unsteadiness. But for the first month after this stroke he spoke with what the doctor called a 'Nordic' accent.

4 Everything else, including reading, writing, comprehension and the ability to talk fluently, was normal. But he had this accent, and the rhythm and tone of his speech had become altered: it was sing-song, with misplaced stresses on words, and inappropriate tones, rising at the ends of sentences instead of falling. So he would say, 'canoe' with the stress on the first syllable: 'CA-noo'. Pronunciations were wrong: 'hill' became 'heel', 'quite' became 'quiet', and he would stick an 'a' in unusual places like, 'How are you today a?' He even substituted 'd' for 'th' as in 'dat' for 'that'. Put all these together, and you can see where his speech would have taken on what would seem to be a Scandinavian sound, at least to English speakers. Apparently this patient enjoyed having an accent, and just as well, because he didn't seem to have any control over it.

5 What's going on here? Are these people revisiting an earlier life in a foreign country or what? Obviously linguists don't put *that* forward as an explanation for FAS. In fact, it seems clear that these people are not really speaking with a true accent, but rather that these temporary changes in speech are misidentified by listeners as a foreign accent, because there are one or two features that remind us of accented English. People with true foreign accents hear the difference right away.

The human brain has a great capacity for taking in unusual information and making some sort of sense of it, and it's probably true that this altered speech is closest to English as spoken with a foreign accent, so that's how we perceive it. We are very acute at hearing accented speech – one study showed that as little as twenty thousandths of a second of French-accented English is all we need to hear to know there's an accent there.

6 One of those features that would make this kind of speech sound to us like Nordic or German accented English would be changes in vowel sounds ('hill' to 'heel'). There are probably others too: this sort of speech contains grammatical errors and some deletions of syllables, mistakes that are typical of someone whose first language is not English, and this would tend to confirm any perception that there is an accent present, especially since the rhythm and tone changes make the speech more singsong, again something that isn't typical of a native English speaker.

7 The damage to the brain that causes Foreign Accent Syndrome is usually in the left hemisphere, but there doesn't seem to be any one location that causes it. The odd thing is that it happens to relatively young people – two thirds of the cases reported have been under forty-five – yet the strokes that usually cause it are very rare in that age group. It might be that Foreign Accent Syndrome is what we hear as the injured brain recovers from a stroke, an ability that has been lost in an older person.

(Jay Ingram: *Talk, Talk, Talk*)

Reading technique: finding the main ideas

1 Read the text carefully and decide if the points listed below are Main Ideas (MI) in the passage or merely Supporting Details (SD). There are three of each.

 a Medical literature covers many odd cases of people with unusual language abilities. (paragraph 1)
 b A Frenchman began speaking French with an Alsatian accent after his stroke. (paragraph 2)
 c An American began to speak with a Scandinavian accent. (paragraph 3)
 d We are very quick to detect foreign accents in other people's speech. (paragraph 5)
 e A feature of Germanic English is to pronounce 'hill' as 'heel'. (paragraph 6)
 f Two thirds of FAS cases are under the age of 45. (paragraph 7)

2 For each of the Supporting Details above, find and write down the Main Idea.

3 Comment on the style of the text.

4 Read paragraphs 4 and 6 again. You will find four types of pronunciation mistake made by foreign learners of English. Are these typical of your own errors when speaking English? Do you make other errors? Ask your partner or teacher or someone outside the classroom to help you analyse your speech.

Vocabulary development: words for talking about language

1 How many words in the text can you find that are related specifically to pronunciation?

2 Complete the following common expressions using the verb 'say', 'speak' or 'talk'.

 a Come on now. Don't hold back if you have something to say. .... your mind.
 b OK, look at the camera. Ready? .... cheese.
 c You can .... until you're blue in the face. He'll never listen to you.
 d Just .... the word and I'll be round immediately.
 e .... sense! How can we afford another holiday this year?
 f OK. The last chocolate. Who wants it? .... now or forever hold your peace.
 g Darling, can we forget the business for the weekend? You're always .... shop.
 h Our new manager's rather a disappointment, to .... the least.

Writing skill: writing a summary

1 Being able to distinguish between the main ideas and supporting details is a useful skill for summary writing. Go back to the text and highlight the main ideas only, and delete as many of the supporting details as you can.

Example:
<u>In the world of language unusual individuals turn up all the time: sometimes with surprising language abilities</u>, like the young man in England who, although not capable of taking care of himself on a daily basis, is nonetheless conversant in sixteen different languages. Sadly, <u>most of the individuals whom researchers think are worth noting</u> ...

2 Now try to combine the main ideas as economically as you can and by using your own words where possible (paraphrasing).

Example:
There are many cases of strange people with unique language abilities. They are of interest to researchers mainly because ...

3 Now write a summary of the whole text of around 150 words.

4 Compare your summary with someone else's in the class. Did you agree on what the main ideas in the text were? How well did each of you paraphrase the writer's words?

PART TWO
Sign language

Lead-in

How good are you at using your hands to communicate? Using the following manual alphabet developed for the deaf, practise spelling your
own name. When you are really confident, try spelling your home
address (road, home town) for your partner to write down.

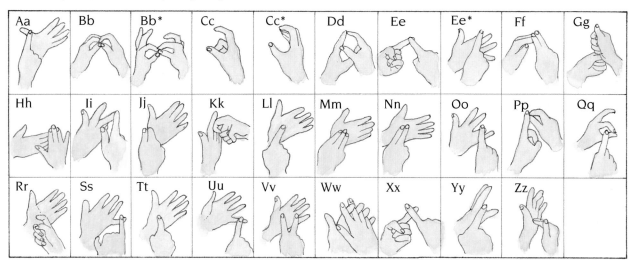

*(This is an alternative version to help fast signing.)

Listening technique:
comprehension and inference

1 You are going to hear an extract from a lecture by Peter Llewellyn-
   Jones, a famous sign-language interpreter. Listen to part one and
   say if the following statements are True (T) or False (F) or if he
   Doesn't Say (DS).

   a Peter had always wanted to work with deaf people.
   b Some of his own relations were deaf.
   c He didn't find his job as a social worker very fulfilling.
   d He used to help deaf people in everyday situations.
   e He now works for the British Deaf Association.
   f He plans to continue in his present job.

2 Correct any false statements.

Listening technique: following instructions

Listen to part two of the tape where Peter goes on to describe
a warm-up exercise that he does when teaching people sign
language. Try to follow his instructions.

Exploring pronunciation: marker words

1 You will notice that when Peter is guiding you through the activity he uses a number of marker words such as 'Okay', 'Right', 'Yeah'.
Listen to the tape again and mark the intonation of the underlined words with a rising tone ➛ or a falling one ➛ . Check your answers with a partner.

Example: a   I want all of you to stand up. Okay. Stand up.

b <u>Right</u>. Now I want you to imagine ...
c <u>Okay</u>. Now I want you to be able to see this clearly.
d <u>Right</u>. Now this is a very simple task.
e All I want you to do is to make a cup of tea. <u>Okay</u>. Something you probably do every morning.
f <u>Right</u>. Visualise it, see it on the surface.
g Is there enough room inside your fist for that handle to fit? <u>Yeah</u>?
   <u>Okay</u>.

2 Which intonation pattern, rising or falling, does he use to check his audience's understanding? What is the purpose of the other pattern?

3 What marker words do you use in your own language?

Listening technique: specific information

1 You are going to hear two students attempting an information gap exercise. Student A is trying to explain to Student B how to organise the shapes opposite into the same arrangement as his own. As you listen for the first time decide how well Student A uses marker words.

2 Cut out the following shapes from a piece of paper. Now listen to the recording again and follow Student A's instructions. When you're finished check your pattern with the answer on page 146.

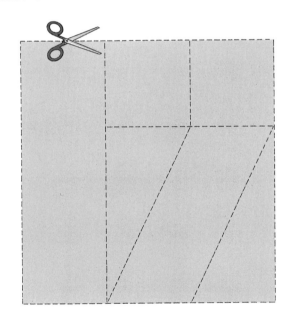

Speaking skill: giving information to complete a task

Work in pairs. Student A – arrange the shapes into your own pattern, without Student B seeing what you're doing of course! When you're ready, describe your pattern to Student B. Try to use marker words, either to check that your partner understands or to signal that you've completed a particular instruction. When you've finished, swap roles and try again.

See Language awareness: formal and informal language

EXAM FOCUS
(English in Use,
Section B)
informal to formal
writing

Read the following informal memo about a forthcoming presentation by Susan Greenaway of the Deaf Institute. Use the
information to complete the formal announcement using one
or two words in each gap. The words you need do not occur
in the informal message.

To: Academic staff

From: John

Just had a chat with Susan Greenaway from the Deaf
Institute. She's agreed to do a talk about teaching
deaf students at the university. She reckons it will
only last about 1 hour and will look at all sorts of
things to do with good teaching practice. She'll start
off with a video about personal delivery: how best to
speak, where to stand in the classroom and that kind
of thing. Then she'll go on to talk about using visual
aids. There'll be a bit on organising activities in lectures and seminars. She'll even give us some advice
about choosing the best rooms. Sounds useful,
doesn't it? She'll finish off with a quick session on
working with an interpreter if she's got time. Shall
we make it next Friday at 12.00? Obviously the talk
won't cost anything to get in. You can get hold of
Susan on Cambridge 453656 (before the 14th) if you
have any suggestions about anything else you need
help with.

P.S. I'll give Catering a ring to see if they can put on
lunch for us.

Presentation by Susan Greenaway
Teaching Strategies to Use with Deaf Students
Friday 14th May, 12pm, The Council Room

Susan Greenaway of the Deaf Institute will be
(a) _____ a presentation on the problems involved in
(b) _____ students with hearing difficulties. The presentation will last (c) _____ 1 hour and will explore
(d) _____ aspects of teaching pedagogy. The presentation will (e) _____ with a video on personal delivery.
There will (f) _____ a brief talk on using visual aids in
the classroom and some useful ideas on the organisation of
lecture and seminar activities. (g) _____ examining the
way teaching accommodation can enhance good teaching
practice, Susan will (h) _____ with a discussion on the
question of interpreting in the classroom (subject to there
being (i) _____ time). All academic staff are welcome.
There will be no (j) _____ for (k) _____ to the session, and a buffet lunch will (l) _____ for all who
attend.

For further details (m) _____ Dr Greenaway on
453656.

1 Read both texts carefully and compare the different styles. How is
   the informal, chatty style in the first text achieved?

2 Underline the words or phrases in the informal text that correspond
   to the gaps in the more formal text.

3 Work with a partner to think of more formal equivalents of the
   expressions in the memo. Compare your suggestions with others in
   the group.

PART THREE
Body language

Lead-in

1 What do you think each of the following gestures might mean?

2 What are the most common gestures in your own country? Are there any that you think tourists should be aware of to avoid misunderstanding?

Reading technique: scanning

1 You are going to read an advertisement that takes a light-hearted look at the possible consequences of such misunderstandings. Read the text and complete the following table. Put a tick in the box if the effect of the gesture is positive or flattering, a cross if the effect is negative or offensive and a question mark if you're not sure. Try to do this in no more than five minutes.

Gesture	The effect on a person from			
Touching lower eyelid	Saudi Arabia ☐	South America ☐		
Tugging ear lobe	Spain ☐	Greece ☐	Portugal ☐	Malta ☐
Thumbs up	Sardinia ☐	Britain ☐		

2 In which countries does this gesture mean the following?

'A-OK'

'money'

'I'll kill you'

'zero'

BODY LANGUAGE

I'm never bored at airports. Quite the reverse. I visit them like other people go to the ballet. To a Manwatcher, there's nothing more fascinating than observing citizens of different countries *mingling* and exchanging body signals. And nowhere is the performance so enjoyable as at Heathrow, the world's top international airport.

Day and night they pour in, a cast of 36 million a year from every corner of the globe. Where else but Heathrow could you hope to see Brazilians rubbing shoulders with Brahmins. Poles with Polynesians, Madagascans with Minnesotans and Neapolitans with Nepalese?

Each nationality has its own language of posture and gesture. But since these body-lingoes are often mutually incomprehensible, an innocent gesture made in an airport lounge may well be an *unwitting* insult.

Something in your eye? Think before you touch the lower lid. If a Saudi sees you, he'll think you're calling him stupid but a South American señorita will think you're *making a pass at* her.

There is no greater insult you can offer a Greek than to thrust your palms towards his face. This gesture, called the 'moutza', is descended from the old Byzantine custom of smearing filth from the gutter in the faces of criminals as they were led in chains through the city. So vile is this insult that in Greece even the Churchillian Victory-V is taboo, as it looks like a half 'moutza'.

It's so easy to give offence. Suppose a passenger asks at the Information Desk where he should go to pay his airport tax. Now the good news is that at Heathrow, unlike many airports I could name, passengers don't pay any taxes*. But just as the Information Assistant begins to say so, she is *assailed by* a tremendous itch and tugs at her earlobe.

Astonishing though it may seem, this simple gesture means four different things in four different Mediterranean countries. Depending on his nationality, the Assistant has offered the passenger the following insult:
TO A SPANIARD 'You rotten *scrounger.*'
TO A GREEK 'You'd better watch it mate.'
TO A MALTESE 'You're a sneaky little so-and-so.'
Only a Portuguese (to whom the gesture signifies something *ineffably* wonderful) would hang around long enough to hear the answer.

Happily, I can report that BAA's information staff are trained in body language.

A Sardinian woman asks if it is easy to find a taxi at Heathrow. The answer she gets is a *cheery* British thumbs up. Immediately, she *clonks* the unfortunate man with her handbag for making such a devastatingly obscene suggestion. This is why, incidentally, it's inadvisable to hitch-hike in Sardinia.

Isn't there at least one truly international gesture? Don't bet on it! A Japanese asks an American passenger whether Heathrow has a luggage trolley service. It has. And, as it happens, this service is not only first class, but FREE! So the Yank replies with the famous 'A-OK' ring gesture. But to the Japanese this signifies 'money' and he concludes there is a large charge for service.

Meanwhile, a Tunisian on-looker thinks the American is telling the Japanese that he is a worthless rogue and he is going to kill him.

The ring gesture can have further meanings. A Frenchman has just read a BAA advertisement. Glancing around the restaurant in Terminal 4, he remarks wonderingly to his wife, ' You know how much zis aeroport cost the British taxpayer? Not a sou.' And he makes the finger and thumb ring which to him means zero.

Of course I am exaggerating to make a point, but I do find it astonishing that Heathrow receives only 8 complaints per 100,000 passengers. Keeping the lid on this simmering rum-punch of international emotions must take every bit as much diplomatic skill as running the United Nations.

But even if you're never treated to such a choreography of misunderstandings, the Heathrow ballet is never dull. Eyes peeled next time you're there. And if you spot anything really unusual, like the South American Goitre Sign, or the Hawaiian Missing Bottle Waggle, do write and let me know.

The world's leading international airport group.

*Since November 1994 Heathrow has charged a departure tax.

Vocabulary development: guessing unknown words

Match the following words or phrases from the text (in italics) with the correct definition in the right - hand column. Be careful, as there are three extra definitions.

1 mingling	a someone living at the expense of others
2 unwitting	b attacked by
3 making a pass at [slang]	c someone who is kind
4 assailed by	d lively, merry
5 scrounger [slang]	e unintentional
6 ineffably	f kisses
7 cheery	g mixing
8 clonks [slang]	h indescribably
	i making (possibly unwelcome) sexual advances to
	j hits
	k followed by

See **Language awareness: expressing time**

Speaking skill: giving a talk

1 How does a good speaker make use of his/her voice and body language? Categorise the following points as either good or bad public speaking techniques.
(There may be some debate about these points!)

- speaking quickly
- pointing your finger at the listeners
- looking directly at your audience
- lowering your eyebrows (frowning)
- making a joke at the start
- keeping your body still throughout
- maintaining eye contact with your audience
- speaking in a loud, booming voice
- using hand gestures
- smiling at your audience
- standing with your hands in your pocket

2 Imagine you have been asked to give a talk either in English or in your own language. To what extent would the above factors be influenced by any feelings of nervousness you might suffer from?

3 Choose a topic that you feel you could talk about for about five minutes. It could be something you have personal experience of or just something that interests you. Prepare a speech in note form making use of some of the phrases below. When you're ready, give your talk to a small group of colleagues.

Introduction
For those of you who don't know me, let me introduce myself. I'm ...
The theme of my presentation is to introduce/explain ...
My talk is divided into two/three ... main parts.

Theme
Let's start by looking at ...
Now let's move on to ...
Finally, I'd like to finish by looking at ...

Conclusion
Well, I hope you enjoyed this talk on ...
If there are any questions, please don't hesitate to ask.

LANGUAGE AWARENESS
formal and informal language

1 Read the following two letters. Underline the words or phrases in each that are examples of formal and informal language. What conclusions can you draw about formal and informal language?

Dear Sir

I am writing to complain about the treatment I received in one of your hotels during a recent visit to London.

On arrival on my first day I was rather disappointed to learn that my room had been given to another person, despite the fact that I had reserved and paid for the room in advance. Although I was immediately offered alternative accommodation, the room was situated on the top floor and had neither a television nor telephone.

Moreover, despite the fact that I have complained on several occasions, I have yet to be reimbursed for the cost of these services. Consequently, I have decided to put my complaint in writing. Should I receive no satisfaction, I will be forced to take further action against your hotel.

I look forward to hearing from you soon.

Ms Rebecca Jones

Dear Tom

Just a quick note to let you know about the trip to London. The trouble we had!

Can you believe it? When we turned up at the hotel on the first day, the receptionist told me they'd given our room to somebody else even though I'd reserved and paid for it in advance. I was furious! They did offer us another room, but it was right up on the top floor - no telly, no phone.

If that isn't enough, they keep refusing to pay me back the money they charged me for extras. Anyway, the long and short of it is I've sent them a letter and told them if I don't get my money back I'll be taking them to court.

Anyway, write back soon,

Becky

2 Read the letters again and comment on the way the following are used in formal and informal writing:

- Idiomatic English
- Understatement
- Missing out words
- Punctuation
- Vocabulary
- Phrasal verbs
- Contractions
- Passives
- Inversion
- Length of sentences

3 Many of the Language Awareness sections highlight formal/informal possibilities. Keep a record of them all on page 147.

4 In English, many informal words have formal synonyms. The informal words are often of Anglo-Saxon origin. Their Latinate equivalents can be used to create a more formal effect.

Example:
eat (Anglo-Saxon/informal)
consume (Latinate/formal)

Can you find the pairs of synonyms from the following list? Indicate which words are informal and which are formal.

ask	proceed
inform	talk
gear	equipment
purchase	children
tell	go
vehicle	buy
enquire	offspring
converse	car

5 Fill in the missing word in each of the sentences below. Decide whether you need the informal word or its more formal equivalent.

a This product must be .... within three days of purchase.
b Can you .... some tissues when you go to the shops?
c Candidates will be .... of exam results by post.
d My .... are usually well-behaved. What about yours?
e Unauthorised parking of .... is strictly prohibited.
f She sat .... with the Prime Minister.
g Did you remember to bring your .... for badminton tonight?
h I think we ought to .... to the next item on the agenda.

EXAM TIP: Extremely important in Paper 2 (Writing) and Paper 3 (Use of English) Section B.

LANGUAGE
AWARENESS
expressing time

1 Can you solve the following puzzle? Ignore the brackets for the moment.

Sharon and Tracy went off one day to do their daily exercise routine. When they'd changed into their kit they started jogging (B) and ran for 15 minutes. 'Let's have a rest,' said Tracy. When Sharon looked at her watch she noticed it wasn't working ( ). 'What's the time, Tracy?' she asked. '6.15,' Tracy replied. 'Let's stop for a minute.'

Once they'd rested for a few minutes, Sharon decided to do some more running ( ). 'OK,' said Tracy, 'I'll do some cycling. When we've finished, I'll meet you in the changing room ( ).'

When Sharon started running, Tracy started cycling ( ). By the time they stopped, Sharon had run another 3 km. and Tracy had cycled 10 km. Both of them had started from the same place, and neither of them had turned any corners or bends. However, neither of them looked at all surprised when, a few minutes past 6.50, both of them entered the changing room together. How on earth could they have arrived at the same time?

2 Many of the sentences contain two separate actions. Write A in the brackets if one action happens immediately after or as a consequence of the other, or B if one action is obviously completed before the other. The first has been done as an example.

3 Now complete the following general rule regarding the use of time clauses with the Past Simple, Past Perfect and Present Perfect.

When one action is the result of another or one action happens immediately after another, you should use the .... in both clauses. If you want to emphasise that one action was (will be) completed before another one began (begins), you should use the .... or the .... to describe the first action.

4 Which statement in each of the pairs below corresponds to the sequence of events in the puzzle?

a They changed into their kit when they started jogging.
b They didn't start jogging until they had changed.

c Sharon's watch had stopped before she looked at it.
d Sharon's watch stopped when she looked at it.

e When they had rested for a few minutes Sharon decided to do some more running.
f When they rested for a few minutes Sharon decided to do some more running.

g They had decided to meet when they started running and cycling.
h They decided to meet again once they had started running and cycling.

i Tracy started cycling as Sharon started running.
j Tracy started cycling after Sharon had started running.

5 Re-write the incorrect sentences using the time adverbials below.
a Once ...
d By the time Sharon looked at her watch ...
f After Sharon ...
h They ... until ...
j As soon as Sharon ...

6 Steve and Tom are late for school again – for the third time this week. Read the following conversation. How many times does Tom contradict Steve?

Teacher: So, what's the excuse today?
Steve: Well sir, as we left the house the bus drove past.
Tom: Yeah, it drove past when we'd left the house.
Steve: Let me do the talking Tom. Then, sir, after we'd waited about 30 minutes another bus came.
Tom: We had to wait another half an hour until another one arrived.
Steve: Then, sir, once we'd got on the bus we remembered we'd forgotten our homework.
Tom: Yeah, we remembered we'd forgotten it by the time we got on the bus.
Teacher: So you haven't got your homework either?
Steve: No, sir, sorry. Tom ... Shut up! Anyway, while we were sitting on the bus we decided we'd bring it tomorrow.
Tom: Yeah, we'd decided when we sat down.
Steve: So anyway, we realised we'd be late once we got caught in this terrible traffic jam.
Tom: Honestly, sir. We didn't know we'd be late until we'd got caught in it.
Steve: Then when we got to school we talked about how we should tell you.
Tom: Yes, sir. We talked about what we should tell you until we got to school.

7 Tom obviously didn't get his story straight! Correct his statements that are inconsistent. In each case use a different time conjunction from the one used by Steve, but don't alter the meaning.

Your review of Unit 5

Vocabulary:

Topic related

General

Reading

Writing

Speaking

Listening

Exam skill

Grammar

UNIT 6

Food and Drink

PART ONE
Garlic

Lead-in

Are you fond of garlic? Is it commonly used as a cooking ingredient in the cuisine of your country? Do you know of any interesting recipes containing garlic? Does it have any special properties? Discuss with a partner.

YOU ARE WHAT YOU EAT

<table>
<tr><td>EXAM FOCUS
(Listening, Section D)
extracts for global
understanding</td><td>🔊 Listen to five people expressing different views about garlic. As you listen, try to identify the occupation of the speaker in each extract. Put a number in the box, according to the order in which you hear the speakers. (Three of the occupations below are not mentioned.)</td></tr>
</table>

A doctor ☐ ....

B cookery writer ☐ ....

C radio presenter ☐ ....

D farmer ☐ ....

E housewife ☐ ....

F advertiser ☐ ....

G chef ☐ ....

H lecturer in cinema history ☐ ....

What words or phrases helped you to decide? Write them in next to the boxes as you listen.

🔊 Listening technique: specific information

1 Look at these five photographs and listen to the extracts again.
What do the speakers say about each of these items?

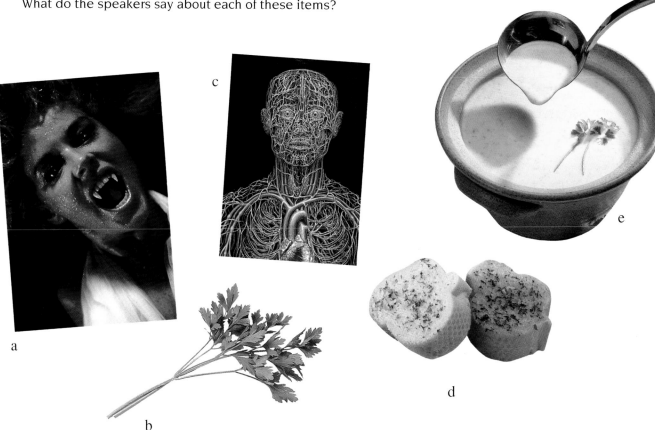

a

b

c

d

e

2 Do you agree with any of the opinions or beliefs
expressed by the speakers? Share your views
with the class.

Reading technique: predicting

1 Now read the first paragraph of a newspaper
article about garlic.

> As Elizabeth David* says, 'Eating garlic is a
> question of habit and digestion'. Get into the
> habit and you'll have no problem with diges-
> tion seems to be the lesson. And what better
> way of enjoying this gastronomic routine than
> to have your own supply.
>
> * A famous cookery writer

2 What do you think the theme of the text is going
to be?

a How eating garlic can improve your digestion
b How to grow garlic in your garden

3 Now continue with the second paragraph and
check if your prediction was correct.

> When I first tried to grow garlic I went to the
> greengrocer one chilly February morning and
> bought some bulbs; one or two went in the din-
> ner, the rest went in the garden. I enjoyed the
> meal, but the crop from the garden was truly
> humiliating, weedy little bulbs that were hardly
> worth lifting.

4 Why do you think the writer's effort was a failure?

Listening technique: specific information

The rest of the text has been recorded. As you listen fill in the chart below.

What he did	What he should have done	Reason
Stage 1 buy garlic from a shop	....	....
Stage 2 plant garlic in February	....	....
Stage 3 harvest in May	....	....
Stage 4 eat straight away	....	....

Vocabulary development: collocations

Many items of food and drink are uncountable nouns, e.g. honey, rice, sugar. Therefore, when wishing to express them as quantities we often need particular words that collocate with the food item.

Example: a jar of honey.

1   Box A contains either measures of food or containers. Use your dictionary to check each word.

2   Match the types of food and drink in box B with an appropriate measure or container, using the structure a __sprig__ of __parsley__.

    For some items there is more than one match.

3   Some collocations can be reversed to become compound nouns.

    Example: a bottle of milk – a milk-bottle

    Make a note of similar examples.
    What is the difference in meaning between the two structures?

4   Say 'a bottle of milk' very quickly. How should you pronounce 'a' and 'of'? Why?

    Most native speakers of English will say 'a jar of honey' with a linking /r/ sound. Practise in groups until you are happy with your pronunciation.

A

pint	clove	knob
carton	pinch	pot
sprig	bottle	jar

B

beer	milk	water
garlic	parsley	salt
jam	yoghurt	butter

Writing skill: describing a process (formal)

1 Look at the following examples from the tapescript of the previous text about garlic:

growers create a strain specially suited to their own climate ...
you can hardly expect garlic to thrive here ...
you can't grow good garlic unless you plant ...

You will notice that much of the description is in the active voice. What effect does this create?

2 Write a short paragraph (around 120 words) with the heading 'Successful garlic growing' which is to be included in a book called *Making the Most of Your Garden*. Your set of instructions will need to be more formal than the writer's. Discuss with a partner some of the grammatical constructions and vocabulary you can use.

The following notes will also help you:

> Each country/own climate/strain/specially suited/create/growers
>
> Garlic/other countries/can hardly/expect/thrive/Britain
>
> Strain/develop/flourish/Britain
>
> Good garlic/grow/unless/plant/autumn
>
> Necessary/garlic/harvest/July

3 Ask your partner to grade your work out of 20 in the following way:

- Appropriacy of style (5 pts)
- Use of connecting devices (5 pts)
- Accuracy (5 pts)
- Impression on the reader (5 pts)

PART TWO
Drink

Lead-in

1 Read these dictionary definitions of the three main types of alcoholic drink.

Spirit / spɪrɪt / strong distilled alcoholic drink e.g. whisky, brandy, gin, rum

2 Dictionary definitions, however, only give the meanings of individual words. What associations do the above words have for you? Spend five minutes thinking and jotting down your thoughts about any or all of these drinks. Then form a small group to discuss your opinions.

Beer / bɪə(r) / alcoholic drink made from malt and flavoured with hops

Wine / waɪn / alcoholic drink made from the fermented juice of grapes

Reading technique: skimming

Quickly skim read the following text (about one minute) to answer this question. Which two of the categories 'spirit', 'beer' and 'wine' are the writer's main concern?

Mine's a pint of wine, thanks

Drink divides Europe. While the old split between East and West becomes increasingly blurred and countries outside the EC queue up to join an expanding economic club, drinking habits die hard. Despite all the integration, despite all the talk of an emergence of a pan-European culture, grapes and grain still mark one part of Europe as different from another.

Beer-drinking nations describe an arc from the Atlantic through Eire, Britain, Belgium, Germany, Denmark and into the Czech Republic. To the south lie the big wine-consumers - France, Italy, Portugal and Spain. The gulf between these two drinking cultures is vast.

When it comes to beer, the Germans knock everyone else into a pintpot. In 1988 they consumed 143 litres a head on average. Czechs clocked up 132 litres. Denmark's average was 126 litres, Belgium managed to drink 119 litres and Britons drank 111 litres each – the equivalent of 195 pints. Drinkers in Eire were close behind with 94 litres each on average.

In southern parts of Europe, wine predominates. The British increased their wine-drinking during the 1980s. In 1988, it stood at 12.4 litres each. But that was eclipsed by France (74 litres a head), Italy (65 litres), Portugal (58 litres) and Spain (41 litres) None of this is too remarkable. Grapes grow better in Bordeaux than they do in Britain. Barley is better suited to the east coast of England than to Italy. But, strangely, the traditional beer-drinking countries are drinking less of the brew with which they are normally associated. East Germany is the only one of the traditional beer drinking countries whose consumption increased during the 1980s. Most of them – the exception now being France – are now drinking more beer.

In general, Europeans seem to be abandoning their traditional, national tipple in favour of the other person's favourite drink. Beer-drinkers want more wine. And wine-drinkers want more beer. Why? No one explanation is sufficient.

There have been several attempts to rationalise the shift – ice-cold, fizzy lager seems to be more appropriate in a hot climate than a glass of red wine. By an accident of climate and botany, the raw material of beer is better produced in cooler climates. Only with the advent of cheaper and more efficient transport have drinks from further afield become available in any one market. Thus beer has invaded the south and at the same time wine has become more readily available in the north. More plausible is the idea that things from overseas are generally regarded as more chic than things from home.

'In Europe, as people gradually increase their standard of living, they seek drinks which are different – drinks from other countries,' Richard Hall, drink analyst, said. 'Undoubtedly, the increase in travel has had an effect. So has the increasing internationalisation of marketing.

'We are witnessing a very slow, very gradual convergence of drinking habits across Europe'.

But what of the countries who have hitherto been big spirit drinkers?

There is little sign of pattern. Most striking, though, is the effect of vodka price rises in the Soviet Union, encouraged by their teetotal ex-leader, Michail Gorbachev. In 1980, the average Russian citizen drank 5.7 litres of spirits. By 1988, Soviet consumption had fallen to 1.8 litres.

(Independent)

Reading technique: information transfer

1 Look at paragraphs 2 and 3 more closely and consider the type of information they contain.

2 Work with a partner or in a small group and draw two graphs entitled 'European consumption of beer, 1988' and 'European consumption of wine, 1988'.

3 Underneath your graphs, complete the following summary, using the information from elsewhere in the text:

- As you can see from these two graphs, traditionally ...
- However, drinking habits in Europe appear to be changing. What this means is ...
- One possible reason could be ...
- In addition, it appears that ...
- The result is ...

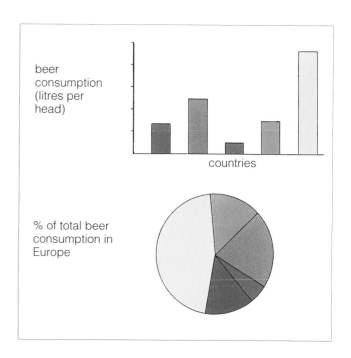

beer consumption (litres per head)

countries

% of total beer consumption in Europe

Vocabulary development: using synonyms

1 Good writers will always find ways to avoid repeating the same words or phrases within a single piece of writing.
Look at the examples opposite:

> they *consumed* 143 litres a head ...
>
> Czechs *clocked up* 132 litres.
>
> Denmark*'s average was* 126 litres, Belgium *managed to drink* 119 litres and Britons *drank* 111 litres ... Drinkers in Eire *were close behind* with 94 litres ...

2 In the text find and highlight the phrases below. Then find their equivalents.

grow better in/_____

beer/_____

tipple/_____

has invaded/_____

average Russian citizen drank/_____

3 Note that, although these phrases mean much the same thing, the writer mixes formal, neutral and colloquial words. Put all of the words and phrases from Activity 2 under the appropriate heading. The first one has been done as an example.

Formal	Neutral	Colloquial
consumed	average was/managed to drink/ drank/were close behind with	clocked up

Exploring pronunciation: vowel sounds

1 The following words are also taken from the text on p67. Look at the underlined vowel sounds and put them into the appropriate category. (Clue: there are two words for each category.)

a gr<u>a</u>pes   b c<u>u</u>ltures   c It<u>a</u>ly   d transp<u>or</u>t
e pl<u>au</u>sible   f s<u>ou</u>thern   g Belg<u>iu</u>m   h gr<u>ai</u>n

1 / ɔː /	2 / ʌ /	3 / eɪ /	4 / ə /

2 Compose a similar activity yourself, for the following vowel sounds, using words from the text.

5 / iː /   6 / aɪ /   7 / æ /   8 / eɪ /

3 Now test your partner.

4 The text you have just read states that 'things from overseas are generally regarded as more chic than things from home.' Do you agree with this statement with regard to your personal drink preferences?

An international magazine has organised a competition asking readers to submit letters describing the role of 'social drinking' in their society. Your letters should not be more than 250 words and entrants are expected to give an account of customs and habits particular to their country (and not just an account of personal behaviour).

1 Work with a partner (not necessarily from the same country) and decide on what aspects of social drinking you are going to focus on. The following questions will help you to get started.

- What are your country's main alcoholic drinks or beverages?
- Why are they so important to your society?
- When are they drunk? Regularly? On special occasions?
- Do people of all ages drink them?
- Where do people drink? At home? In a bar or restaurant?
- Are they made, served or drunk in a special way? With food? As part of a ceremony?

2 Don't forget to make clear exactly what country, region or society you are writing about.

PART THREE
The hamburger empire

Lead-in

1 What types of food from other countries have you tried? If you were going for a foreign meal what type of restaurant would you choose? Do you like to experiment by cooking foreign food at home?

2 Work in groups of three or four. Test your knowledge of food around the world with this quiz.

1 What are the main ingredients of a Greek 'souvlaki'?
2 Japanese 'sushi' consists of rice topped with what?
3 What is a 'wok' used for?
4 What is included in an 'English breakfast'?
5 What is a 'chapati'? A type of bread, rice or potato?
6 With what country do you associate the brandy 'palinka'?
7 What is the country of origin of 'paella'?
8 What is a 'McDonald's'?

3 Add up your group's total of correct answers, and compare with other groups.

Speaking skill: sharing information

1 In your groups, discuss your country's national dish. Do you agree about what it is, where it originated and how it is made? If you have a mixture of different nationalities in your group, take it in turns to explain your national dish to each other.

2 Look at the following quote from Michael Quinlan, chairman and chief executive of McDonald's:

'We're proud that over the past two decades the British people have elevated hamburgers and french fries to the same league as fish and chips among your national favourites.'

Discuss whether the concept of a national dish will still be valid in 20 years' time, given the increasing internationalisation of food throughout the world.

Reading technique: summary skills

McDonald's abroad

1 Since McDonald's burst onto the American scene in the mid-1950s it has become a leading institution and symbol of popular American culture. The McDonald's Corporation has expanded rapidly both at home and abroad and is now the world's largest fast food restaurant chain. Currently located in 72 foreign countries, this far-flung "hamburger empire" has over 14,000 units in operation in the United States and throughout the world, including 526 outlets in Britain.

2 When McDonald's first moved abroad, it began to export more than just hamburgers and french fries. McDonald's, like Coca-Cola and Levi's jeans, has come to represent the popular image of contemporary American culture. Some suggest that McDonald's foreign outlets stand as "embassies" or "consulates" of American culture, offering Americans travelling abroad a comfortable respite – a home away from home – while providing the local population with an opportunity to sample American cuisine. (A typical meal will consist of hamburger, french fries, and apple pie, all washed down with a strawberry-flavoured milkshake.)

3 McDonald's takes great pride in the uniformity of its cuisine; a cheeseburger should taste the same in Paris, France, as in Paris, Tennessee. However, in its expansion abroad, the company has also found it desirable to make certain minor concessions to regional food and drink preferences. New beverage items on the menu include beer in Germany, wine in France, tea in Britain, and tangerine milkshakes in Japan (to take advantage of that country's surplus of fruit). New food additions to McDonald's regular line include fish and chips served in Britain, apple sauce and chicken croquettes in the Netherlands, soup in Japan, and tomato and beetroot in Austria.

4 McDonald's is only one – albeit the most significant – of a number of large American fast-food chains that have expanded abroad. Kentucky Fried Chicken, Burger King, Wendy's and Pizza Hut, for example, all have well-developed international growth strategies. The success of such ventures depends on their financial ability to command prime, highly visible locations in city centres. The possible displacement of smaller, traditional eateries, as a consequence, is a phenomenon which often accompanies the growth of McDonald's abroad.

5 Advertising is a critical concern that has frustrated and challenged McDonald's expansion abroad. The importance of advertising to McDonald's phenomenal success in the U.S. cannot be understated. McDonald's saturates the American market with a barrage of multimedia advertising – primarily television – that costs the company in excess of $100 million annually. Overseas this marketing strategy has been seriously undermined in the many countries where television is strictly controlled by the state and commercial advertising is either limited or non-existent.

6 Ultimately, the international expansion of American (and European and Japanese) fast food enterprises must be seen as one small aspect of an emerging process of world cultural convergence. With growing frequency, culture groups in widely separated regions of the world are now using identical products, listening to the same music, watching the same movies, wearing similar clothing, and eating like foods. This expanding set of common experiences often includes the sharing of identical landscape elements. One can only speculate on what this portends culturally. In respect to the landscape, diversity must certainly suffer as these common features are diffused around the world and gradually replace, or at least diminish, those distinctive elements that traditionally have given character to and helped define the essence of a place. The growth of McDonald's abroad both reflects and contributes to this process.

---

1 Read the text and then match each paragraph (1–6) with an appropriate paragraph summary from the list opposite. You will have three summaries left. Check your answers with a partner.

2 With a partner make notes under the three remaining headings about what the writer might have said about these points. Save these notes as you will need them later.

A   The international culture
B   The role of fast food in a healthy diet
C   The spread of McDonald's throughout the world
D   How all fast-food chains succeed
E   Local objections to McDonald's
F   The McDonald's menu around the world
G   What McDonald's symbolises
H   McDonald's as a major employer
I   The financial cost of promoting McDonald's

Reading technique: understanding the purpose of a text

Read the text more carefully and answer the following questions.

1 The main purpose of the text is to:
   A criticise the spread of McDonald's
   B account for the success of McDonald's abroad
   C persuade the reader to go to McDonald's restaurant
   D explain how McDonald's food is cooked

2 The text is taken from:
   A a tabloid newspaper
   B an academic journal
   C an information booklet produced by McDonald's
   D a leaflet from an environmentalist group

3 The writer's attitude towards McDonald's is one of:
   A admiration
   B hostility
   C detachment
   D cynicism

See **Language awareness: participles (1)**

Vocabulary development: recording vocabulary

1 Highlight the following words from the text:

   respite   displacement   concessions   critical
   ventures   saturates   barrage

2 In pairs, write a glossary for each word, giving information about the following: part of speech (noun, verb, adjective, etc.), a phonetic transcription, an explanation of the meaning in the context of the passage, and an indication of some of the word's collocations.

   Example: Critical
              adjective, / ˈkrɪtɪkl /
              crucial, decisive, of great
              importance
              a critical concern/
              moment/time, critical
              timing

   Use this technique when you record other vocabulary in the future.

Speaking skill: taking part in a debate

As a class, you are going to debate the following motion:

'The class believes that the spread of fast-food hamburger restaurants across the major cities of the world should be stopped immediately.'

1 Before you begin the debate you will need to prepare notes exploring all of the issues surrounding the motion. In pairs, think about what views the following people might express:

   • a nutritionist talking about the dietary value of hamburger meals
   • a conservationist talking about the effect on the local landscape
   • a local restaurant owner offering food that is traditional to the area
   • a tourist development minister wanting to attract more visitors
   • a marketing manager of a fast-food hamburger chain

   (Look back to the notes that you made after reading the McDonald's text.)

2 Select two speakers to speak in favour of the motion and two to speak against. Then select a chairperson. While these speakers prepare what to say, members of the audience must think of three questions to ask the panel members.

3 Conduct the debate in class. At the end, take a vote to see if the motion is won or lost.

1 Can you identify the student's error?

Do we have to study participles? I'm boring!

Yes, I know you are.

2 The following verbs can all be used as adjectives in the form of past or present participles. Supply the appropriate participle to the following sentences. There may be more than one answer.

disappoint   confuse   excite   tempt
irritate   worry   terrify   shock
enthrall   amaze   astound   embarrass

a My parents were really .... when they heard I was thinking of going on holiday with my boyfriend.
b His exam results have been rather .... lately. He's obviously not working as hard as he could.
c The manager came in just as I was complaining about the pay rise. It was so ....
d He's really .... about his birthday party. He can't stop talking about it.
e Stop tapping your fingers! It's really ....
f They won the championship without a single defeat, an .... achievement.
g I found the book quite .... I couldn't put it down.
h I'm .... to have the day off work today. I feel exhausted.

3 Many compound adjectives are formed from participles. Look at these examples from the text on p 71.

... this *far-flung* 'hamburger empire'
... washed down with a *strawberry-flavoured* milkshake
... all have *well-developed* growth strategies

Using a good dictionary, see how many compound adjectives you can find by matching words in column A and B.

A	B
narrow	grown
wide	powered
empty	sighted
full	fetched
big	reaching
small	minded
long	headed
short	flying
heavy	playing
light	handed
high	eyed
near	lying
low	pitched
far	winded

4 Examine the sentences below. Can you supply the correct compound?

a I came away from the auction .... I was out-bid on everything I wanted and ended up with nothing.
b Can you read that sign at the end of the road? I'm not wearing my lenses and I'm really .... without them.
c The new arms agreement will have .... consequences for arms manufacturers who fear thousands of job losses.
d Don't try discussing anything liberal with him. He's so .... and set in his opinions.
e She's always boasting about how expensive her house is and how intelligent her children are. She's become so ....
f She's got herself a really .... job in the city. Lots of money, lots of travelling and she meets so many important people.
g .... of the country are likely to suffer flooding later this evening.

LANGUAGE AWARENESS
expressing possibility

1 Read the following dialogue.

(Tony's girlfriend has gone to Spain for two weeks)

Steve: Lucky Sue, eh? Two weeks in the sun! What do you think she's doing now?

Tony: She might be having dinner.

Steve: She can't be. It's 12 o'clock at night!

Tony: No, stupid! They're five hours behind us. Anyway, don't talk to me about Sue. She's been there a week and she hasn't phoned me yet.

Steve: She might have phoned while you were out.

Tony: Well, she can't have phoned today, I've been in all day.

Steve: I'm sure you've got nothing to worry about. She might call you later.

Tony: Nothing to worry about? What do you mean? Do you think she could have met someone else?

Steve: Don't be silly! She won't forget to phone. Anyway, you should be due for a postcard soon.

Tony: No! I can see it all now. She must have met someone else. I would have heard from her otherwise.

Steve: Listen! There's the phone now! That'll be Sue.

Tony: Hello? Sue! ... What do you mean, 'How are you?' Listen, we're finished! How dare you be unfaithful?

Now underline all the structures that express degrees of probability. When you've found them all draw a table like the one below and put them in the appropriate section.

certain ◄————————► possible		
Past		
Present		
Future		

2 Here's a brainteaser for you. A man is lying face-down in a field unconscious. He has a bag strapped to his back. Have you any idea what happened?

3 Here are some ideas. Re-write each one using an appropriate modal verb, paying particular attention to tenses.

a He probably had a heart attack.
He ....

b Perhaps he was robbed.
He ....

c There's no way he was robbed because his bag's still there.
He ....

d Maybe he's meditating!
He ....

e It's more likely to have been an accident
It ....

f There's bound to be a very logical explanation.
There ....

g I'm certain the bag has something to do with the answer.
The bag ....

h I'm fairly certain he'd been flying just before this.
He ....

i In fact I bet anything you like the local flying club are looking for him.
The local flying club ....

j It's odds on he didn't check his parachute.
He ....

4 Look at the picture below.

The man lying in bed is dead. Your job is to work out the story behind the picture! Put a piece of paper over the list of clues below, and reveal each one only after you have made a deduction about the one before. You should write your deduction down and pass it to your partner.

Example:

1 There is a gun on the floor next to the man.
   Perhaps somebody shot him.

2 The man outside didn't own a gun.

3 Later the police found the dead man's fingerprints on the gun.

4 There was sawdust next to the bed.

5 The man outside had a key to the room.

6 The man outside had sawdust on his shoes.

7 The man outside didn't kill him.

8 The man in the bed had been the shortest man in the world.

9 The man in the bed had been famous and very rich.

10 The man outside hated the dead man.

Your review of Unit 6

Vocabulary:

Topic related

General

Reading

Writing

Speaking

Listening

Exam skill

Grammar

UNIT 7

The Human Condition

PART ONE
A gifted child

Lead-in

1 Test your intellect. Try the short intelligence test below:

a **Can you write your name in the square provided?**

b **Some months have 31 days, some 30. How many have 28?**
c **Divide 30 by 1/2 and add 10.**
d **How far can a dog run into a forest?**
e **If two peacocks lay two eggs in two days, how many eggs will one peacock lay in one day?**
f **You are alone in a deserted house at night. There is a lamp, a fire and a candle. You only have one match. Which would you light first?**
g **Why can't a man living in Paris be buried west of Berlin?**
h **Is it illegal for a man to marry his widow's sister?**

2 Did you have any particular skills or talents as a child? Can you remember the first book you read? Or the first musical instrument you learnt to play? Did you learn any unusual skills? Share your memories with the group.

3 At what age would a person of average ability be able to do the following things:

- Count up to 20?
- Read and appreciate Classical literature?
- Play the piano proficiently?

4 Read the following newspaper extracts to find out about three people who caused great excitement as children.

Having problems with homework? Trouble telling your Shakespeare from your Tolstoi? Have a word with Everton Williams of Shirley, Birmingham. He's read most of Shakespeare's works, is quite an expert on Zola and has more than a superficial knowledge of Freud. Not impressed? His friends and relatives certainly are, for this well-read little wonder is only seven years old.

How many of you remember our article on child prodigy Jamie Sutton whose talents on the piano were making quite a stir? Two years on, we can now report that Jamie, now seven, is making steady progress, so much so in fact that he will be giving a concert performance, accompanied by a professional orchestra.

Two year old Stephanie Peters has become quite a celebrity in her home town of Huddersfield. She has astounded her parents with her many talents like counting up to twenty, spelling her own name and reciting nursery rhymes by heart. 'We don't know where she gets it from,' said her father, John Peters. 'Her memory is quite incredible.'

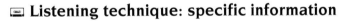

Listening technique: specific information

These three people, now adults, were recently interviewed on a radio programme. Listen to the interview and fill in the table below.

	Stephanie	Everton	Jamie
job now			
parent's attitude or decisions			
education			
relating to people			

Listening technique: inference

1 Listen to the interview again. Do all three sound happy with the way their lives have turned out?

Share your ideas with a partner.

2 What are the problems of being or having a gifted child? What would you do with a child of your own who showed a particular talent?

Vocabulary development: collocation

1 The adjectives in the table all refer to intelligence or ability. However, they can only be used in certain collocations. Use a dictionary to fill in the chart, indicating in which circumstances they can be used.

2 With a partner, try to explain the use of these words. For example, 'good' is a general term that goes with many words, whereas 'fluent' is mainly concerned with speech.

3 Do similar collocations exist in your own language?

	Speaker	Athlete	Artist	Business person	Musician
good					
gifted					
fluent	✓				
skilled					
agile					
clever					
efficient					
talented					
shrewd					
astute					

Writing skill: an article for a newsletter

You have been asked to write an article for a newsletter produced by 'The Society for Parents with Gifted Children' which highlights some of the benefits and problems of having gifted children in a family (250 words) and offers some suggestions for parents on how to deal with these problems (200 words).

1 Start by listing some of the benefits and problems, and their causes. Refer to the tapescript on pages 160–161.

Example:

Action	Effects	
	Benefits	Problems
Parents pushing a child to achieve success	encourages the child	makes the child feel anxious ▶ rebelliousness

2 Look at the use of the cause and effect expressions in the model paragraph below and try to use some of them in your article:

Example:
As a parent, you can often – quite unintentionally – put your child under immense pressure to succeed. This may serve to encourage your child to apply herself even more enthusiastically to her special talent. Too much pressure, however, and you risk your child feeling anxious and unhappy. This could lead to your child losing interest or even rebelling against you.

As a consequence/result ...
Consequently ...
This can result in/may serve to/might lead to/could lead to ...
If ..., you ...
Because/Since/As ...
... as a result of which ...

3 Work in groups of four. When you have finished the first part of your article, show your work to others in the group. Can they think of solutions for the problems you have identified? Exchange ideas for Part 2.

PART TWO
Memory

Lead-in

1 How good are you at revising before an important exam? Tick those points that best describe your own methods.

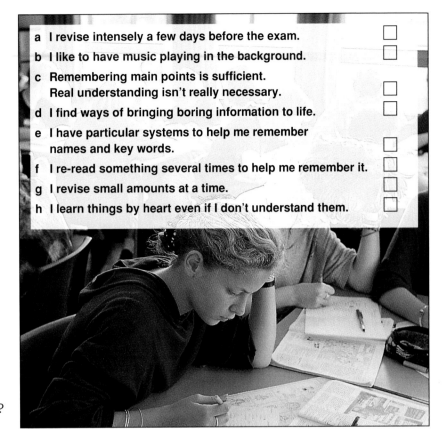

a I revise intensely a few days before the exam. ☐

b I like to have music playing in the background. ☐

c Remembering main points is sufficient.
   Real understanding isn't really necessary. ☐

d I find ways of bringing boring information to life. ☐

e I have particular systems to help me remember
   names and key words. ☐

f I re-read something several times to help me remember it. ☐

g I revise small amounts at a time. ☐

h I learn things by heart even if I don't understand them. ☐

2 You are going to read a section from an article giving advice on how best to revise. All of the points above are mentioned. Which do you think are strongly recommended and which are not? Give reasons for your choices.

Reading technique: skimming

Form two groups. Group A read text 1, group B text 2 (over). Read your text quickly (one minute). How many of the points above are dealt with in your text?

Text 1

Sadly, there is no memory system which can bypass the need to really understand your material. You simply have to get to grips with the arguments, the information and ideas that are central to your subject. You need to establish the material in your long-term memory. You forget things much more quickly in the first few hours than you do in subsequent days or weeks

It might seem easier simply to rely on reading and re-reading your material. But no matter how many times you read through your material, you won't get it into your long-term memory. The information will stay in your head for a few seconds, or even a few minutes, but most of it will be forgotten by the time the examination papers are handed out. Memorising needs to be much more active: you need to seek out the meaning of what you are reading. Once you have read a chapter, run through it in your mind. Write down the key points. This reinforces the information and helps you to restructure it in your mind. Don't be tempted to prepare answers to specific questions. You need to organise your material by topics, making sure you are equipped to deal with a range of questions you could be asked about the topic. Familiarise yourself with the first letter system.

Learn your material over a period of time. Intensive effort the night before the exam really does not produce good results. However, starting your revision several months in advance, regularly reminding yourself of the key factors, will help you feel confident of your material. Every time you re-read material it will take less effort to recall the facts and you will be storing the information in your long-term memory.

Breaking up your material into manageable chunks is equally essential. Pick up a vast file of revision and you will instantly feel daunted. Break your material into smaller units, keeping it in its proper context. Remember that you will have to be able to link these smaller blocks back together.

(*Daily Mail*)

Text 2

The biggest obstacle to learning is boredom. Try to become truly interested in the subject as it is always easier to remember something that fascinates you. For a clear example of this look no further than the encyclopaedic knowledge most football fans have about their sport. If, however, the book is dry, you will have to employ extra effort. Ask challenging questions; dispute what the author has written. If you can find points of debate within the material, it will start to become more interesting.

Finding images to illustrate dull facts is one of the most successful ways of committing potentially boring knowledge to memory. Whether it is a series of statistics or details about an historical character, the process is the same – translate your facts into concrete images. In her book 'Memory Power' Ursula Markham suggests the following technique for revision via visualisation.

Once you have written notes and established key words of what you have to learn, close your eyes and relax. Now see, in your mind's eye, the words being written by a giant unseen hand. The writing must be performed very slowly, one letter at a time; each word should be written in capital letters and there must be a stark contrast between the words and the material on which they are written. Work on a maximum of five key words at a time.

It does not matter whether it is The Beatles or Bach, music is unlikely to help you study for exams. It might make your revision time more bearable but there's not much evidence that putting on a tape or CD helps your concentration, soothes your mind or cuts out background distraction. One study of 40 law students in the United States showed that they remembered information better if they were not listening to music.

The First Letter System is useful for complicated titles of organisations, short lists of names or key words that have to be kept in the right order. Research has shown that as many as one-third of students sitting high-level examinations use this technique.

Say you need to remember the names Johnson, O'Hara, King and Ellis. All you would need to do is make a word out of their initials, in this case JOKE, and you have the first letters of each name firmly fixed in your mind.

(Daily Mail)

Reading technique: specific information

1 Read your text again, this time making any notes that are relevant to the points in the previous activity. Use your own words rather than copying out chunks from the text.

2 Using your notes, and without looking at the original text, share your information with someone from the other group.

3 Have you any strategies of your own for recalling information? Is the advice offered in the text suitable for students revising for language examinations like CAE?

See **Language awareness: verb forms (1)**

EXAM FOCUS
(English in Use, Section B) proof-reading

Here is another extract from the same article. Read it carefully as there is one incorrect word in most of the lines. Write the incorrect word in the space provided or put a tick if the line is correct. The first two have been done as examples.

So there you are. You've met the man next to you before   0 ✔

and you've acknowledged him with a nod across from the crowded   0 _from_

room. Any moment now you are going to have had to start talking   1 _____

to him, and although his name is on the tip of your tongue, so it   2 _____

simply won't come in to mind. Lapses of memory like this are   3 _____

hardly life-threatening, but when they are highly embarrassing and   4 _____

could even lose us business. Is not there anything we can do to   5 _____

help ourselves or do we have to remain at the mercy of our   6 _____

memories? Remembering people's names is quite about motivation.   7 _____

You don't forget people's names because you've got a bad   8 _____

memory for names, but you do rather forget names because you are   9 _____

not sufficiently interested in them. When you turn round to someone   10 _____

you have met on numerous occasions with and admit you can't remember 11 _____

their name, the sub-text is clear and the person who knows that the truth 12 _____

of the matter is that, since you last met, you have simply not thought   13 _____

enough about this person for to keep them in your mind.   14 _____

Speaking skill: describing in detail

How good are you at remembering names? Try this activity to test each other's memory.

1 Form two groups. Group 1 look at picture A, group 2 picture B. Decide on the names, personalities, jobs and possible relationships between the people and make brief notes.

2 Think of several questions based on your description that you could ask members of the other group to test their memory.

Example:
Who's the woman standing next to the man with blonde hair?
What's the name of the doctor?
Who's the woman who's married to the shy teacher?

3 Pair up with a student from the opposite group. Describe the people in your photograph and when your partner is ready ask him or her your questions. You might find some of these expressions useful:

In the foreground
In the background
In the middle
On the left/right of
The man standing behind/
in front of/on the left of
The woman smiling/laughing/wearing

PART THREE
Phobias

Lead-in

1 Read the following extract from George Orwell's '1984':

'You asked me once,' said O'Brien, 'what was in Room 101 ... the thing that is in Room 101 is the worst thing in the world ... The worst thing in the world varies from individual to individual. It may be burial alive, or death by fire, or by drowning, or by impalement, or fifty other deaths. There are cases where it is some quite trivial thing, not even fatal ... In your case,' said O'Brien, 'the worst thing in the world happens to be rats.'

2 What would be in your Room 101? Any of the following ... or something even more frightening?

3 Match the following phobia descriptions with their proper medical names. You may recognise some of the Greek roots on which these words are constructed.

   a fear of spiders   hypnophobia
   b fear of poison   geraphobia
   c fear of water   arachnophobia
   d fear of light   opthalmophobia
   e fear of old age   hydrophobia
   f fear of eyes   toxiphobia
   g fear of needles   photophobia
   h fear of sleep   belonephobia

4 Which phobias from this list seem particularly irrational to you? Which ones have an understandable basis?

5 What do you think causes phobias in the first place? Share your views with a partner.

📻 You will hear a radio interview with a doctor who gives some advice on how to deal with common phobias. For questions A–K complete the notes using a few words. You do not need to write full sentences.

**Advice sheet No 1:
Overcoming Your Fears and Phobias**

Most people at some time in their life will experience feelings of fear and anxiety. Unpleasant though these feelings are, they are also perfectly normal. However, when these feelings begin to cause (A) _____ or even (B) _____ then you may feel it is time to get help.

A phobia is 'an irrational fear of certain objects or situations', and they range from the common to the highly unusual. Many tens of thousands of people suffer from agoraphobia, which stops them (C) _____, and makes this the most disabling of all the phobias. However, although many people are nervous about flying, only 5% have a chronic fear of (D) _____, or the medical term, aerophobia. More unusual phobias that have been recorded are the fear of (E) _____!

It is usually, but not always, possible to trace the cause of the phobia. Claustrophobia, the fear of enclosed space, has in most cases two main causes. It is often linked to the distressing childhood experience of being locked (F) _____. Another cause is being given (G) _____, where the person experiences fear and a sense of being suffocated.

Men and women are (H) _____ to develop a phobia, although it seems that women are less ashamed and embarrassed about admitting to feelings of anxiety than men. The good news for everybody is that phobias can be successfully cured with the right treatment. Options currently available are behaviour therapy, (I) _____, alternative medicine such as (J) _____, and hypnosis, yoga and of course, will-power. Get help from a trusted friend or a (K) _____ . There is no need to suffer in silence.

1 Make sure you read through the text first to give you an idea of the type of information that you need to listen for.

2 Listen to the tape and complete the answers. Your answers should be short: no more than three words. Make sure these are key words containing important information.

3 Compare your answers with a partner. Did you agree on all the information?

See Language awareness: will, would and used to

Vocabulary development: word-building

Recognising some of the common Latin and Greek elements in many English words can help you a great deal in working out word meanings.

1 Look again at the list of phobias in the Lead-in activity. Use a dictionary to find out which ones you can use to build further English words. You will find it useful to indicate where the stress occurs on these words.

Example: toxiphobia

Element	Meaning	Other English words
toxi-	poison	toxic (adj.) toxin (noun)

2 Fill in the meaning of the Latin and Greek elements in the chart below.

Element	Meaning	English words
ambi-	_____	ambidextrous, ambiguous
ante-	_____	antenatal
anti-	_____	anticlockwise, antisocial
circa-	_____	circulation, circumference
micro-	_____	microphone, microscope
peri-	_____	perimeter

Can you add any other words based on these elements?

LANGUAGE AWARENESS
verb forms (1)

1 Look at the following extracts from the text on memory on page 79 and page 80. How do you explain the use of the gerund? Consider their grammatical role in the original sentence.

... starting your revision several months in advance ...
Breaking up your material into manageable chunks ...
Finding images to illustrate dull facts ...

2 Re-write the following sentences using the gerund form as the subject of the sentence.

Example:
It is important that you understand the material you want to remember.
Understanding the material you want to remember is important.

a   It is common to forget things you haven't understood.
....

b   It is not a good idea to prepare answers to particular questions.
....

c   It takes less effort to recall facts from material learnt over a long time.
....

d   It is easier to remember something that fascinates you.
....

3 Now re-write the sentences below using one of the words from box A, a preposition from box B and a gerund form.

Example:
I don't really think children should be allowed to stay up late.
I don't believe in allowing children to stay up late.

Manuela's scared that she might fail her exams.
....

Philip paid me even though I told him not to.
....

Katie was able to drive well.
....

The teacher arrived late and didn't say sorry.
....

Jenny often turns up uninvited.
....

I was so annoyed that I'd missed the party.
....

Some people aren't concerned if they upset others.
....

Many people would love to retire early.
....

A		B	
	apologise		about
	afraid		of
	habit		in
	believe		of
	dream		on
	angry		of
	insist		about
	care		at
	good		for

4 Some of the sentences below are incorrect. Which ones and why?

You shouldn't put off to revise until the last minute.

The article suggests visualising dull material.

You should avoid to listen to music whilst studying.

You can't expect to remember large chunks of material.

Consider to bring your material to life.

Attempt establishing a system of key words.

Learn translating facts into memorable images.

Don't risk to try to memorise too much.

5 Can you now give three reasons for using the gerund?

EXAM TIP: The expanded notes exercise in English in Use, Section C, often requires a knowledge of dependent prepositions and verb forms

1 How many uses of 'will' and 'would' can you think of? Give an example for each.

Example:
to make a future prediction
I think it'll rain later.

2 Match each of the sentences below with the appropriate use.

I'll be home about 6.00.

I'm sure she'll give you a lift home.

Grandfather would always bring me a bar of chocolate.

She will insist on smoking (stress on 'will')

Is that the phone? I'll answer it.

Will you give me a hand?

Little did he know, this woman would be his wife.

You would do that, wouldn't you? (stress on 'would')

I'd like a cup of tea.

I wouldn't if I were you.

Request
Future in the past
Criticism
A past habit
An offer
A prediction
To show willingness
Advice

3 Look at this extract from the listening text on page 83. Which of the above functions does it correspond to?

Yes, every time she bought an item of clothing she'd remove any buttons ...

4 In which of the sentences below can 'would' replace 'used to'?

a I used to own a lovely little Ford Escort.
b My uncle used to bring me chocolate whenever he visited.
c Every Christmas we used to sit round the fire and open our presents.
d I used to live in London before I moved to Birmingham.
e My Grandfather used to be a taxi driver until he retired.
f Dad used to spend hours in the garden before he injured his back.

5 Look at the following extract from a magazine which has invited people to write about fond memories from their childhood.

CHILDHOOD MEMORIES

I suppose my childhood was a happy one. My parents never used to have a great deal of money but we generally managed to keep ourselves entertained. My father used to be very busy but would always take the time to read bedtime stories to us. I also remember the way my grandfather ...

Do you have a similar story to tell? Write and let us know and you could win a hundred pounds.

Write a similar piece of about 100 words in which you fondly describe memorable events or people from your childhood.

Your review of Unit 7

Vocabulary:

Topic related

General

Reading

Writing

Speaking

Listening

Exam skill

Grammar

UNIT 8 Leisure

PART ONE
Armchair entertainment

Lead-in

The following list of words are all associated with books, films or television. In small groups sort the words into the correct categories. (Some words can fit in two or all three categories.)

soap (opera)
blockbuster
comic novel
cult movie
remake
thriller
Mills and Boon romance
(spaghetti) western

complete works
documentary
autobiography
telethon
repeat
cartoon

chat-show
comedy
weepy
whodunnit
sitcom
new edition
sequel

EXAM FOCUS
(Listening, Section D) identifying topics and opinions

1 ▭ You are going to hear five people talking about different types of books they have read recently. As you listen, put the books in the order in which you hear them being talked about by filling in the boxes (1 for the first speaker, 2 for the second speaker, etc.) with the appropriate number.

a a feminist novel ☐
b a competition winner ☐
c a royal romance ☐
d a foreign language textbook ☐

e a whodunnit ☐
f a travel guide ☐
g a book made into a film ☐

2 Here is a list of the opinions of the speakers about the various books they have read. Listen to the extracts again and put the opinions in the order in which they are expressed.

a divided opinion ☐
b disappointing ending ☐
c attractive design ☐
d hard to put down ☐

e uninformative ☐
f difficult to follow ☐
g uplifting ☐

Reading technique: skimming

Read the book and film reviews as quickly as you can. What type of work is being reviewed? Use the list from the Lead-in to help you.

A The Joy Luck Club

Every mother and daughter should see this film: a marvellous distillation of feminine hopes and hurts across the generations. Experiences every woman can connect with are explored through the relationship of four Chinese friends and their American daughters. The older women recount spellbinding tales of their early lives, and the younger ones work through amusing and tearful confrontations to reach a new understanding of themselves. Adapted by Amy Tan from her novel for director Wayne Wang and producer Oliver Stone, it's skilfully symmetrical and emotionally overwhelming - wonderful. Bring a big box of tissues.***

The Joy Luck Club (15) opens in London on April 6, nationwide May 8.

(New Woman)

B Century

Clive Owen makes a welcome appearance on the big screen in Stephen Poliakoff's intense drama of progress, morality and class in nineteenth century England. Owen's Paul Reisner is a newly-qualified doctor whose ambitious mentor Professor Mandry (Charles Dance) seems to share his excited zeal for scientific and social change. But a medical mystery reveals human guinea pigs being used in an experimental programme with chilling implications. Paul finds himself torn between hero worship, his hopes for the future, ethics and his growing attachment to Clara (Miranda Richardson) in a thoughtful blend of romance, intrigue and philosophical debate. ***

(New Woman)

C Charlotte Brontë: A Passionate Life

Few women seem as completely out of step with their time as Charlotte Brontë. Equipped with all the attributes of talent and passion that are considered laudable in the twentieth century, she had the misfortune to be born into an age when it was thought women should be married and not much else. What was passion without beauty? Talent without money? Charlotte had neither of these and suffered for it, as Lyndall Gordon shows in her new biography (£15.99, Chatto and Windus), a moving and intelligent study of the woman who, with her two sisters Anne and Emily, produced some of the greatest, most passionate books in the English language. Charlotte's life can sometimes seem like a catalogue of misfortune. By the age of thirty-three she had lost four sisters, a mother and a brother; her surviving father required constant companionship. Gordon's book is the story, first and foremost of a writer; a novelist out of her time and, frequently, out of her depth socially, but never at a loss when it came to setting down the thoughts of a woman's heart.**

(Marie Claire)

D Lovers and Liars, Sally Beauman (Bantam Press, £14.99)

Don't let the dreadful cover put you off this latest offering by the author of the best-selling Destiny and Dark Angels. And if you weren't a fan of those particular novels don't let that put you off either because this one marks a departure from her usual style to accomplished thriller with a difference. It's one of those explosive reads that hooks you from start to finish. Investigative journalist Genevieve Hunter and her one-time lover Pascale Lamartine, are assigned to unearth a scandal about a would-be US president. However, this is no straightforward assignment - nothing is what it seems and the two soon find themselves over their heads. Mystery, mayhem, bugged phone calls, love, sex and secrets are all there. Compulsively delicious. ****

(New Woman)

E The 39 Steps. 11.10pm - 12.35am BBC1

Hitchcock's marvellous romantic comedy thriller stars Robert Donat as the archetypal innocent man on the run from a spy ring, handcuffed to Madeline Carroll. The quintessence of wit, pace and style, packed with sparkling dialogue, alluring acting, terrific suspense and typical Hitchcock touches. It's Hitchcock's most famous British movie, the one which made his name internationally known and landed him his first Hollywood offers, thus paving the way for better-known classics such as 'Psycho' and 'Dial M for Murder'.****
(Black and White)

(Radio Times)

**** Unmissable   *** Very good   ** Fair   * Terrible

Reading technique: scanning and inferring

1 Which review:

  a suggests the type of people who would be likely to enjoy it?
    (Write down the phrases that are used.)
  b gives examples of other works by the same person?
  c has a historical focus?
  d describes storylines which are set in America?
  e suggests a close male/female relationship?

  There may be more than one answer to each question. For each answer, try to underline the relevant information in the text.

2 Do any of the reviews reveal how the book or film ends?

Writing skill: the language of reviews

1 Now that you have read some authentic book and film reviews you can examine some of the main language features. Which of the following sentences (a or b) would you find more interesting to read in a review? Make a note of why.

  a The book I am going to write about is called A *Judgement in Stone* and is written by Ruth Rendell. I found the book shocking and fascinating …
  b Ruth Rendell's A *Judgement in Stone* is a fascinating and sometimes shocking read …

  a Set in 18th century England, this tale explores the relationships …
  b The story is set in England in the 18th century and is about the relationships …

  a The film is called *Presumed Innocent* and is adapted from the book by Scott Turow. It …
  b *Presumed Innocent*, a successful adaptation of Scott Turow's novel of the same name, is …

  a After a traumatic experience in Colombia, Mary decided to move to France where she would be able to build a new life …
  b After a traumatic experience in Colombia, Mary decides to move to France where she can start a new life …

  a Tara Fitzgerald's Polly is a strong, forceful character.
  b The character is played by Tara Fitzgerald; Polly is a really strong character.

2 You have been asked to write a review of around 250 words, for an English magazine, of a book you have read recently or a film that you have seen. Before you start, try the following:

  a Quickly read the reviews again and make a note of any adjectives (e.g. 'marvellous', 'overwhelming') or other phrases (e.g. 'a welcome appearance', 'this latest offering') that you particularly like and would use yourself.
  b Make a list of the language features of reviews (e.g. expressing points economically, use of the present tense).

3 Write a first draft and ask your partner to comment on how interesting your review is!

PART TWO
Sport

Lead-in

How good is your knowledge of English sporting vocabulary? Try the short quiz below:

a Referees and umpires do the same job. But in which sports?
b What's the difference between a competition, a contest and a championship?
c Can you explain the difference between a prize, a trophy and a title?
d Name the sports that take place on the following:
   a track, a ring, a pitch, a court, a course, a rink
e Can you name the following pieces of sports equipment and the sports in which they are used?

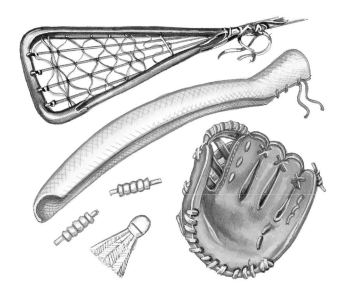

🔲 Listening technique: specific information

1 You are going to hear two students who are practising for Phase B of the speaking exam. In Part 1 Student A will describe one of the photographs opposite and Student B will try and identify the correct one. Listen to the recording and decide if Student B is correct.

2 In Part 2, a native speaker chooses one of the photographs and describes it in detail. Another native speaker then talks about the similarities and differences in his/her choice of photo. As you listen, try to decide which two photographs are being described.

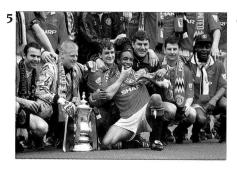

3 The examiner will mark your speaking skills using the following criteria:

- Fluency
- Accuracy
- Pronunciation
- Achievement of the task
- Interactive communication (involvement and turn taking)

4 Listen to Part 1 again and give each student marks (1–5) for the first four criteria (Interactive communication is not applicable to Phase B). When you've finished, share your views with the class.

Exploring language: ways of improving fluency

In Unit 5 we looked at the way native speakers often use marker words and fillers when speaking. Listen to Part 2 again. Can you hear any of the following markers or fillers? Tick each one every time you hear it mentioned.

let's see	☐	well	☐
anyway	☐	mm	☐
OK	☐	er	☐
right	☐		

EXAM FOCUS
(Speaking, Phase B) describing a picture

Work with a partner. Student A should choose one of the photographs and describe it in detail for about one minute. Student B should listen carefully and then decide which picture was being described. You may ask questions if you're not sure.

Student B should choose a photograph and describe it in detail for about one minute. Student A should listen carefully and then talk about two things that are similar and two things that are different in his/her choice.

Work in groups of three. Student A and B should do the activity. Student C should monitor the discussion and check how well each person uses the marker words and fillers listed above.

See Language awareness: questions (2)

PART THREE
Theme parks

Lead-in

Have you ever been to a theme park? Some people go on every ride no matter how frightening it might be. Others prefer to watch! What about you? What's the most thrilling ride you've ever been on?

Reading technique: skimming

The text below gives a personal account of one person's visit to Alton Towers, one of the most famous theme parks in Britain.

I Skim read the text and tick which of the points below are dealt with by the writer.

   a The cost of building Nemesis
   b An interview with somebody who has just ridden on Nemesis (look at the punctuation)
   c A description of the design of Nemesis
   d People who shouldn't ride on Nemesis for health reasons
   e An invitation to the writer to ride on Nemesis
   f A description of the Log Flume
   g A statistic about how dangerous Nemesis is to ride

2 Now put the five points in the order in which they are mentioned by the writer. Check your answers with a partner.

Aaaaaaargh ... I'm with Diana on this one!

Mick Brown declines to meet his Nemesis at Alton Towers

There is a certain ritual to approaching thrill-rides. You look at the height of the drop and the angle of the twists and turns. You measure the screams. You read the warning signs at the entrance: not suitable for expectant mothers, people who suffer from heart conditions, back or neck prob-lems, vertigo. Curiously, there is no mention of cowardice.

The Princess of Wales' anxiety about riding Nemesis when she visited Alton Towers recently with Princes William and Harry is understandable. In the publicity handout, Nemesis is the ride which threatens to 'take all your senses to the very limit'. Riders are suspended under the track, four abreast, in chairs, not unlike a ski-lift, their legs dangling, bodies seemingly secured only by a fragile-looking harness and the power of prayer.

They are then hurtled down a 90ft incline, around a series of twists and turns, narrowly avoiding collision with rock-faces and blood-coloured waterfalls, and through a series of upside-down loops. Nemesis is the only thrill-ride in Europe on which you ride on the *outside* of a 360-degree loop.

It cost £10 million to build and is designed with the sole inten-tion of scaring you witless. It may reach only 50mph but it's emotionally exhilarating. Get your body used to the sensa-tion of leaving your stomach behind.

The Brown children – Clem-entine, 11, Dominic, 13, and Celeste, 15 – and I started gently. The Log Flume ride is a standard theme-park attrac-tion in which you sit in a log-shaped carriage and are car-ried along a water trough, to be eventually deposited down a 100ft incline through a plume of water. Well, I enjoyed it.

Next we experienced the Beast and the Thunder Loop (which left me with some difficulty in walking) but none of this, it seems, was quite enough. The Brown children approached Nemesis at a gallop. At the entrance, people were queuing with an expression of bravado seen on the faces of South American revolutionaries about to face a firing squad. I had a thought: how do people look *after* the ride? Nemesis is designed so that those going on and those coming off do not cross paths. I went to investi-gate. People were stumbling out of the exit like Californian earthquake victims, ashen-faced, legs trembling. Some looked close to tears.

'Are you coming, Dad?' asked my 11-year-old. I bravely kissed her goodbye. Well, *somebody* had to stay behind to take notes.

(Daily Telegraph)

1ft = 0.31metres
1mile = 1.61kilometres

Reading technique: scanning

1 Read the text more closely to decide if the following statements are True (T) or False (F). Underline the evidence in the text for your answer, as in this example:

Statement: 'There are five members of the Brown family present.'
Answer: F
Evidence: 'The Brown children – <u>Clementine, 11, Dominic, 13, and Celeste, 15 – and I</u> started gently.'

a Pregnant women are prohibited from riding on Nemesis.
b The aim of Nemesis is to terrify you.
c The design of Nemesis is copied from other European rides.
d The Brown children were not as excited by the other rides.
e The writer thinks people find it difficult to walk after coming off one of these rides.

Reading technique: appreciating the writer's tone

1 Look at the following extracts and, working with a partner, decide whether you think the writer's tone is Serious and Factual (S/F), or more Humorous and Ironic (H/I).

a 'Curiously, there is no mention of cowardice.' (line 11)
b 'The Princess of Wales' anxiety about riding Nemesis ... is understandable.' (line 13)
c 'Nemesis is the only thrill-ride in Europe on which you ride on the *outside* of a 360-degree loop.' (line 36)
d 'Well, I enjoyed it.' (line 58)
e 'Nemesis is designed so that those going on and those coming off do not cross paths.' (line 72)

f 'People were stumbling out of the exit like Californian earthquake victims, ashen-faced, legs trembling.' (line 76)
g 'Well, somebody had to stay behind to take notes. (line 83)

2 How does the writer's description of Nemesis make you feel about this type of ride? Do you think he exaggerates too much? Does it make you want to experience the thrill of Nemesis or does it put you off altogether?

See **Language awareness: future forms**

Exploring language: punctuation marks

Draw a table like the one below. Complete the sections 'Name' and 'Use' from the list provided and find your own examples from the previous text in order to complete the table.

Punctuation mark	Name	Use(s)	Example from text
'	apostrophe	used in possessive forms	'The Princess of Wales' anxiety.'
:			
-			
' '			
–			
( )			

Names
colon
brackets
dash
hyphen
quotation marks
apostrophe

Uses
1 used to show where letters have been left out in contracted forms of words
2 often used before an explanation
3 used when quoting speech
4 used commonly in linking compound words
5 used in possessive forms
6 used before a list
7 used to give additional but not essential information
8 used instead of colons or brackets to create an informal style

EXAM FOCUS
(Writing, Section A)

You and your family recently spent a day at Leisureworld Theme Park. However, despite the publicity material, you were disappointed by the standard of the facilities. Read the documents below and use the information in them to write:

a a formal letter of complaint to the manager of Leisureworld expressing your disappointment with your day, with a suggestion of how you can be compensated (175 words).

b an informal letter to a close friend who is planning to visit Leisureworld next month (75 words).

You should lay out your letters in an appropriate way but you do not need to include addresses.

L E I S U R E W O R L D

Do you want a fun day out for the whole family AND great value for money? For a day you'll never forget come to Leisureworld Theme Park. Experience the thrill of old favourites such as the Log Flume or try our new ride The Danger Zone – if you dare!

Make your children's dreams come true and a few of your own!

HELP US TO HELP YOU!

We hope that you enjoyed your visit to Leisureworld.
Please take a few minutes to complete the following questionnaire.

			Comments/suggestions
Were you able to park near to the entrance?	Yes ☐	No ☑	I had to wait half an hour to get into car park. Suggest you expand car park.
Were all the Leisureworld staff you encountered			
Polite?	Yes ☑	No ☐	
Helpful?	Yes ☑	No ☐	
Wearing a name badge?	Yes ☑	No ☐	
Were the toilets well-stocked and clean?	Yes ☐	No ☑	No toilet paper or soap. Air dryer out of order. Suggest they're checked every hour.
Did you have to wait more than 30 minutes for any ride?	Yes ☑	No ☐	We were advised to come back later.
Were you thanked for your custom?	Yes ☑	No ☐	

If you have any further comments please write them below.

Poor selection of food. Only fries and hamburgers. Why not introduce other menus?

LANGUAGE AWARENESS
questions (2)

1 Can you supply the correct question tags in the exercise below? Sentences c and i can have more than one answer.

a The shop opens at 9.00, ...?
b It's your turn, ...?
c Close the door behind you, ...?
(to a stranger)
d Don't be late, ...?
e Nobody called me, ...?
f You couldn't do me a favour, ...?
g I'm next, ...?
h Make sure you're home by 11.00, ...?
i Give me a hand, ...?
(to a friend)
j Everywhere's closed now, ...?
k You haven't got the time, ...?

2 Listen to the tape and check your answers.

3 Generally speaking, the verb in the question tag mirrors the auxiliary verb or the verb 'to be' used in the main clause. 'Do' is used in the question tag when the main clause does not contain an auxiliary verb or 'to be'. A positive statement usually carries a negative question tag and a negative statement usually carries a positive question tag.

Do question tags that follow imperatives differ? When the imperative is a request, what happens to the 'positive/negative, negative/positive' model?
What must be used after a negative imperative?

4 Listen again and mark the intonation pattern on each of the question tags:

Example:
The shop opens at 9.00, doesn't it? ↗

The shop opens at 9.00, doesn't it? →

5 Match each sentence (a–k) with the appropriate function (column A) and then fill in the intonation in column B.

	A	B
question	e	↗
confirmation		
request		
polite order		

6 Complete the gaps in the following conversation with a question tag. When you've finished, mark what you feel is the appropriate intonation pattern for each tag.

Dad: So, we've left the cat next door, (a) ....?
Mum: Yes, and I've finished packing the suitcases.
Dad: Hey, kids. Give me a hand, (b) ....? The bags have got to go in the car.
Susan: I'm just going to the bathroom Mum.
Mum: Well, don't take too long, (c) ....? We're leaving in a minute.
Dad: Right. I've remembered everything, (d) ....? Passports – tickets –, you haven't seen my glasses, (e)..................?
Steven: Ooops! I've just sat on them.
Dad: Great! 6.30. Everywhere's closed now, (f)..................?
Steven: Dad, I can take my bike with me, (g)..................?
Dad: Don't be stupid! Is your sister still upstairs?
Steven: Please Dad? You let me take it last year, (h)..................?
Dad: We didn't go by plane last year, (i)..................? Where's that sister of yours? She is coming on holiday, (j)..................?
Mum: Of course she is! What about these suitcases?
Dad: Oh, I'll do it myself! Don't forget to lock up behind me, (k)..................?
Susan: I'm ready! I'm sitting in the front of the car, (l)..................?
Steven: No! It's my turn. You sat in the front last week. Mum, tell her, (m)..................?
Dad: I don't know why we bother going on holiday, I really don't!

7 Now read the conversation in groups, paying attention to your intonation. When you've finished, compare your performance with the conversation on tape.

8 Test your memory. In groups of three or four, tell each other the following things:

Your birthday
The name of the last place you went on holiday
Something you're going to do next Saturday
The number of brothers and sisters you've got
The name of a famous film you've never seen

Take it in turns to try and remember things about each other. Use question tags with falling intonation if you're sure, rising intonation if you're not sure.

Example: Your birthday's on the 15th of July, isn't it?

EXAM TIP: Question tags, like reply questions examined in Unit 2, are very useful in making a conversation interactive and might prove useful in Section C of the Speaking Paper.

LANGUAGE AWARENESS
future forms

1 Read the following dialogue and underline the examples of future verb forms:

A: So ... it's your birthday on Friday, is it?
B: Yeah ... I'll be 21.
A: Well, that calls for a celebration. I'm not doing anything then so ...
B: Hang on. My girlfriend's coming round in the evening. I'm cooking her a meal.
A: Very nice! So you're not going to celebrate your birthday with your mates then?
B: Of course I am! She'll probably leave about 9.00 so I'll be free after that.
A: OK. What time shall we meet?
B: Well, my train gets in at 9.30. Is that too late for you?
A: No. There's some things I need to do in the office on Friday, so I'm going to stay till late anyway. I'll meet you at the station. We can try that new restaurant in town.
B: Saturday night though, it's going to be busy, isn't it?
A: No problem. I'll phone and book a table.
B: Great! Dave comes back from his holiday on Friday so I'll give him a ring too.
A: OK. See you Friday.

2 How many examples of the following can you find in the dialogue?

a   a simple prediction
b   a planned intention
c   an arrangement
d   a future fact
e   a firm prediction
f   requesting information or a decision about the future
g   a timetable or calendar event
h   a spontaneous decision

3 Here is some information from the authors.

a   Fiona will have been living in Birmingham for three years next September.
b   Peter will have smoked about 15 cigarettes by the end of the day.
c   Don't phone tonight. We'll be watching the football.
d   In a few minutes' time it will have been raining for two hours.
e   Hopefully by 2020 we'll both have retired.
f   We'll probably be moving this time next year.

4 Match each sentence with the appropriate time line.

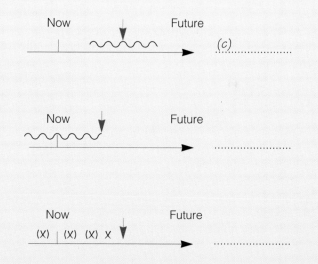

5 Write some sentences about yourself, friends or relations using the same structures.

6 Underline the correct verb form in each of the sentences below.

a   You look exhausted! Sit down. I ('ll/'m going to) do the washing up.
b   I've made an appointment with the dentist. I ('m seeing/going to see) her tomorrow.
c   I feel dizzy. I think I ('m going to/'ll) faint.
d   Trains to London (are leaving/leave/are going to leave) from platform 2.
e   I've had enough of this cough! I ('m going to/'ll) give up smoking.
f   By the time she takes the exam, she ('ll be/'ll have been) studying English for 6 years.
g   I hope I ('ll be/'ll have been) feeling confident on the day of the exam.
h   You can have the tape later. I ('ll have listened/'ll listen/'ll be listening) to it by then.
i   I ('m going to/'ll) see you later. What time (shall we/will we/are we going to) meet?
j   I ('ll have read/'ll read) the book by the time we (will leave/leave)
k   You ('ll like/are going to like/are liking) it in Spain. The weather's beautiful.
l   Don't phone him at six. He ('ll have eaten/'ll be eating/'ll have been eating) his dinner.

Your review of Unit 8

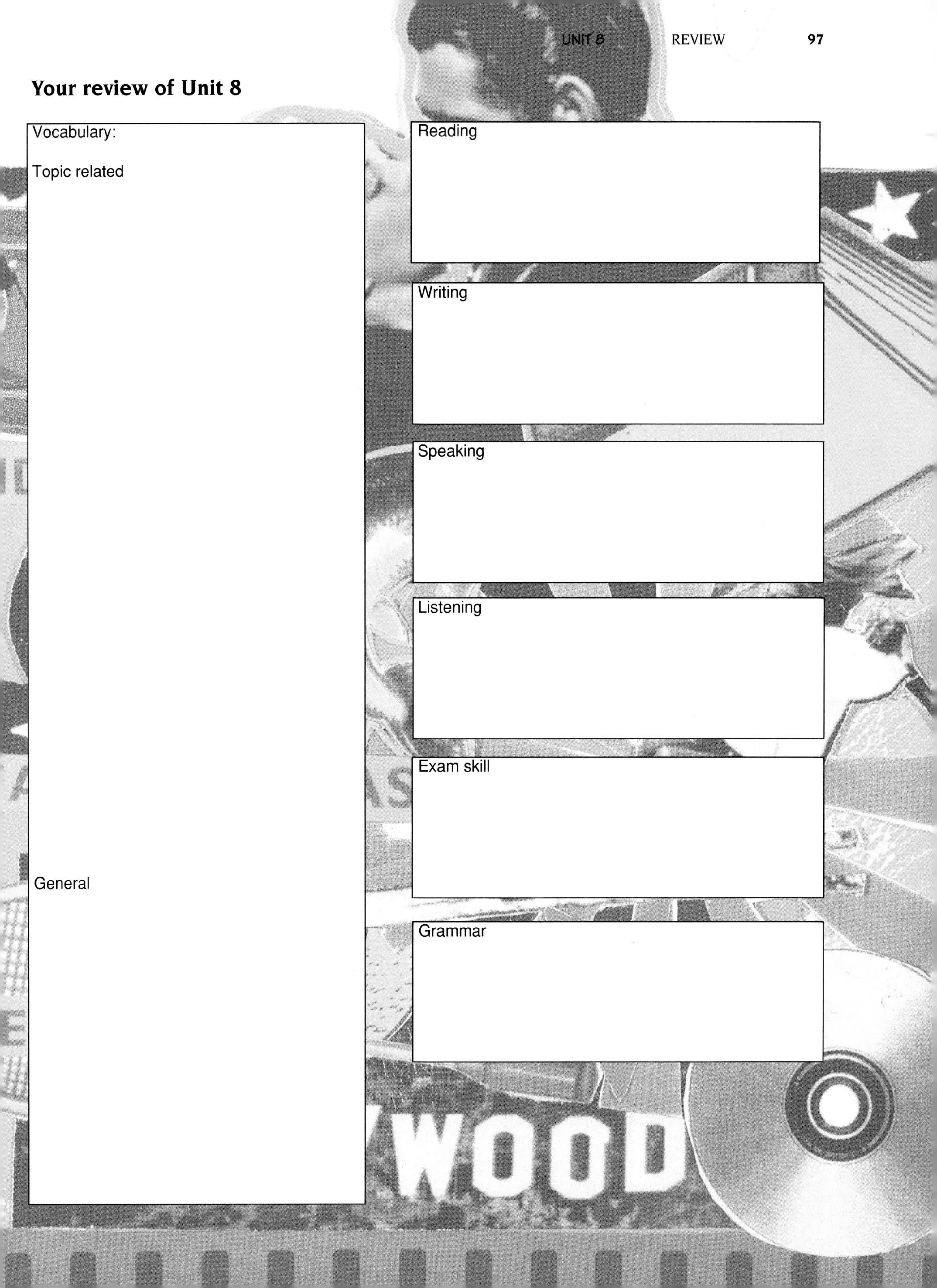

Vocabulary:

Topic related

General

Reading

Writing

Speaking

Listening

Exam skill

Grammar

UNIT 9

Human Relationships

PART ONE
An ideal family?

Lead-in

1 How much freedom do you think parents should give their children? What dangers are there in being too strict or too lenient? At what age should young people be treated as adults? Share your views with a partner.

2 Try the questionnaire below from a parent's guide-book to discover what kind of parent you are or would be.

You agree strongly with the statement	5 points	You disagree	2 points
You agree	4 points	You strongly disagree	1 point
You neither agree nor disagree	3 points		

Parents should:

- shield their children from disappointments
- always know exactly what their child is doing
- take important decisions on behalf of their child
- expect complete loyalty from their child
- never let children question parental judgements
- never tolerate criticism from their child
- expect total obedience from their child
- feel free to read their child's private diary

- be able to enter a child's bedroom without permission
- not let their child see distressing TV programmes
- not let children get their way too often
- demand respect from their children
- always have the last say

Check your scores with the key on page 146

Compare your score with a partner.

EXAM FOCUS
(English in Use,
Section C)
discourse cloze

Read through the following text and then choose from the list A–L the best phrase to fill each of the gaps.

All parents want to protect their children (1) **a** .... **b** .... Restricting a child's freedom does not imply (2) **a** .... **b** .... In fact a parent's desire (3) **a** .... **b** .... from life's dangers and disappointments probably indicates very understandable concern. It is important however that children should be allowed (4) **a** .... **b** .... , that they should make mistakes, get into and out of difficulties, (5) **a** .... **b** .... , feel the pain of rejections and cope with 'normal' human unhappiness. By allowing your child to experience (6) **a** .... **b** ...., within a caring and loving family, you are more likely to encourage the development of an assertive, (7) **a** .... **b** .... person. If your child is over-protected, he or she may well grow up (8) **a** .... **b** .... , but may also be too passive. (9) **a** .... **b** .... Excessively dependent children are at the mercy of others, whether they be parents, teachers or other children – their self-esteem can be shattered so easily. They may also be easily influenced by other children.

A	to shield her child	**G**	to face up to the problems of living
B	There are real dangers in this	**H**	quiet and well-behaved
C	more of the world	**I**	rebellious
D	But this is not a problem	**J**	self-reliant and independent-minded
E	from harm and distress	**K**	experience disappointment
F	a genuine love	**L**	any lack of warmth or love

1 Before you attempt the cloze yourself, read it through quickly for a general understanding.

2 Listen to a recording of Claire (a native English speaker) who was given the text and asked to guess some of the missing phrases. Write down her suggestions in the longer numbered gaps (1a, 2a, etc.). What strategies does she use for attempting to complete the passage?

3 Now read through the text again and choose the best phrase or sentence from the box above to fill in each of the gaps. Write one letter (A–L) in each of the short gaps (1b, 2b, etc.). Take care as there are nine gaps but twelve choices.

Writing skill: a magazine article

1 Conduct a class survey. What is the average number of brothers and sisters that people have? How many people in the group have no brothers or sisters?

2 Work in a group. Hold a brainstorming session and try to complete a table like the one below with the pros and cons of being an only child and having brothers and sisters.

| A BROTHERS/SISTERS | | B AN ONLY CHILD | |
advantages	disadvantages	advantages	disadvantages
1a	2a	3a	4a
1b	2b	3b Lots of attention	4b
1c	2c Feeling left out	3c	4c Can be spoilt
1d	2d	3d	4d

3 Look at the points your group has listed. Group together any related points and give each group a suitable title. These titles will serve as paragraph topics.

Example: 2c, 3b, 4c – love and attention

4 Look at the paragraph based on the example points above. Choose the correct connecting word or phrase from the list supplied to complete the paragraph.

> The amount of attention a child receives from the parents will to a large extent depend upon the number of brothers and sisters there are. (a).................... , a child from a large family might sometimes feel neglected while the parents tend to their other children. (b).................... , an only child will probably find itself being showered with attention. (c).................... , it is not always beneficial for a child to receive lots of attention. (d).................... , this could lead to the child becoming spoilt.
>
> a   on the one hand/to begin with/however
> b   in contrast/on the contrary/nevertheless
> c   however/moreover/although
> d   in addition/in conclusion/on the contrary

5 Students sometimes overuse connecting words in their writing with the result that the text seems unnatural. Could any of the phrases you supplied be omitted?

6 Working with a partner, write the following article for couples planning a family, in which you examine the advantages and disadvantages of large and small families (200–250 words). Concentrate on the organisation of paragraphs and sentence construction and making use of the connecting phrases you practised in 4 above.

'Planning a family.'

PART TWO
Family conflicts

Lead-in

Look at the two photographs of Helen and Tom Phillips. The first was taken 30 years ago; the second is a recent snapshot. What kind of things do you think they argued about when they first got married? What do they argue about these days? Discuss your ideas with a partner.

Reading technique: skimming

Helen and Tom's problem appeared in a magazine. Read the text quickly (three minutes) to find out what the source of their argument is, and whether you were correct in your prediction.

Helen's view:

Since my husband Tom retired last year, our home has been turned into a battleground. He's trying to take over my kitchen and I'm determined not to let him. I know it sounds trivial, but it's making my life a misery.

We'd been happily married for 35 years before Tom retired from his demanding job as a bank manager. We always knew where we stood with each other. I've never worked, at least not outside the home. My job was to look after the house and children and make sure Tom could relax when he came home from work.

Each morning, once the family had gone, I was able to get on with things in my own time, in my own way. Tom never intruded. We both had our own territories. I didn't interfere with his work, so I expected him not to interefere with mine. However, when Tom retired he seemed to think I should take a back seat in the home. I had managed on my own all these years. He wanted to be the boss.

My comfortable routine was shattered. Tom tried to reorganise my household schedule, telling me I was not doing things the best way. He offered to show me how to do things better. I couldn't believe it! For 35 years he hadn't noticed what I did at home and now it was suddenly all wrong.

At first it seemed easier to let Tom have his way. I let him reorganise the cleaning and actually felt relieved when he took over the cleaning of the bathroom and toilet. It was when he started in the kitchen that I knew things had gone too far. This was definitely the last straw. Every day he peers over my shoulder as I try to get on with the cooking. If he doesn't stop interfering I'll end up screaming the place down and flinging pots and pans at him.

Tom's view:

All my married life I've worked hard and supported the family and Helen has looked after everything at home. It always worked well. I've never understood how these new-fangled mar-riages work, where the woman has a career and they both come home exhausted in the evening.

Before I retired I didn't really pay much attention to Helen's routine. I suppose I was too absorbed in my own work in the bank. I just took it for granted that things always ran smoothly at home. Now I'm around all the time and I can't help noticing that certain things could be done more efficiently. Take the cleaning for example. Until I stepped in Helen didn't do the rooms in a logical order, one after another. She would do a bit in each room in a hap-hazard way. It's much better since I've taken over.

I've also tried to sort out Helen's cooking. I've noticed she misses odd ingredients out of recipes and sometimes lets things boil over. I've tried to work out a way of avoiding this, but she goes mad if I say anything.

It's strange, but we have this terrible tension at home. Helen shouts at me as soon as I come into the kitchen. I'm only trying to help organise things prop-erly. Even though she won't admit it, my suggestions are always good. How can I make her see sense?

(*Bella* magazine)

> Summarise the problem in one sentence.

Vocabulary development: describing personal characteristics

1 Read the text more closely and state which of the following characteristics belong to Helen (H), Tom (T), both (B) or neither (N). Use your dictionary to help you if necessary.

gentle	patient	bossy	conventional	bored
forceful	humorous	passive	exasperated	kind
tender	bullying	arrogant	patronising	fussy
affectionate	resentful			

2 Where possible, underline the relevant lines in the text where you find evidence for your views.

Example:
Resentful (H)
My comfortable routine was shattered.

Writing skill: a report for a magazine

1 A counsellor gave some advice to Tom and Helen. What do you think she said about the following points?

a What the problem was
b What the reason is
c Helen's point of view
d Tom's point of view
e A list of solutions for the couple

2 Using the notes your have made, write a reply (200–250 words) for the readers of the magazine, giving your opinion of:

a the problem
b its cause
c how the couple can resolve their difficulties

Use some of the words from the Vocabulary Development exercise in your report.

After 20 years I want him back

Two weeks ago I came face to face with the first boy I'd ever loved. We first got together when I was 16 and we went out together for two years. I'm now 30 and I couldn't believe the way I felt when I saw him. Since then, I haven't been able to stop thinking about him and wondering how I could meet him again.

I've been out with lots of men in the meantime and was married for 8 years, although we split up last year. Do you think there's any point in trying to get him to go out with me again?

You may still be feeling vulnerable after the end of yo marriage. Seeing your firs

MY HUSBAND'S JEALOUSY IS DESTROYING OUR MARRIAGE.

He makes scenes in front of everyone and it's so embarrassing. In the beginning I flirted on purpose to make him show how much he cared. He was protective and passionate but now it's all gone wrong and I blame myself. He used to like the way I dressed, but now he only lets me wear loose-fitting clothes. He's thrown away all my other clothes. If I even talk to another man he gets cross. One day I think he might attack someone. How can I show him I love him?

● Games like the one you have been playing can get out of control. Realising that this was partly your fault is a big step. But it will take both of you to improve things. The best thing is to tell him how you feel, and try to reassure him. Sometime jealous reactions stem from when we were young. For example fear that a new baby might take all Mum's attention can develop into a r of losing someone you e to someone else.

I WAS LOOKING FORWARD TO MY RETIREMENT BUT MY HUSBAND WON'T STOP WORKING.

There are so many exciting possibilities open to retired people nowadays and I was really looking forward to the chance for us to enjoy ourselves. I gave up my job at 60 and did voluntary work for 4 years, but now I feel the need to relax. I want to go somewhere hot and sunny for a holiday but my husband won't even hear of it. I'd be happy to spend relaxing weekends in the garden or enjoying a late breakfast but my husband has other ideas. He's decided to continue working part time, and he's r than he was before. so cross!

when I m
I thought that if I told him I was 20 years older than him, it would scare him off. The only problem is that I've fallen in love with him and he feels the same. My secret is always at the back of my mind and it's starting to spoil things. I want to tell everyone how happy I am, but I worry that someone will tell Tom the truth. Half of me wants to tell him myself but I can't find the courage. Sometimes I dream he's left me and wake up crying.

● Honesty is always the best policy. There will plenty of opportunities for him to discover your secret, especially if you decide to get married. And there are always plenty of busybodies around to tell him your real age. My advice is to tell Tom now; before he finds out some other way.

Family dilemma

I was 4 months pregnant when my husband and I got married. We weren't pressurised at all into marrying, but I was only 18 and my family wanted me to finish my education first. I didn't get pregnant on purpose, but it did stop our parents who are devout Irish Catholics opposing the marriage. After my first pregnancy we never had any more children. My daughter has never asked what year we married, but next year is our 25th wedding anniversary, and my daughter will be 25 – she'll realise we weren't married when I got pregnant. Lots of family are coming over from Canada and I don't know what to do. Should I tell her?

I think that there are three separate issues here; your guilt over being pregnant before you were married; the fact that you kept this a secret from your daughter and who decides how to celebrate your wedding anniversary. Your daughter was obviously a wanted baby and you love her dearly. So why would she reject you if you told her the truth? I think that you are confusing her reaction with your own feelings about the pregnancy. I think that you need to talk to someone about your feelings. When you see that your daughter is unaffected by your news you will be able to celebrate your 25 years of marriage in the right mood.

ould have been wonderful husband could have gone king holidays with you ately, but perhaps he little breathing space. e's settled into his new then you could try to e him to spend more u you. Many people feel nless they fill their day ork. Psychologists at it takes a long time to n after years of a full

PART THREE
The colours of love

'Love's just a game between two people; you shouldn't take it too seriously.'

'I couldn't eat or sleep for the first three months.'

'Physically and emotionally I felt as if I'd met my other half; we were like two pieces of a jigsaw.'

'Love is finding someone more important to you than yourself.'

Lead-in

1 How do you know when you're in love? Which of these statements opposite do you most identify with?

2 What do you feel when you're in love? Is it portrayed the same way in books and films?

Reading technique: prediction

1 There is not just one type of love. Researchers have identified six styles or categories of love. In groups, try to decide what some of these categories might be.

   Example: love where friendship is the most important element

2 Listed below are six groups of statements from a psychology journal that reflect the six categories of love. Read through them quickly. How close were you in activity 1 to identifying the categories?

A
1 We were attracted to each other immediately after we first met.
2 We have the right physical chemistry between us.
3 I feel we were meant for each other.
4 We became emotionally involved rather quickly.
5 We really understand each other.

B
1 I try to keep my partner a little uncertain about my commitments to him/her.
2 What my partner doesn't know about me won't hurt him/her.
3 I like to keep secret my other relationships/partners.
4 I could get over my relationship/affair with my partner quickly and easily.
5 My partner would get upset if he/she knew of some of the things I've done with other people.

C
1 I'm not sure when our friendship turned to love.
2 I expect to always be friends with my partner.
3 Our love is the best kind because it grew out of a long friendship.
4 Our love first required caring for a while.
5 Our love isn't mysterious, just a deep friendship.

D
1 I won't choose a serious partner unless I've first tried to plan my life carefully.
2 If my partner had come from a different background, I might not have chosen him/her.
3 It was important that he/she would be a good parent of my children.
4 My partner's choice of career is important to me.
5 I might not have chosen my partner if my family hadn't approved.

E
1 My stomach gets upset if things aren't going well between us.
2 If we broke up, I might even consider killing myself.
3 Since I've been in love I find concentrating on anything difficult.
4 I wish I could relax when my partner's with someone else.
5 If my partner ignores me for a while I do stupid things to get his or her attention.

F
1 I always try to help my partner through difficult times.
2 My partner's happiness is more important than my own.
3 I would sacrifice my own wishes if they stood in the way of my partner's.
4 I would put up with anything provided it's in my partner's best interest.
5 Were I to win a fortune, it would be my partner's to use.

3 Read the statements again. Which ones most apply to you? Do you belong to more than one category? Which category would you like your ideal partner to correspond to?

Reading technique: comprehension

Now read the six definitions from the psychology journal. In pairs, quickly match the definition below with the appropriate set of statements (e.g. A = 1, B = 2, etc.).

1 Agape: Sees love as all-giving, selfless and non-demanding. Associated with kind, committed, idealistic love.

2 Storge: Sees love as an extension of friendship. This love is solid, down to earth and presumably enduring. It is evolutionary, not revolutionary and may take time to develop.

3 Mania: Sees love as possessive and dependent. Associated with high emotional expressiveness but low self-esteem. Associated with negative relationship satisfaction.

4 Eros: Sees love as passionate and intimate, with commitment. It is strongly correlated with relationship satisfaction. Eros gives fully, intensely and takes risks in love.

5 Pragma: Sees love very logically, like a shopping list. Focuses on the desired attributes of a lover. Suited to computer match dating.

6 Ludus: Sees love as an interaction game to be played out with various partners. Relationships do not have great depth of feeling. Ludus is wary of and rather cynical towards emotional intensity in others. Associated with negative relationship satisfaction.

See **Language awareness: conditionals**

Vocabulary development: emotions

1 Not all emotions are to do with love! Here is a list of words to do with emotions. Organise them into six categories of similar meaning.

   Example: fear, terror, horror

2 Think back over the past five years of your life. Can you remember any moments when you felt any of these emotions? Choose three or four and, in groups, share some of your memories with each other.

dislike	contentment	sorrow
irritation	terror	serenity
sadness	infatuation	adoration
tranquillity	fear	rage
grief	disgust	anger
horror	calm	love
hate		

Listening technique

1 Global understanding: Tony, an English teacher, has just returned from a year's contract in Greece. His friend Steven has just received a letter from him. As you listen to Steven reading the letter, number the pictures below in the order that you hear them mentioned.

2 Specific information: Listen to the tape again but this time pay attention to the phrases and tenses used. As you listen, number the pictures in the order in which the events actually happened.

See Language awareness: past tense forms

EXAM FOCUS (Speaking, Phase B) information gap

Work in pairs.
Student A – look at the picture below of a romantic scene in a restaurant.
Student B – turn to page 146 where you will see a similar picture.

Student A, describe your picture to student B for about one minute. Student B then describe some of the similarities and differences in your picture.

1 Why not get into the habit of beginning this type of activity with a personal comment about your picture?

Example:
'This looks like a nice restaurant.'
'This is/isn't the kind of place I'd like to go to.'

2 Try to make your description as clear and detailed as possible. Don't worry if you don't know a particular word. Try to describe it!

Example:
'It's like a ... '
'It's how you look when ...'
'It's a thing you use for ...'

LANGUAGE AWARENESS
conditionals

1 Look at the extracts from the article on love opposite. What do they tell you about the commonly held belief that 'will' and 'if' always appear in conditional sentences?

2 You will probably have learned that there are four basic types of conditional sentence. Group the sentences above into the four types (there are two sentences in each).

3 Now decide which refer to 'real' and which to 'unreal' situations.

4 Finally, can you explain how the following 'mixed conditionals' differ from those above?

See the Grammar Reference section (page 171) for an explanation of mixed conditionals.

5 Unfortunately love isn't always about romance and flowers! Look at the dialogue opposite and put the verb in brackets into the correct tense. There are examples of zero, first, second, third and mixed conditionals.

---

1 I would sacrifice my own wishes if they stood in the way of my partner's.
2 Were I to win a fortune, it would be my partner's to use.
3 I'll put up with anything provided it's in my partner's best interest.
4 I probably wouldn't have chosen my partner if my family hadn't approved.
5 My stomach gets upset if things aren't going well between us.
6 I won't choose a serious partner unless I've first tried to plan my life carefully.
7 If my partner had come from a different background, I might not have chosen him or her.
8 If my partner ignores me for a while I do stupid things to get his or her attention.

---

1 Our love wouldn't be so strong now, if we hadn't first been friends.
2 We would have had a lot of arguments by now if we weren't so easy going.
3 If I'd married my previous boyfriend, I'd be living with him in Spain now.
4 If I were less independent I'd have got married years ago.

Woman waiting for her boyfriend at the cinema:

Woman About time too! Where have you been? I've been waiting half an hour. I (a) .... (not rush) if I (b) .... (know) you were going to be so late.

Man Sorry darling. My car wouldn't start and I had to get a bus.

Woman If you (c) .... (take) my advice last week and put the car in the garage, we (d) .... (sit) in the cinema now watching the film. Unless we (e) .... (hurry) , we (f) .... (miss) the beginning.

Man Look, I've said I'm sorry! If you (g) .... (know) the trouble I (h) .... (have) getting here, you (i) .... (be) a little more understanding. If you (j) .... (not stop) moaning, we (k) .... (miss) the end of it.

Woman Come on then. I (l) .... (get) some chocolate if you (m) .... (buy) the tickets.

Man But I thought this was going to be your treat! I've left my wallet at home. If you (n) .... (tell) me earlier, I (o) .... (bring) it with me.

Woman If only you (p) .... (can) do something right for once.

Man Sorry darling. Have I told you lately how much I love you?

1 Look at the short extract from a love story below.

There he was again! The tall, middle-aged man (who had been) into the bank only two hours earlier was standing in front of her waiting to be served. He was still wearing the exquisitely tailored suit that had caught her attention earlier. Helen, the cashier, (stopped) what she was doing, (greeted) him politely and (made) a little joke about the frequency of his appearances. In actual fact, she'd (been thinking) about him all afternoon. She'd been so preoccupied with the thought of his rugged but sensitive features and those wonderful green eyes that she'd been unable to concentrate on her work. This second visit seemed to confirm what she'd been hoping for all along. 'Would it be possible to change this into something smaller?' he asked. As he handed her a five pound note Helen couldn't help noticing that his hand (was shaking). 'Was he blushing) as well?' she asked herself. Helen (had carried) out a similar transaction only ten minutes earlier so why did this one seem so obviously contrived? 'I was wondering ...' he continued. He (was looking) at the counter rather nervously. 'I hope you don't mind my asking ...' Helen knew this was the moment. 'Yes,' she said to herself, 'ask me, the answer's yes.' She (was preparing) her response to the question that she knew (would) turn her world upside down, when from the manager's office she (heard,) 'Helen, can you come here a moment. There's something I'd like you to do for me.'

2 Work in pairs. Can you match the following uses of past tenses with the circled verbs?

a long action or event in the past interrupted by a shorter action or event
b a past action in progress at the same time as another
c an action in progress in the past
d one of a sequence of completed actions in the past
e action in an earlier past
f activity in progress or repeated action in an earlier past
g future in the past

3 Can you find any other examples of these uses in the story?

4 'Time lines' are often useful ways of understanding the uses of tenses. Look at the example below and then try to construct time lines for the other uses listed above.

Action in an earlier past   Past   Now

5 🔲 Turn to the tapescript of the love letter on page 163. Many of the past forms have been omitted. Put the verb in brackets into the correct form. When you have finished, listen to the tape to check your answers.

6 'Past' and 'past modal' forms are used widely in English to create 'distance'. Discuss what kind of distance the use of 'past' forms convey in each of the groups of sentences below.

a Provided Manchester United win this evening they will go top of the league.
b If I won the lottery I'd buy a house abroad.
c I would have phoned if I'd known.

a Close the door!
b Can you close the door?
c Could you close the door please?

a I live in a terraced house in Birmingham.
b Last year I was living in Coventry.
c I'd lived in London for 27 years before I moved to Coventry.

a Hundreds of years ago scientists had argued the earth was flat.
b Today the Prime Minister claimed unemployment was his number one priority ...
c ... yet statistics indicate his Government's policies are making matters worse.

7 Which of the above groups are examples of 'past' forms used to show:

a social distance?
b distance in terms of what you believe to be true?
c distance in terms of time?
d hypothetical distance?

Your review of Unit 9

Vocabulary:

Topic related

General

Reading

Writing

Speaking

Listening

Exam skill

Grammar

UNIT 10

The World of Work

PART ONE
Work values

Lead-in

1 Look up the meaning of the following phrases in your dictionary. Which, if any, best describe your feelings towards your choice of career or your general attitude towards work?

I'm in a rut	I'm a bit of a plodder
I'm a go-getter	I'm at a loose end
I'm a high flyer	I'm on the way up

2 Very few people are lucky enough to find the perfect job. However, the search can be made easier if you can identify the things you like to do. Work in small groups and identify which of the following activities appeal most to each person.

contributing to society	having contact with people
working alone	working with a team
competing against others	making decisions
being creative	solving problems
gaining security	supervising others
using your intellect	taking risks
gaining recognition	constantly learning
being active	being able to travel

3 Would you make a good Careers Officer? From what you have learnt about the other members of your group, work alone and think of three or four jobs that might suit each of them. When you're ready, share your opinions with each other.

▣ Listening technique: specific information

1 Read the extract from a pop music magazine below. Then listen to the interview and complete the information for questions 1–13. Use no more than three words for each answer.

P O P   P R O F I L E

Danny Price, jazz dancer and choreographer, gave us the low down on the life of a dancer.

Qualifications	Believe it or not, you need to have experience in (1) _____ and have a good voice apart from being a good dancer.
Equipment	You need to invest a lot of money in equipment (clothes, shoes, etc.) You may even need your roller skates for particular shows.
Food and fitness	You'll need to exercise daily for about (2)_____ in total. Stock up on the pasta. A dancer's metabolism often (3) _____ . So you can afford to eat a lot without worrying. Dancing's a great way to de-stress.
Current projects	Lots of things! Some choreographing, some video work, a module for N.W.A.B. Soon I'll be touring with a band called N-Joi and every week I'm doing some (4) _____ in Leeds, York and London.
Ambitions	I've discovered I could never be a (5) _____ . I stick out a bit too much for that. I would settle for a long-running (6) _____ .
Background	I'm of mixed race. I was born in Jamaica, as was my dad. Mum's from Edinburgh. I've got (7) _____ and an absolutely adorable sister who's like (8) _____ .
Pets	I've got (9) _____ Armani!
Training	In England, Paris and LA. I enjoy training, apart from not (10) _____.
Breaking in	You need to be a member of Equity, the union for actors and dancers, to get good contracts. But it's not easy. My advice? Go out into (11) _____ and see if you can find anything else you'd like to do first. If not, take up dancing.
Personal beliefs	Thanks to dancing, I've visited (12) _____ so far. This has opened my eyes to the world, and I've been able to come to terms with issues like (13) _____ and hopefully have become a better person as a result.

2 Listen again if necessary. Have you made any spelling mistakes? When you're satisfied, check your answers with a partner.

3 From what you've heard, does the lifestyle of a professional dancer appeal to you? What are its advantages and disadvantages?

Vocabulary development: some common expressions

1 Rewrite the following words and phrases to show that you understand their meaning. Look at the tapescript on page 162 if you cannot remember the context.

you can pig out on pasta   like a household name

a cocktail   into a vicious circle

2 In natural speech you will hear the schwa / ə / sound very frequently. Mark in the schwa sounds in the expressions opposite. Which schwa sounds are contained in the word? Which ones become schwas in connected speech?

EXAM FOCUS
(Writing, Section A)

A friend from overseas has sent you the letter opposite asking for help in finding a course in professional dance. Following your enquiries, you've been sent a prospectus of which an extract appears below. You've also come across Danny's article in the magazine.

Using this information, write a reply to Debbie, giving her the information she requires about the college and any appropriate advice from Danny's article. You may invent information of your own but do not change any of the information given. You are advised to write approximately 250 words.

The London College of Dance and Drama is pleased to be able to offer a one year course in modern dance and drama. There are no formal qualifications required for entry onto this course. However, successful candidates will have already gained some experience in either dance or drama and will have a level of fitness necessary for an intensive course in the performing arts.

The course will run from September 12th to July 20th. Fees £2000. For an application form, contact Sarah Tomlinson:

London College of Dance and Drama
Marlborough Street London EC1

and my family sends their love. I've just returned from another holiday. You know me, I'd travel for the rest of my life if I had the chance! It was Spain this time. Anyway, could you do me a really big favour? I'm hoping to come to Britain during the summer - I'm not sure when yet - to do a course in professional dancing. You know I've always loved to dance and I still study and perform with my part-time dance group twice a week.

The problem is, I can't get my hands on any information over here. I'd be really grateful if you could find some details on a good college, preferably in London. Sorry to be a nuisance, but I really haven't got the faintest idea what you need to start a course like this. I expect it'll be quite expensive, what with the course fees, any clothes I might need to buy and then of course living in London! I'm hoping the course will be quite short, two years at the longest. I should be able to afford that.

What do you think? I haven't got any qualifications but what's the use of a Maths or Geography certificate if you want to be a dancer? Could you write and let me know what you find out?
Write back soon

All the best
Debbie

1 Highlight exactly what the task is in the Exam Focus instruction.

2 Working with a partner, underline all the points in the letter that need to be answered.

3 Now look for the information from the college and the magazine article that should be included in the letter.

4 Consider the following: the level of formality (who are you writing to?), the layout and the organisation of the letter.

PART TWO
Finding the right person for the job

Lead-in

1 Do you believe that graphology (the study of people's handwriting) can reveal important aspects of an individual's personality? If you are not sure how graphology works then try the following questions which have been designed by a graphologist to convince you of its effectiveness:

a   Which person has the moodier character? Why?

A   **or   B**

I couldn't wait any longer.   I couldn't wait any longer.
– See you tomorrow.   – See you tomorrow.

b   Who likes to be in the middle of everything? Why?

A   **or   B**

                                     Just a note to let you know
                                     I can't make it tonight.

        Just a note
        to let you
        know I can't
        make it tonight.

c   Who is lying about his/her age? Why?

A   **or   B**

    I am 36 years old.   I am 36 years old.

2 | Please submit a typed CV and a handwritten letter of application |

How would you feel if you applied for a job and discovered that handwriting analysis was one of the methods used for selection? Discuss as a class.

1 A interviewee	B applicant	C employee	D looker
2 A undertake	B give	C performing	D embark
3 A finding	B realising	C searching	D evaluating
4 A worldly	B practical	C useful	D efficient
5 A useless	B unable	C incapable	D incompetent
6 A in-built	B inside	C deep	D real
7 A ability	B aptitude	C skill	D quality
8 A upper	B best	C high-level	D big
9 A understood	B agreed	C approved	D accepted
10 A validity	B advantage	C truth	D good

A Read the article below and then decide which word best fits each space.

Selection Tests

Trade Tests

Simple attainment tests are usually possible in most jobs. A/An (1) .... for a secretarial position would be asked to (2) .... a typing and/or shorthand test, or be given an audio tape to transcribe. Similarly, an electrician could be asked to go over a circuit diagram or answer a few questions on apparatus used in the working routine. Not to take this opportunity of (3) .... a candidate's (4) .... knowledge of the job could prove very embarrassing if he/she is later found to be (5) .... of doing the job.

Psychometric Tests

These are designed to evaluate a person's (6) .... characteristics and discover his/her rating in either general intelligence, personality or (7) .... for a certain type of work. However, they are only generally suitable for (8) .... jobs and care must be taken to ensure that the candidate is able to understand what is required and is up to taking the test.
The use of this type of test is not universally (9) .... and there are certain doubts about the (10) .... of the results.

B Complete the following article by writing the missing words in the space provided. Use only one word in each space.

Write-on, but is it a science?

Job applicants (1) .... find their handwriting says more about them than they reveal in an interview. David Guest reports.

You will know that you have stumbled into the hands of graphologists if, in the course of an application for a job, you are asked to submit anything handwritten. The question (2) .... what can you do?

   According to Dr Fritz Cohen, a graphologist, the use of handwriting analysis (3) .... selecting candidates for jobs is growing. Unfortunately, the employers putting it (4) .... practice are shy and reluctant to declare themselves.

   (5) .... that can be said for sure is that if you apply for a job with a French company you will almost certainly (6) .... asked to provide a sample – but this will not necessarily happen with a British subsidiary. The Germans and Swiss are also more receptive to the practice.

   The case (7) .... graphology is strongly urged by Dr Cohen. 'Coupled (8) .... well worked-out job descriptions and structured interviews, handwriting analysis by experienced analysts is the (9) .... reliable method of candidate selection,' he claims in *Handwriting Analysis at Work*. 'I suggest that employers conduct their interviews to form their own opinions, then get a graphologist's report and compare the (10) .... They will be sure to find points in the report that do not come out of the interview.'

Before attempting this activity, read the notes on page 114

1 Work in pairs. One of you should complete cloze A, the other cloze B.

2 When you have finished, answer the following questions about your text.

- How easy or difficult did you find the activity? (You can put an asterisk * next to any answers you're not sure of.)

- What kinds of words were you required to fill in? 'Grammatical' words, e.g. prepositions/auxiliary verbs or 'content' words, e.g. nouns/main verbs/adjectives?

- What type of knowledge were you being tested on? Vocabulary and collocation or knowledge of grammatical structures?

- Summarise the content of your text in one or two sentences.

3 Share the above information with your partner before checking the answers with your teacher. Can you work out any strategies to help you with these types of questions in the CAE exam?

Listening technique: specific information

1 What personal experience have you had of applying for jobs or training courses? Did you have an interview or some form of test or exam? Have you had any disastrous experiences? Tell your partner.

2 Peter, one of the authors of this book, had a rather unfortunate experience with a psychometric test. Listen to the tape once and tick each point as it is mentioned. Make sure you understand the context in which each point is made.

a a heating engineer
b it was a chance to meet lots of people and the working day wasn't too long
c 40 with three or four choices each
d four weeks
e the graphs didn't correspond at all
f when he felt like it
g it was unfair because he would have been a good milkman

3 Working in pairs, write suitable questions which correspond to each of the answers above. Try to ensure grammatical correctness in your question forms.

4 Based on the texts in this unit and your own knowledge or experience how should we go about finding the right person for the job?

See Language awareness: verb forms (2)

PART THREE
Trade unions
Lead-in

1 Look at the list of statements below. Give each
   one a score of 1–5 depending on your opinion.
   (1 = strongly disagree, 5 = strongly agree)

   Every worker should be made to join a trade union.

   If you let them, trade unions would take over the country.

   Workers should negotiate individual pay rises, not collectively through trade unions.

   Everybody should have the right to strike, even policemen, soldiers, doctors, etc.

   Without trade unions, people's working conditions would be a lot worse.

   Management should be allowed to ban trade union membership in their company.

   Trade unions and management can work together quite easily.

   Trade unions are no longer as necessary in a modern economy.

2 How well can you argue your case? Work in a
   group and see if you can persuade the colleagues who disagree with you to change their
   scores.

Read the following trade union handout and then answer the questions which follow.

A NEW DEAL FOR YOUTH

A

Mass unemployment among young people remains a blight on our society. Yet thousands of needs go unfulfilled. There are many jobs to be done, both in industry and in the public services – for instance caring for the old, sick and the very young. These jobs must not just take young people off the streets, but should carry proper pay and sound training. Anything less would be a waste of our most valuable resources – the country's young people.

B

School studies should help young people understand and take their place in society, including preparation for working life and an understanding of the major social, economic and political issues of our time.

C

Every 16-year-old should have a genuine choice of a place on a training scheme, a place in full-time education, or a job.

And this does *not* mean a job with pay kept deliberately low.

D

The priority is to create jobs, but until we can achieve this: Young people completing a year on a training scheme without finding a job must have the chance of further education and training. All 19–25-year-olds who have been unemployed for over six months must be given a guarantee of a training place as part of a massive expansion of special programmes for unemployed adults.

E

All 16–19-year-olds must have the chance of continued study courses suited to their needs and interests. Grants must be guaranteed for all 16–19-year-olds in full-time study. The number of places in higher education must be expanded with better grants. There must be no discrimination against overseas students on course fees.

F FOR YOUNG BLACK PEOPLE

Young black people's chances at school must be improved and all forms of racial bias rooted out of our education system. Racial discrimination against young black people in getting jobs and promotion must end. Unions at every level must work to achieve this goal. Young black people who have missed out at school must be given the chance of training and education both on leaving school and at 18 plus. Police harassment of young black people must stop and local control of the police must be improved. There must be no racial bias in the courts.

G

Sex discrimination must end in schools, and in further and higher education. There must be positive action to improve opportunities for young women in employment, promotion and vocational training, and particularly access to skills training. There must be new training programmes for young unemployed women disadvantaged by past education failures.

For questions 1–6 choose the most suitable heading for each of the sections of the handout (A–E, and G).

For questions 7–11 answer by choosing from the sections of the handout A–G. Note: When more than one answer is required, these may be given in any order.

1 Students ☐
2 Wasted resource ☐
3 The young unemployed ☐
4 Young women ☐
5 School pupils ☐
6 School leavers ☐

Which section refers to:

student finances	7 ☐
the wages young people should receive	8 ☐ ☐
examples of jobs in the community	9 ☐
prejudicial treatment of groups in society	10 ☐ ☐ ☐
offering a second chance at education or training	11 ☐ ☐ ☐

When you have completed the exercise, work in groups and share your ideas. There are sure to be differences of opinion! You should therefore underline evidence in the text to support your decision. Insist that your colleagues also find evidence if they disagree with you.

See **Language awareness: participles (2)**

Use the following notes to write a leaflet from the management of a company to its employees warning them of the consequences of strike action. Write in complete sentences for each numbered set of notes, adding connecting words or phrases as necessary. Write one sentence only for each set of notes. You may change the forms of words given but do not give any extra information. The first one has been done as an example.

1 Working in pairs, fill in as many words as you can. What type of grammatical words/constructions do you have to supply in this type of question? Discuss with your teacher if necessary.

2 Expand the notes into full sentences and try to focus on how you link clauses together in different ways.

3 It is important that your ideas make sense so check that the meaning of your full sentence is logical in the context of the question.

0 Come to our attention, your T.U. called for strike action, support – demand, more pay.

Example: It has come to our attention that your Trade Union has called for strike action in support of their demand for more pay.

1 Company concerned, turn of events; believes necessary, explain situation, you make correct decision.
2 Company profits up last year, strike action very damaging, threaten productivity .
3 Competition in this industry, suffered through economic recession, never fiercer.
4 Your T.U., refuse enter negotiations, act irresponsibly, ask you to strike.
5 Strike goes ahead, we warn you, redundancies happen.
6 Company's 5% offer, above national average, final.
7 We move into 21st.C, T.U.s realise, a need for more responsible behaviour.
8 Company hopes, employees understand seriousness of situation, refuse take strike action.

Vocabulary development: common abbreviations

When tackling an English in Use question like the writing activity above, it is necessary to know common abbreviations or to be able to work out their meaning from the context.

Example: We move into 21st C, T.U.s realise

As we move towards the twenty-first century, trade unions must realise ...

1 The following abbreviations are commonly used in the world of work. Write out their full equivalents.

a Re your letter of September 14th ...
b And furthermore we would be pleased ... PTO
c Yours sincerely,
Mrs. Burke
Enc. Report
d To: Mike
From: Joanne
cc: Head of Personnel
e Head of GTL Banking req.
50k + benefits

2 What do the abbreviations in the following extracts stand for? Where do you think each extract might come from?

1 Has anyone phoned about the ad you put in the paper yet?
2 Fantastic hols. V. hot and loads of good food. Fave place so far: Prague, esp. monuments.
3 Fully furnished accom. to let, £45 pw. Non-smoker pref.
4 To order this magazine send £12 to the address below (p+p inc.).
5 Coats, hats, etc. may be left in the cloakroom.
6 Cap. Budapest. Pop. 6m approx.
7 Parking 10m from entrance.
8 Read pp. 10–14, ch. 2 for next week.

LANGUAGE AWARENESS
verb forms (2)

1 Look at the following extracts from the interview with Peter. Categorise the uses of 'to + infinitive' under the five headings below:

as the subject of a sentence
to show purpose
after the object of certain verbs
after certain verbs
after most adjectives

a I'd given up my job as a heating engineer to have a nice long holiday.
b ... to cut a long story short.
c ... and why I'd always wanted to be a milkman.
d ... he gave me this questionnaire and asked me to fill it in.
e ... what does it take to be a milkman?
f It's one thing to fail an interview, but to fail it without knowing why ...
g I'd be interested to know just how successful they are.
h I'm pleased to see you got over the experience.

2 Convert the following notes of a letter into full sentences using 'to + infinitive' constructions. You will also need to concentrate on prepositions and tenses.

a It/great/receive/your last letter.
b This/just a short note/tell you /my recent holiday.
c My friends/persuade/me/go/holiday to England.
d I/never/be/to England before/and I/determine/have a good time.
e On the first day/we/go/to London/see/the sights.
f Unfortunately/I/not remember/take/an umbrella. It/rain/all day.
g Still/it/interesting/see/all the famous buildings.

3 Certain verbs can be followed by either a 'to + infinitive' or '...ing' form but with a change of meaning. Look at the sentence pairs below and then complete the third example.

a I remember feeling very nervous on my first day at school.
b Did you remember to lock the door?
c You were sleep-walking last night. Do you remember (walk) .... into my bedroom?

a I'll never forget seeing my first football match. I went with my dad.
b I forgot to tell you Jim phoned earlier.
c I forgot (pay) .... the gas bill. Do you think they'll cut us off?

a He was totally lost so he stopped the car to ask the way.
b I stopped smoking three years ago.
c Can we stop (argue) .... all the time? Let's be friends!

a The team went on to win the Cup the following year.
b He went on doing the garden even though it started to rain.
c She was so lazy! Her tutors never realised she would go on (become) .... famous.

4 Here's a chance to revise verb forms. Read this reply to the letter in activity 2 which contains several mistakes. Can you find them all and correct them?

Dear Fabio

Thanks very much for your letter. I was sorry hear about your holiday ... it didn't really rain every day, did it? Next time you go to England remember taking an umbrella! Actually, I had the opposite problem on my holiday ... sunburn. Everybody told me avoid the sun in Greece, but you know me, I'd rather to lie on the beach than go sightseeing and to visit boring old buildings.

I'm working very hard at the moment for passing my English exam. I passed First Certificate last year and a friend of mine suggested me to try CAE. It's quite a nice exam actually, but there's so much work to do. That reminds me, I'd better to finish this letter soon, I've got loads of homework! My tutor goes mad if you don't hand in your work on time. She doesn't even allow that students finish it a bit late.

Anyway, I must to go now. Write back soon, you know how much I enjoy to read your letters. And don't forget the telephone, it would be nice talking to you.

I hope hearing from you soon

5 Think of somebody very famous who all your colleagues will know. Complete the following sentences (using 'to + infinitive') in the way you think this person would finish them. When you're ready, read your sentences to the class. Can they guess the person?

I once attempted ...   In the near future I hope ...
I took up my career ...   I would never allow my partner ...
I would hate ...   I was once very pleased ...

EXAM TIP: Useful for expanded notes in English in Use, Section C.

1 Read the following newspaper article. Can you explain the headline?

TESTS IN THE DOCK

Tests used by companies to identify high-flyers came under attack yesterday from leading psychologists. According to the latest issue of 'Perspectives in Psychology,'companies turning to psychometric tests as a means of identifying potential ability could be choosing the wrong candidates. Controversy has raged over the suitability of these tests since their introduction over a decade ago. However, reservations expressed during the 1980s have lately turned into major doubts.

People attending interviews over the past few years have found themselves having to overcome yet another obstacle on their way to a successful appointment. In addition to forms, references and final interviews, they now face questionnaires concealing investigations into their psychological health.

However, psychologists argue that tests compiled and analysed incorrectly are doing more harm than good.

2 The article contains several examples of present and past participles used as 'reduced relative clauses'. Can you find them? How would they be expressed as full relative clauses?
Example: Tests used by companies
Tests which/that are used by companies

3 Supply the correct participle in the sentences below. Each verb is used twice, but you must decide whether the past or present participle is necessary.

a 1 Any luggage .... unattended will be removed by the police.
  2 Employees .... the premises should ensure all lights are extinguished.

b 1 People .... duty-free goods must show their boarding passes.
  2 Goods .... during the sale cannot be returned.

c 1 Plants .... under artificial light tend to grow much quicker.
  2 Gardeners .... sensitive plants should beware of an early frost this year.

d 1 Students .... examinations should report to Room 101.
  2 Photographs .... within the restricted area were confiscated by officials.

e 1 Anyone .... company property will be dismissed.
  2 Buildings .... by the storm may have to be demolished.

4 Participles can also be used to express many different ideas:

If this is done	because
after	when
with the result	

Match these meanings with the participles in the following sentences.

a The oil tanker ran aground, polluting rivers and coastline over a wide area.
b Putting his hand in his pocket, he noticed his wallet was missing.
c Used regularly, this product can alleviate symptoms of stress.
d Having turned off the light, she went to bed.
e Having turned off the light, she couldn't see where she was going.

5 Using participles in this way creates a formal style often found in written English such as literature, instructions and reports. Make the following informal sentences more formal using participles.

a He missed his flight because he turned up late.
b If you take the tablets regularly they should clear up the infection.
c When he arrived at the ground he realised the game had been called off.
d The government did away with state pensions, with the result that many people were left penniless.
e After he left university he went into the legal profession.

6 The sentences all contain phrasal verbs which are often avoided in formal writing. Find a more formal equivalent for each multi-word verb.

EXAM TIP: Participles used in these ways will be useful for the expanded notes in English in Use, Section C.

Your review of Unit 10

Vocabulary:

Topic related

General

Reading

Writing

Speaking

Listening

Exam skill

Grammar

Power Relationships

PART ONE
At the top

Lead-in

What do you know about these four people? Which person is the odd one out?

Do you know of any other people who have shared the same fate?

KNOWLEDGE IS POWER

MONEY IS POWER

POWER CORRUPTS

32 — 40 BALLARD & MARLIN

Reading technique: identifying paragraph topics

Look at the sentences opposite, which have been extracted from the article on assassination (below). Read the article and try to place the sentences in the correct spaces. Two of the sentences are not used.

1 America is naturally very aware of this threat.

2 Assassinations of political leaders have occurred for thousands of years.

3 But why has murder become so popular as a means of bringing about political change?

4 Some look at it in terms of numbers.

5 The dictionary definition of 'assassinate' is to kill a political or religious leader for religious or political beliefs.

6 Although a lone gunman, Lee Harvey Oswald, was arrested for the murder, he denied the charge.

7 By the Middle Ages, a Christian doctrine had been developed to justify murders in order to save the Christian world from 'evil rule'.

8 Sometimes, assassins' efforts have backfired.

9 But as Professor Wilkinson points out, only a relatively small number of assassinations have been politically successful.

WHEN FANATICS OPT FOR MURDER

Public figures are all well aware of the dangers faced from political extremists or individual fanatics. One of the most publicised examples is of President Kennedy, who was shot dead while travelling in a motorcade through Dallas, Texas.

a

He was shot dead by an outraged citizen before he could be brought to trial, and rumours persist that Kennedy was killed by more than one gunman in a conspiracy which involved criminal organisations, federal agencies or foreign governments

b

In 44 BC, Julius Caesar was killed by senators unhappy about his use of power. But it was only in the 11th century that the term 'assassination' came to be used. It gained its name from the Nizari Ismaillis, a politico-religious Islamic sect, based in Persia, which considered the murder of its enemies a religious duty. The name derives from the Arabic *hashishi* (hashish eater), since members of the sect were believed to take the drug before carrying out the murders.
From 1094, Hasan-e Sabbah, the sect leader, commanded a network of strongholds all over Iraq and Persia. Assassin power ended in 1256, after a continued assault by the Mongols and the Mameluke Sultan of Egypt.

c

And followers of theological philosopher Thomas Aquinas (1224–1274) as well as radical thinkers such as Marcilius of Padua (1280–1343), began to argue powerfully for the overthrow of rulers who defied the laws of God.
Assassinations continued and, in the 100 years up to 1870, over 20 political leaders were killed by revolutionaries in Europe alone.

d

According to Professor Paul Wilkinson of the Research Institute into the Study of Conflict and Terrorism, the most common justification used by assassins is that the end justifies the means. 'Assassins believe that their objective is a positive goal which overrides the negative aspects of killing,' he says.

e

If, for example, a tyrannical ruler were responsible for deaths on a large scale, it could be argued that his or her death would help save future lives. This argument was used during the English Civil War and The French Revolution, where King Charles I and King Louis XVI had been seen as tyrants and their removal, it was believed, would end widespread repression in these countries.

f

'It is easy to remove a tyrant,' says Professor Wilkinson, 'but far more difficult to remove a system of government. The only examples of long-term success in recent years have been assassinations by groups fighting against colonialism, for example in Cyprus, Aden and Algeria. Otherwise, the assassins' "victories" have achieved only short-term goals – for example, extorting large sums of disruption and a general air of tension.'

g

This occurred in Russia in 1881. Tsar Alexander II, who had already abolished serfdom, was about to announce a move towards a new, more democratic constitution. But he was blown up by anarchists and his son, Alexander III, cancelled the liberal reforms and imposed a tougher, more authoritarian regime on the population. The rest is history.

(Guardian)

How successful were you? How did you make your decisions? Circle the words or phrases that helped you and discuss your answers in groups.

**Read the text again and answer the questions
by choosing A, B, C or D.**

1 President Kennedy was
A shot dead by an outraged citizen
B murdered by more than one person
C involved in a conspiracy that led to his death
D assassinated for reasons as yet unknown

2 The Nizari Ismaillis
A carried out assassinations as a consequence of taking hashish
B and their use of hashish gave rise to the term 'assassination'
C were the first to use the term 'assassination'
D took hashish out of a sense of religious duty

3 Many Christians in the middle ages
A began to develop a doctrine to justify assassination
B disagreed about the justification for murdering non-Christian rulers
C assassinated more than 20 people
D found it possible to justify the murder of their opponents

4 Professor Wilkinson believes
A assassins have had no success in removing systems of government
B groups fighting against colonialism have only achieved short-term goals
C gaining publicity is not a worthwhile objective
D assassinations have tended to have limited success

5 The purpose of the text is to
A Outline briefly the history of assassinations
B argue that assassinations are often justifiable
C argue against politically motivated murder
D explain why assassinations can rarely be justified

1 Look back to Unit 3 (page 31) to remind yourself of how multi-choice questions generally work. Then, with a partner, try to narrow down your choices by rejecting those answers that are obviously incorrect.

2 When you've finished underline evidence in the text for your choices and discuss your answers in a group.

3

'If, for example, a tyrannical ruler were responsible for deaths on a large scale, it could be argued that his or her death would help save future lives.'

Do you agree? Can politically motivated murder be justified in certain instances? Have there been any cases of political killing in the news recently?

See **Language awareness: emphatic structures**

Vocabulary development: guessing unknown words

1 The following words all appeared in the article, many of which are probably new to you. How sure are you that you can guess their meaning correctly? Tick the appropriate answer:

	no idea	perhaps	fairly sure	sure
motorcade	☐	☐	☐	☐
outraged	☐	☐	☐	☐
conspiracy	☐	☐	☐	☐
sect	☐	☐	☐	☐
derives	☐	☐	☐	☐
strongholds	☐	☐	☐	☐
doctrine	☐	☐	☐	☐
overthrow	☐	☐	☐	☐
overrides	☐	☐	☐	☐
backfired	☐	☐	☐	☐

2 What factors helped you to make informed guesses?

Writing skill: revision of narrative tenses

Every year on November 5th in England people 'celebrate' Guy Fawkes Day. A 'Guy' is put on the top of a bonfire and fireworks are set off.

1 Imagine you have been asked to write an account of this custom for an encyclopaedia. Look at the following picture story of Guy Fawkes. In pairs, using the past simple and past continuous, quickly tell the story chronologically as illustrated. Use the following words or phrases in your story:

1 to give birth
2 to be outraged
3 to convert to (catholicism)
4 to enlist in
5 courageous

6 to plot
7 a cellar
8 to plant, barrels of gunpowder
9 to torture, the rack
10 to try, to find guilty, to sentence to death

2 Is the story interesting? Does it grab the listeners' attention? One way to create interest and dramatic effect is to re-arrange the sequence in which events are described. Try re-writing the story following the sequence below. You will now need to think about using the past perfect simple and continuous as well. Try to join the events together imaginatively.

Sequence: Picture 4, 1, 2, 3, 5, 10, 6, 7, 8, 9

Example:
Picture 4,1. In 1593, Fawkes left England to join the Catholics who were fighting in the Netherlands. 23 years previously, Guy had been born in Protesant England ...

3 Read this new version to the other students. Ask them to comment on how you have linked events as well as your use of past tenses.

PART TWO
Between the sexes

Lead-in

1 Look at the list of words below. How would you score the average man and woman on the scale? Put an M (man) and a W (woman) under the appropriate numbers.

Example:

	6	5	4	3	2	1	
Aggressive		M		W			_____

	6	5	4	3	2	1	
Emotional							_____
Aggressive							_____
Caring							_____
Sensitive							_____
Expressive							_____
Talkative							_____
Assertive							_____
Sentimental							_____
Selfish							_____
Tender							_____
Innocent							_____

2 How do your scores compare to other students', particularly those of the opposite sex?

3 Working with a partner, can you supply the opposites to these words? Quite often more than one word may exist. List as many as you can but be careful to choose words with the correct contextual meaning.

Speaking skill: sharing opinions

1 Are there real differences between the sexes? Are they more to do with nature or nurture?

2 In groups discuss the ways society might influence the behaviour of men and women. Consider the following points:

- the toys children are given
- examples set by parents
- stereotyped images of men and women on TV

3 The role that men and women generally have in society can vary from culture to culture. Look at the topics in the box opposite and discuss how they relate to men and women in your country. Put an M (man) W (woman) or E (either) in the box.

4 Do you agree with these gender roles?

	Your country	Trikeri
Proposing marriage	☐	☐
Deciding on the children's education	☐	☐
Controlling the family budget	☐	☐
Inheriting land and property	☐	☐
Being the breadwinner	☐	☐

Reading technique: scanning

The following article describes life for men and women in an isolated Greek village called Trikeri. Scan the article for information to complete the second section of the box above. How quickly can you do it?

Where Women Rule

Eleni Kotta, 33, is blonde and cheerful. 'Here,' she says, 'it's not the boys who propose. They wait to be asked. Like objects.' 'Here' is Trikeri, a Greek village of 2,000 perched on a rock at the tip of a peninsula in the Aegean Sea. For centuries, people say, the Earth here has spawned seamen who go out to fish or ship out on cargo vessels, far across the ocean. So, in this closed society bound by traditions, it is women who have the last word. 'They're the queens of the village,' says Kotta, with a gleam in her eye.

The women of Trikeri are anything but striking. The old women, like mysterious silhouettes, stiffly wend their way along the mule paths that pass for streets. They go to cook their bread and pastry at the baker's oven. They sit crocheting in the shade of a terrace, or scrub laundry in old tubs. The young women, with '*Dallas*' style hair-dos, spend their time chatting, first at one house and then at another, or at a cafe, with lazy expressions and childish giggles.

They do not make much of an impression, but they decide everything: the children's education, housework, the purchase of land, the family budget. And they decide on the unwritten laws that have always governed Trikeri. The men come home from the sea after weeks or months with arm-

loads of gifts. They rest or drink *tsipouro* (a powerful liqueur) at the bar, and the women spoil them until they go to sea again. No one would dream of changing the division of roles. This system, formerly widespread in the Aegean, has been lost to modernity except in Trikiri, where people have always been wary of strangers.

The social system in Trikeri is 'matrilocal'. A marriage or even an engagement means that the man goes to live with the woman, and it is the girls who inherit land and houses. The family has to own or build as many roofs as there are female children. The boys inherit the boats. But a boat does not last – the land is eternal. And it is the maternal family that serves as a nest for infants and provides a social framework for the husband.

When Kotta got married, she received the house that had belonged to her maternal grandmother and then to her mother. 'It's my eldest daughter who will inherit it when she gets married,' she says. 'My youngest daughter will have another house. As for my mother, she settled nearby so she can continue taking care of me.

'Boys,' says Kotta, 'are like lamps that light other people's houses, not your own. The good that comes from boys is never for you, it's for other

women. When you give birth to a boy, you raise him, you help him to study, and then you give him to the sea ... But my daughters and I always stay together.' Without daughters, women in Trikeri feel unfulfilled.

Men are not scorned in Trikeri – far from it. They play an economic and symbolic role. It is the father who gives his daughter away in marriage. But it is the mother who chooses the groom. Even community affairs, theoretically handled by men, are not settled without the women. 'If you ask a man whether the road needs repair,' Beopoulou says, 'he often answers, "What do I know? Ask my wife."'

Wrapped in her black shawl, Kotta's daughter Malamatenia approves of this: 'The men exist to work and bring home money. It's a system we like.' Boys are raised with only that goal in view, and they go to sea when they are eight or ten years old. Since 1988, Trikeri has had a school where boys can study to become seamen, but with higher qualifications.

The girls are raised at first like the boys, just as free. But when the girls are four or five years old, their grandmothers, godmothers and mothers begin preparing their trousseaus. At age twelve, the girls leave school. Not long ago, they were kept at home and put to work embroidering. That is less common today. If they show talent, they can now go to high school. But many of them, like many boys, prefer to stop after elementary school.

(Observer World News)

Reading technique: inferring meaning

1 'The women of Trikeri are anything but striking.' What is the purpose of this paragraph in the context of the overall text?

2 'This system ... has been lost to modernity.' Does the writer give any impression that this is a good or a bad thing?

3 'Boys ... are like lamps that light other people's houses, not your own.' What do you infer from this statement?

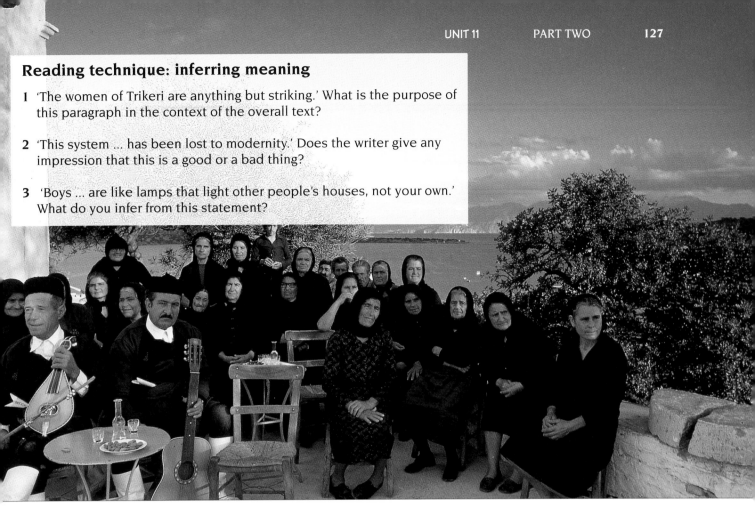

EXAM FOCUS
(English in Use, Section A) open cloze

Read the final three paragraphs of the article and then decide which word best fits each space.

Fourteen-year-old Angela, for example, wears jeans torn at the knees – the latest fashion – but spends her days at the sewing machine, embroidering her trousseau, just (a) ..like.. her great-grandmother did. 'I'll get married when I'm 25,' she says. And meanwhile? 'I'll embroider.' She does not seem bored. She laughs with her sisters, her aunts, her mother and her friends. The bride's trousseau (b) .... one wedding in Trikeri included 100 pillow-cases, 50 sets of sheets, 50 tablecloths, piles of woven blankets and clothing for the bride as (c) .... as for the couple's future children.

Even today, (d) .... all marriages are arranged, but an effort is made to ensure (e) .... the two young people like (f) .... other. Women are engaged at age 14 or 15. Yet marriages in Trikeri tend to be successful. 'The men are gone (g) .... much to have time to fight,' says an old woman.

Women in Trikeri talk (h) .... fatalistic ease about love and relationships. Some find their husbands' constant absence hard to bear. But most agree with Assimina, 24, who says, 'I prefer for him (i) .... go to sea. When he comes home, he's all honey and flowers. It's (j) .... like an eternal honeymoon.'

1 Look back to page 113 to remind yourself of the the open cloze question. What kind of words are gapped?

2 When you've finished compare answers in groups and try to reach agreement.

PART THREE
Campaign groups

Lead-in

1 Are you the kind of person who tries to make a stand against the establishment? Have you ever been involved in a campaign? Alternatively, do you believe trying to get politicians and civil servants to change their minds is a waste of time?

2 Have you ever done any of the following:

gone on a march   signed a petition
gone on strike   joined a political group
written a letter of protest to a newspaper

3 If not, would you be prepared to? What issues might make you angry enough to take some kind of action?

Reading technique: predicting

Look at the following headlines from a local newspaper in England. What do you think the stories are likely to be about?

1 **MOTORWAY STORM** ☐
2 **YOUTH CLUB DANGER** ☐
3 *Wildlife threat* ☐
4 SUPPORT FOR NURSERIES ☐
5 Shelter Alert ☐

Reading technique: scanning

Look at the extracts from the stories that accompanied the headlines. Read them quickly and try to match them with the appropriate headline. Try to finish within a minute. Don't worry about the gaps in the text.

a Homeless organisations are warning that people will face great hardships this winter unless urgent action is taken to offer shelter. This warning follows publication of figures showing an increase in homeless people, particularly amongst (1) ....

Pam Whitecroft of 'Homes for All' warned; 'With a shortage of rented accommodation, more people are having to sleep rough in (2) .... With a cold winter predicted this year these people will have to put up with sub-zero temperatures. Action must be taken urgently to offer these people shelter.

b Residents of Shildon were last night preparing for a night of protest to save their village from Government planners. Proposals for the new M29 have caused uproar amongst residents who claim that insufficient time was allowed for consultation.

The proposed new motorway will run within (3) .... of Shildon. Tony Fellows, spokesperson for the (4) '..................................' campaign, explained yesterday:

'The planned route cuts across some of the most picturesque countryside in the region. Shildon plays host to thousands of tourists each year. Many of the shopkeepers depend on this trade and would almost certainly face ruin if tourists were put off coming by the damage this road is likely to do.'

c Youngsters in the City-Centre are to lose out on a much loved project if substantial funds aren't found. The (5) '..................................', open to young people from the ages of 10 to 17, is threatened with closure by Health and safety officials who claim the building is unsafe.

The club, built in 1973, was badly damaged by heavy storms last year and city engineers estimate that (6) .... pounds is needed to repair structural damage. With only limited funds at their disposal, organisers fear the club will have to close.

d A rare species of butterfly and many (7) .... face extinction if the Lea-Valley Office Complex Project goes ahead, claim local environmentalists. They argue the proposed 10 acre development, to be built on the site of woodland dating back hundreds of years, will rob the country of several rare species of wildlife.

'Local people would be horrified if they knew of the consequences of this project,' claimed environmentalist Ian Wilson yesterday. 'We need a (8) .... to alert everyone of the dangers. The developers must not be allowed to do this.'

e Mums and dads throughout the city are signing up for our (9) '..................................' campaign. Readers have been jamming our switchboard all week supporting our demand for cheap nursery care for children between the ages of 3 and 5. At the time of going to press, (10) .... people had signed our petition.

'Married couples', single parents and their children are facing severe financial problems due to a lack of child care facilities,' explained campaign organiser Sue Shipmen. 'Parents are not able to take up paid employment because of parental responsibilities. Society should be there to lend a hand.'

Listening technique: global understanding

You are going to hear a local radio programme which invites listeners to write letters commenting on issues of current interest. Read the articles on page 128 once more and then listen to the broadcast. How many letters do each of the news items receive? For each letter, tick the appropriate headline below.

MOTORWAY STORM   ☐

YOUTH CLUB DANGER   ☐

WILDLIFE THREAT   ☐

SUPPORT FOR NURSERIES   ☐

SHELTER ALERT   ☐

EXAM FOCUS
(Listening, Section A) gap fill

You will have noticed that the articles on page 128 were gapped. For questions 1–10 listen to the radio programme again and supply the missing information. Use no more than three words.

Vocabulary development: homophones

Homophones (words that have the same pronunciation but which are spelt differently and have different meanings) are often used in British newspaper headlines, particularly with reports of a lighthearted nature.

1 Look at the three headlines below. What exactly is the 'play' on words? What do you think the stories are about?

SUITE SUCCESS

COURT IN THE ACT

NOW YOU SEA IT – NOW YOU DON'T

2 Can you find homophones for the following words?

four	wait	made	heal
steal	sight	been	through
peer	stair	rain	tear
sauce	night	bread	morning
sought	blue	meet	lead

3 Working in pairs, invent headlines like the examples above, making use of some of these homophones. Make up stories to go with them. When everyone is ready read your headlines to the group. See if they can guess the content of your story.

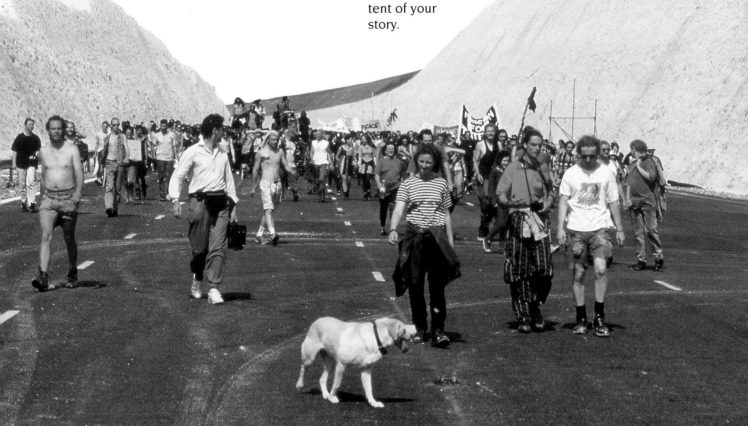

Speaking: role play

A local businesswoman has recently died and left eight thousand pounds to the campaign group who can put the money to the best use. She has instructed her solicitor to decide who should receive the money. You are going to take part in a meeting to decide who should get the donation.

1 Form six groups. Each group should nominate a speaker.

2 Groups 1–5: choose one of the issues dealt with in the newspaper articles on page 128. Think of all the reasons you can why your campaign is the most deserving of the money. What uses could you put the money to if you had it?
Work together and write a speech supporting your bid for the money.

Group 6: you are representatives of the solicitor. You should prepare a short speech giving an outline of the businesswoman's life, her interests and why she decided to leave this money in her will.

(Groups 1–6: Refer to the language awareness section: emphatic structures)

3 When everybody is ready nominate a chairperson.

4 Before starting the meeting, look at the feedback sheet on page 146. While listening to the speakers, make comments in the appropriate sections. You are allowed to comment on positive as well as negative points!

5 Start the meeting. Make notes of any questions you might want to ask the speakers when they have finished.

6 When the meeting is finished and all questions have been asked, the solicitor's representatives should decide who receives the money.

Writing skill: a formal report

Groups 1–5: write a report of the meeting (200–250 words) for your campaign group. Include summaries of the speeches and any decisions that were made. Goup 6: write a similar report for the businesswoman's next of kin.

See Language awareness: multi-word verbs

Nurseries for all

- Help mothers return to work
- Cheap nursery care for the under fives
- Greater provision needed in

SAFE HAVEN

More than 2,000 people sleep rough on the streets of Manchester every night of the year.

With another cold winter approaching they need your help more than ever.

HOMES FOR ALL aims to renovate 30 flats for homeless people - paid for by donation

- £1000 buys a new damp proof course
- £250 buys plumbing for a flat
- £100 buys roof insulation
- £15 buys paint for the kitchen
- £10 buys a smoke alarm

PLEASE HELP US TO BRING THE HOMELESS IN OUT OF THE COLD

If you would like to contribute to the appeal please fill in the form. Thank you for your support

Mr/Mrs/Miss/Ms _____

Address _____

_____

Postcode _____

Telephone _____

Please send your donations to:
Homes For All
18 Paddenswick road
Manchester
M24 6NB

Wildlife Watch

Don't let our wildlife become extinct

- threat to butterflies
- rare species in danger
- unique plants face extinction
- precious woodland will be destroyed
- recreational area will be lost forever

ACT NOW TO OPPOSE THE DEVELOPERS

Stop the Lea Valley office complex project

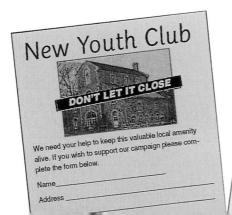

New Youth Club

DON'T LET IT CLOSE

We need your help to keep this valuable local amenity alive. If you wish to support our campaign please complete the form below.

Name _____

Address _____

SAVE OUR VILLAGE

Say 'No' to the road builders

The figures speak for themselves. Over 20 million cars are registered in D...
and road traffic...

LANGUAGE AWARENESS
emphatic structures

1 Look at the sentences listed below. What feature do they all share?

Not only has this Government reduced inflation, but unemployment has also fallen.

No sooner had I got in the bath than the phone rang.

Rarely does one find such fine examples of 17th Century furniture.

Should you wish to discuss the matter further, I will be pleased to assist you.

Only when the power is off should you attempt to dismantle the machine.

On no account must you open this document.

Had we known the criminal's whereabouts we would have arrested him sooner.

2 All the sentences have inversion of subject and verb. Which word or words are stressed in each sentence? Write the sentences without inversion and compare the difference.

Structures like these are generally employed when a degree of emphasis and/or formality is required, such as in anecdotes, speeches and literature.

3 Frank has upset his bank manager again. The manager made the remarks below to Frank during their last meeting. A letter needs to be sent confirming the same points in writing. Using the structures above, re-write the comments, making them more formal and emphatic.

a I don't often have customers with such an irresponsible attitude.
b You've extended your overdraft and also made some expensive purchases with your credit card.
c Immediately we finished our last meeting you went away and bought a new hi-fi.
d If I'd known about your other debts, I would have asked you to see me sooner.
e Don't use your credit card again until you have paid off your overdraft.
f And whatever you do, don't use your cheque book.
g If you have any more financial problems contact the bank as soon as possible.

4 Look at the political speech below which has been written without making any use of emphatic structures. Proofread the speech using the structures provided and inverting subject and verb where you think this is appropriate.

On no account ...	Rarely ...	Were ...
Had ...	So ...	Not until ...

'Good evening Ladies and Gentlemen. The attempted assassination of the Prime Minister this morning has shocked the nation. One doesn't often receive news of such a distressing nature. It showed a shocking disregard for human life. If we had been less fortunate, many innocent lives could have been lost. The people who committed this crime must be left in no doubt: the nation will not be satisfied until those responsible have been severely punished. The terrorists demand that we enter into discussions, yet the population are so outraged by this terrible act that we could not consider talking with these people. We really will not give in to such pressure. If we weakened, the very foundations of our democratic system would be threatened.'

5 🔈 Now listen to an improved version on tape. How similar is it to yours?

Pronunciation tip: Read your speech out loud to your partner. By banging your fist on the table at the stress points indicated above, you can give added emphasis to these structures.

EXAM TIP: Emphatic structures can be useful for formal letters or reports in Paper 2 (Writing).

LANGUAGE
AWARENESS
multi-word verbs

Multi-word verbs are notoriously difficult. There are a great many, often with both literal and idiomatic meanings.

1 What are the idiomatic meanings of the multi-word verbs expressed literally in the cartoons below? Check your ideas with these dictionary extracts:

2 Draw similar cartoons representing the meanings of the multi-word verbs in these dictionary extracts. (They might help you to remember them!)

come up with sth find or produce (an answer, a solution, etc): *She came up with a new idea for increasing sales.*

cut down (on sth) reduce the amount or quantity of sth; consume, use or buy less (of sth): cut down one's expenses. *The doctor told him to cut down his consumption of fat. I won't have a cigarette, thanks - I'm trying to cut down (on them) ie. smoke fewer.*

fall off decrease in quantity or quality: *Attendance at my lectures has fallen off considerably. It used to be my favourite restaurant but the standard of cooking has fallen off recently.*

get down to sth/doing sth begin to do sth; give serious attention to sth; tackle sth; *get down to business. It's time to get down to some serious work.*

hand sth out (to sb) distribute sth: *Relief workers were handing out emergency rations (to the survivors).*

pass over sth ignore or disregard sth; avoid sth: *They chose to pass over her rude remarks. Sex is a subject he prefers to pass over, e.g. because it embarrasses him.*

pass sth up (infml) refuse to accept (a chance, opportunity, etc.) *Imagine passing up an offer like that!*

point sth out (to sb) direct attention to sth: *point out a mistake. Point out to sb the stupidity of his/her behaviour. I must point out that further delay would be unwise.*

3 It is important to be able to identify which multi-word verbs require an object and where the object should go. Read the following sentences and then try to answer the questions below. Check your answers in the Grammar Reference section on pages 173-4.

a I can't come this evening. John's car's broken down.

b It would appear that the thieves have got away.

c If I come up with any good ideas I'll let you know.

d Let's get down to some work then, shall we?

e If there's one thing I just can't put up with, it's rudeness.

f Would you like me to hand the homework out?

g No, it's all right. I'll hand it out. You can hand out the test papers if you like.

h He never did get over the shock of his team being relegated.

i Do you mind looking after my cat while I'm away?

Why are multi-word verbs like 'break down' and 'get away' different from others like 'get over' and 'look after'?

What do three-part multi-word verbs like 'come up with' and 'get down to' have in common?

In which of the sentences above can the multi-word verb be separated?

In multi-word verbs that can be separated, where must the pronoun go?

4 In groups, complete the following dialogue, exchanging the formal words with their multi-word verb equivalent from the examples above. If it is possible to separate the multi-word verb, do so.

Situation: an informal company meeting.

Tom: Shall we (a) commence (..........................) business? Sue?

Susan: Right. First of all, John sends his apologies. He can't be here today as he still hasn't (b) recovered from (..........................) his cold. Next, I've got copies of the company reports here, can somebody (c) distribute (..........................) them. Everybody got one? If you turn to page three you'll see a break down of profits for August and September. As you can see, they have (d) decreased (..........................) quite dramatically.

Frank: If I can just (e) highlight something (..........................) for a moment. We should be receiving the exact sales figures for October shortly. Do you think we could (f) disregard (..........................) this issue until then?

Tom: Yes, good idea. Can I ask you all at next week's meeting to (g) make (..........................) some suggestions when you've had a chance to look at the overall picture?

EXAM TIP: Multi-word verbs appear commonly in informal writing but should usually be replaced with a more formal latinate equivalent in formal writing.

Your review of Unit 11

Vocabulary:

Topic related

General

Reading

Writing

Speaking

Listening

Exam skill

Grammar

UNIT 12

Crime and Punishment

Lead-in

1 Look at the following list of crimes. How common are they in your country? Which crimes most affect the business community and which ones the general public?

Ram-raiding ☐ ☐

Joyriding ☐ ☐

Burglary ☐ ☐

Violence against people ☐ ☐

Shoplifting ☐ ☐

Handling stolen goods ☐ ☐

Fraud and forgery ☐ ☐

Vandalism ☐ ☐

Drug dealing ☐ ☐

2 Which of these crimes pose the greatest threat to society? Rank them in order of their seriousness using the first column. (1 = most serious, 9 = least serious)

3 Work in groups. How closely do your opinions coincide with those of your colleagues? Try to reach agreement on the most and least serious crimes.

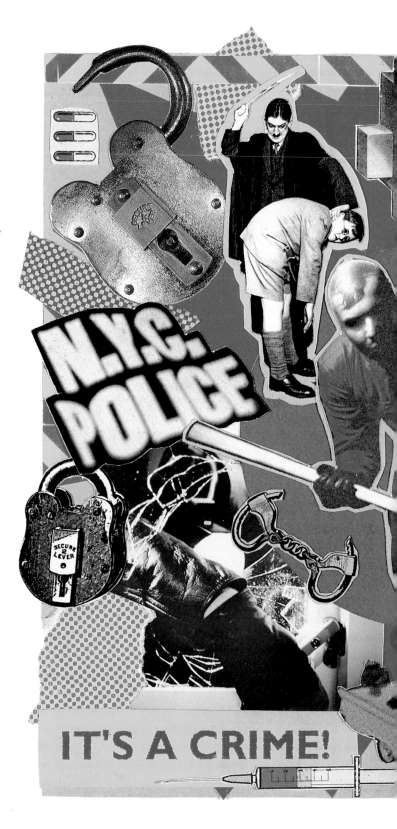

IT'S A CRIME!

EXAM FOCUS
(Listening, Section D) identifying topic and speakers

1 ▣ You will hear some people talking about crime. As you listen look at the crimes listed in activity 1 (page 134) and put them in the order in which you hear them, writing a number from 1–5 in the second column. Four boxes will remain empty.

2 Listen again and put the speakers from the list below in the order in which you hear them, writing a number from 1–5 in each box. This time, three boxes are not needed.

Policeman	☐	Convicted criminal	☐
Concerned citizen	☐	Prison officer	☐
Judge	☐	Priest	☐
Teenager	☐	School teacher	☐

See **Language awareness: perfect tenses**

Exploring pronunciation: word families

1 How are the underlined vowel sounds pronounced in the following pairs of words?

cr<u>i</u>me – cr<u>i</u>minal   m<u>o</u>ral – m<u>o</u>rale   hum<u>a</u>n – hum<u>a</u>ne
/ /   / /   / / / /   / /   / /

2 How does the vowel sound in these adjectives change when they become nouns? Complete the chart.

Adjective	Noun
cl<u>ea</u>r / /	cl<u>a</u>rity / /
n<u>a</u>tural	
s<u>a</u>ne	
v<u>ai</u>n	
cl<u>ea</u>n	

3 Fill in the verb from the following nouns and find the changes in vowel and consonant sounds.

Noun					Verb			
advertisement	/ /		/ /			/ /		/ /
bath		/ /		/ /		/ /		/ /
breath		/ /		/ /		/ /		/ /
cloth		/ /		/ /		/ /		/ /
loss		/ /		/ /		/ /		/ /
reduction		/ /		/ /		/ /		/ /
sign		/ /		/ /		/ /		/ /
supervision		/ /		/ /		/ /		/ /

PART TWO
The right to smack

Lead-in

1 Think back to your early childhood. Were you well behaved or a little terror? Can you remember some of the incidents that led to you getting punished? What kind of punishments did you receive? Work in groups and list the punishments you all received in order of severity.

2 Imagine you look after a friend or a relation's young child on a regular basis. Which, if any, of the punishments you listed would you be prepared to give the child?

Reading technique: skimming

Read the opening and closing sentences of Text A, B and C and complete these tasks in no more than two minutes.

1 Choose the best title for each text:

 a The making of little monsters
 b Campaigners press for ban on minders smacking children
 c Right to smack ruling triggers furore
 d The no-smacking guide to good behaviour
 e Time to stop respecting our children's freedom

2 Which of these pictures (A–E) would you choose to illustrate each article?

3 Try to justify your answers for each question to your partner.

Text A:

We all want good children. Looking after somebody else's children always means effort and stress, but when things go well it can be a lot of fun as well. And when you're taking care of a child whose parents are working, or making a home for children whose parents are unable to look after them for a while, you have the satisfaction of knowing you are doing a vital job.

We'd all rather take care of 'good' children, children who:
– don't do as they shouldn't
– do as they should
– are cheerful, pleasant and polite
– are sensitive to our moods
– don't let us down in public

What kind of discipline will help your charges to be like that as often as possible? The answer is positive discipline which builds on children's desire to please adults who are important to them.

It's NOT the kind that tries to make children good by punishing when they're naughty.

It's CERTAINLY NOT the kind that relies on hurting their feelings .... and it's NEVER the kind that relies on smacking, even if a child's own parents expect it. Because smacking is a short-cut that doesn't lead where you want to go.

A

B

Text B:

A child minder has the right to smack children in her care, the High Court ruled yesterday, renewing a fierce debate over corporal punishment.

Anne Davis, over whom the test case was fought, said it was a victory "for every parent in the land who believes in the reasonable use of physical discipline". Mrs Davis, 34, who has three children, said it was a "victory over the politically correct" who "cannot tell the difference between loving discipline and child abuse".

But the ruling brought instant demands from the National Society for the Prevention of Cruelty to Children and from the National Childminding Association for a change in the law to ban smacking by childminders. Local authorities were alarmed by the comments of John Bowis, a junior health minister, who said: "Clearly what the judgement has done is to underscore common sense."

The court case arose when the London Borough of Sutton refused to re-register Mrs Davis on their books because she refused to sign an undertaking not to smack. She is a former teacher, and had been caring for Luke Formann, then aged three, for two years. She and Luke's mother agreed that young children occasionally require smacking, and that she could, if she thought it appropriate, smack Luke.

Text C:

When did you last stop a youngster from doing something anti-social? I don't mean as a parent or in school, but on the street, as a member of the community – as an adult? And would you do it again? I did last Saturday and I don't know.

Between the Co-op and the baker's the pavement was busy with shoppers and pushchairs. My younger daughter was with me. A boy on a bike came weaving through the human slalom, expertly skidding in front of the post office and doing a wheelie from one side of the pavement to the kerb, to an accompaniment of tuts and mutters and raised walking sticks. The boy on the bike was impervious. He completed a semi-circular return for another skid, when I set a firm hand upon his bars and blocked his way.

I am not of slight build. He was short, thin, and his head reached my stomach.

"Don't use the pavement for bike tricks," I said.

"Get off my bike, you!" and he yanked the bars in my grip.

"Get your bike off the pavement and stop being a nuisance," I said.

"Get your hands off. Don't you touch my bike."

"Don't ride your bike on the pavement."

"Right, I'm telling my dad about you."

He jerked his bike away and sped off, shouting a fricative syllable of abuse. My daughter, observing the hissed exchange from several paces away, said: "Did he say sorry, Daddy?"

C

D

E

Reading technique: appreciating the style of a text

1 Read the texts more closely. Which stylistic description applies to each text? Write the appropriate letter or letters in the boxes below.

neutral ☐   exaggerated ☐

objective ☐   balanced ☐

persuasive ☐   encouraging ☐

factual ☐   cynical ☐

2 Two extracts have been taken from a later section of each of the articles. Match these extracts (a–f) with the correct text.

 a Do expect some showing off and silliness in pre-school children: 'rude' rhymes, noise and boisterous behaviour that tends to send things flying!

 b Even at school ... if you told a kid to pick up the chocolate wrapper they had thrown to the ground you could meet a stare of incredulity.

 c Adults are unwilling or afraid to lay the hand of restraint on children. But unchecked liberty can threaten other people's rights, including those who approve of freedom.

 d The NSPCC said it was "deeply shocked".

 e If you're angry with a child, don't try to bottle it up: tell him or her what s/he's doing wrong, what s/he should have done and what s/he can do to put things right

 f She was evidently highly suitable in all other respects as a childminder, wished to smack only to the extent the parent wished her to do so, and had been successfully minding a child whose parents wished her to have the facility to smack.

See **Language awareness: articles**

EXAM FOCUS
(Writing, Section B)
a letter to a news-paper

Text B, which reports on the true case of a childminder who went to court to argue for the right to smack children in her care, appeared in a national quality newspaper. You have decided to write a letter to the newspaper putting forward your views on the subject. Write the letter (200–250 words) arguing in favour of or against the child-minder's case.

1 Look back at Unit 11 to remind yourself of how emphatic structures can be used in formal writing to state your point of view forcefully.

2 You might find the following formal phrases useful in introducing your points:

It is my belief that ...
It is in the best interests of our children that we ...
Under no circumstances should we ...
There is no evidence to suggest that ...

PART THREE
Living in fear

Lead-in

1 Do people in your country generally live in fear of crime? Is crime a major political issue? To what extent does the fear of crime affect you?

2 Answer the following questions as honestly as possible.

What would you do in the following situations?

a You're lying in bed one night when you hear a noise that seems to come from somewhere in your house or apartment.

b A dangerous criminal has been arrested. Unknown to the police, you were a witness to the crime but if this becomes known you will have to give evidence against the man in court.

c You've left home and are on your way to work. Some 15 minutes from your house, you start to wonder if you closed your front door properly. You think you did but you're not positive. There have been a number of burglaries in your neighbourhood.

d You've recently won an extremely large amount of money on the lottery. The story has appeared in a local newspaper and now everybody knows where you – and all your money – can be found.

e You're due to go on holiday abroad for two weeks tomorrow, when you hear that two of your neighbours were burgled last night.

3 How well do you really know your colleagues? Try to guess what other people in your group would do in these situations.

4 Have you ever felt unsafe in your own home? What have you done (or would you do) to protect yourself from a burglar? Work in a group and list all the precautions that could be taken – rational and irrational – to help you feel secure.

EXAM FOCUS
(Reading)
paragraph cloze

In the following text, the writer gives an account of the fear and insecurity she feels at night in bed when her husband is away from home. Choose which of the paragraphs A–G match the numbered gaps (2, 4, 6, 8, 10 and 12). There is one paragraph which does not fit anywhere.

Home Alone

It is a still, cold night. A silver frost covers the ground, glistening in the light of a perfect full moon. In the distance can be heard the plaintive howling of the wolves in the zoo. One by one all the lights go out.

2

But what was that? I sit bolt upright in bed. I surely heard a door opening? I slide noiselessly out of bed and tiptoe across the landing, my heart pounding, my ears straining for further evidence of intrusion. I sit on the top step and resume my lonely vigil. It is 4 am and I am home alone.

4

I always start the night off well. I watch television to the point where my eyelids are starting to confuse the plot – taking care to avoid all programmes that might possibly provide fodder for my over-voracious imagination. Thus thrillers are out, and even the news – every lunatic and terrorist in the south-east seems to be on the run from prison or mental hospital the night my husband is away.

6

Having satisfied myself that all is secure and that there is no maniacal rapist secreted about the place, I turn on the burglar alarm and make my way upstairs.

8

When we were first married, I used to heave the wardrobe door across the bedroom door – the possible hazards of fire had not at that time occurred to me, although it was a little inconvenient if the phone rang downstairs or one needed the loo in the middle of the night.

10

One friend of mine confided that when her husband is away, she wanders around the house talking to herself in a very loud voice and even stands upstairs and shouts down to him to come to bed. This does not however solve the problem of sleeping.

12

I did once heed my sister's advice to sedate myself with a bottle of wine. I slept like a log, but woke the next morning with a thumping hangover and found that I had been so drunk that I had left the patio doors not only unlocked but open.

I shall definitely sleep tonight. The house is securely locked, the burglar alarm is on and I have taken my neighbour's advice and brought up to bed with me a pot of black pepper to throw in the face of any possible assailant. But what if ...?

A When I must finally switch off – always remembering to pull out the plug – I begin my tour of inspection. All windows and patio doors are checked and doors securely bolted. I then unplug the downstairs phone. I then check behind all interior doors, in the garage, under the stairs – and the beds – and in the wardrobes.

B Another friend always sleeps with a sharp knife under her pillow. Yet another friend suggests getting a dog. A dog? Haven't I got enough to worry about without me and my babies being savaged in our beds?

C By this time, of course, I am wide-awake.

D By day I am an eminently sensible woman. But turn the clock round to midnight, remove my husband to foreign climes and you will see before you a neurotic wreck, whose nerves explode at the slightest creak of a central heating pipe.

E So we eventually decided against the idea of a guard dog even though this appealed to the children.

F The arrival of the children made life more problematic, however. Not only was the wardrobe a no-no, but for heaven's sake, if I was murdered in my bed how long would it be before anyone heard those poor, crying, starving babies the next morning?

G I sit rigid in my bed in the dark. My bedroom door is wide-open onto the large, square, well-lit landing. I have full view of my children's bedrooms, which open onto it, and of the staircase, which rises into it. Every fibre of my being is stretched, taut and alert, listening; the silence roars in my ears. All is well. Eventually I lower my guard, relax back into my pillows and start to drift away from this threatening world.

---

1 Read the text and the extracts first to get a general understanding.

2 You will need to look for clues to the structure of the text. These structural clues might involve general vocabulary, linking words, topics, etc. Here are some words or phrases from the text that will help you identify links. Can you find the connections?

All is well ...   All is secure ...
I watch television ...   I sit rigid in my bed ...

3 Can you and your partner find any more clues? When you think you have finished, compare your answers with the group. If their results differ from your own, insist that they give you evidence of their links.

Vocabulary development: dealing with unknown words

1 Find words from the preceding text that correspond to the following definitions.

   a walk quietly and carefully (verb) *paragraph* 3
   b sound that a wolf makes (noun) *paragraph* 1
   c very anxious and nervous (adjective) *paragraph* 4
   d very eager for knowledge or information (adjective) *paragraph* 5
   e trying as hard as possible to listen (verb) *paragraph* 3

2 Work out the meaning of the following words from the context. Write either a definition as in Part 1 or use the word in a sentence of your own which illustrates the meaning.

   a glistening   e heave
   b fibre   f hazards
   c pounding   g slept like a log
   d fodder   h assailant

Listening technique: specific information

1 Do you have Crime Prevention Officers in your country? If not, what do you think their job is?

2 Listen to this advice from a Crime Prevention Officer and make notes about what the writer could do under the appropriate headings:

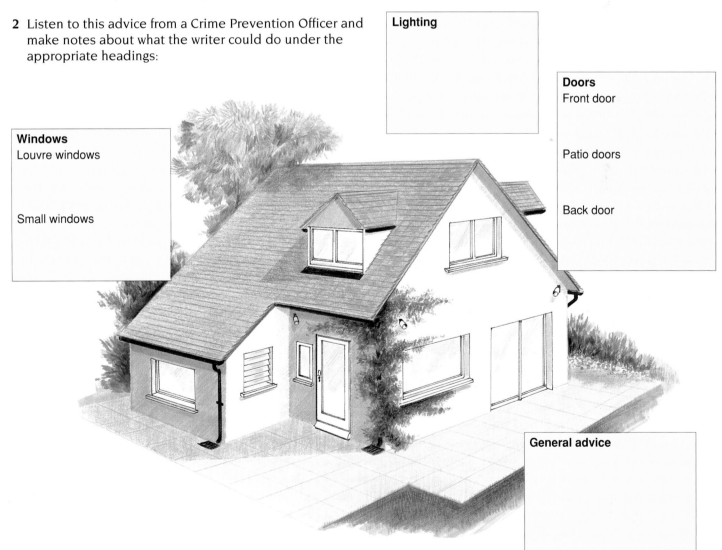

Lighting

Doors
Front door

Patio doors

Back door

Windows
Louvre windows

Small windows

General advice

LANGUAGE AWARENESS
perfect tenses

1 Look at these extracts from the listening activity on page 141. Can you match each one with the appropriate timeline? Refer to the tapescript on page 165 to contextualise the extracts. Two time-lines are not used.

1 ... by next September we'll have been living here for nine years
2 I've been feeling a lot safer since we fitted the alarm
3 I'd bought some jackets off a friend and was selling them in a pub
4 He'd been pleading with me for ages to take them off his hands
5 I've never heard of it happening in our area anyway
6 I'll have retired by the summer

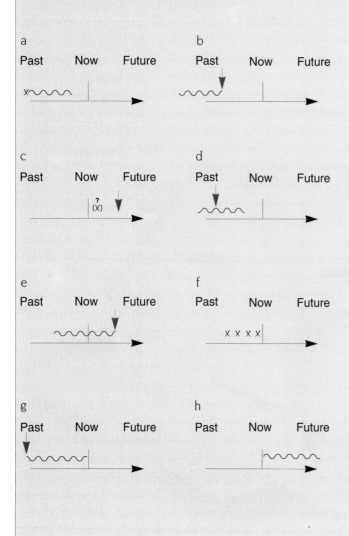

2 Read the newspaper article below and circle all the examples of perfect tenses.

Rise in offences exaggerated in statistics

Statistics showing that the crime rate has doubled over the past ten years are an exaggeration of the facts, the Journal 'British Trends' claimed yesterday. However, prison numbers will have risen by 10,000 by the year 2010.

The study, which has been in progress for the last two years, is due to be published in full next year.

The journal agrees that cases of burglary and theft have been rising steadily since 1984 but points out that recordings of violent crime have only increased by 25 per cent whilst cases of vandalism have scarcely risen at all. 'Until 1987 cases of violence against the person had been growing year by year,' explained Simon Thompson of British Trends. 'However, since then figures have fallen off sharply.'

The study also shows that the number of people given prison sentences last year was the lowest since 1976. Nevertheless, the prison population is expected to increase over the coming years. By 2010 the number of people given custodial sentences will have grown from 47,000 at present to 57,000.

3 Examine the circled verb forms and comment on the following:

a Why has the author used each verb form?
b Could simple verb forms have been used instead of continuous and vice-versa?

4 Most, but not all, of the statements below have mistakes in the verb forms. Can you find them all and correct them?

a Did you read this report on crime statistics yet?
b It's no wonder people have worried a lot about crime lately.
c It seems the newspapers have been exaggerating the statistics for violent crime.
d Statistics for violent crime improved since 1987. Until then they were a lot worse.
e Apparently the crime rate had been a lot lower 10 years ago.
f So far, cases of vandalism didn't rise much.
g They will have been arresting a lot more people in 2010.
h I suppose they'll have been building a lot more prisons by 2010.
i The authors worked on the project for two years.
j By the time it's finished, the study will take three years.
k They'll have collected data for three years.

1 Comment on the use of articles ('a', 'an', 'the' or no article) in the following sentences. Can you find the incorrect sentence in each trio?

Books are expensive.
The books are over there.
I don't like reading the books.

John's in prison .
It's supposed to be worst prison in the country.
John's in the prison.

I've bought a guitar.
I'm learning to play the guitar.
I'm looking for the good guitar.
Do you sell them?

I'll get married one day but I don't think I'll have the children.
You shouldn't give children too much freedom.
You should give a child lots of love and attention.

He put the telescope in the bedroom.
That's a telescope I was telling you about.
The telescope was invented by Galileo.

2 Find examples of the following in the sentences above. Check your ideas in the Grammar Reference (page 174).

a general nouns
   Example: books

b specific nouns
   Example: the books

3 Look at the extract below from Text C on smacking and answer the questions. Do not look at the Grammar Reference section for the moment.

*Have we been told about this community before?**

Why isn't there an article here?

Have we been told about this 'human slalom' before?

When did you last stop a youngster from doing something anti-social? I don't mean as a parent or in school, but on the street, as a member of (the) community – as an adult?
... Between the Co-op and the baker's the pavement was busy with shoppers and pushchairs ... (A) boy on a bike came weaving through (the) human slalom, expertly skidding in front of the post office and doing a wheelie from one side of the pavement to the kerb ... (The) boy on the bike was impervious. He completed a semi-circular return for another skid, when I set a firm hand upon his bars and blocked his way.

***Can you find any other examples of uses like these?*

*Why the change from 'a' to 'the'?**

4 Can you find any other examples of a/the/no article in the text above used in the same way as those highlighted?

5 Another extract from Text B appears below. However, all the articles have been omitted. Supply the articles (where required) and check your answers with the original text. Refer to the Grammar Reference section on page 174.

____ child minder has ____ right to smack ____ children in her care, ____ High Court ruled yesterday, renewing ____ fierce debate over corporal punishment. Anne Davis, over whom ____ test case was fought, said it was ____ victory 'for every parent in ____ land who believes in ____ reasonable use of ____ physical discipline'. Mrs Davis, 34, who has three children, said it was ____ 'victory over ____ politically correct' who 'cannot tell ____ difference between ____ loving discipline and ____ child abuse'.

But ____ ruling brought instant demands from ____ National Society for ____ Prevention of Cruelty to ____ Children and from ____ National Childminding Association for ____ change in ____ law to ban ____ smacking by ____ childminders. Local Authorities were alarmed by ____ comments of John Bowis, ____ junior health minister, who said, 'Clearly what ____ judgement has done is to underscore ____ common sense.'

6 Even if some of your answers differ from the original text, they may not necessarily be wrong. Can you justify all of your choices? For example, examine the difference in meaning between the following:

a junior health minister
the junior health minister

Your review of Unit 12

Vocabulary:

Topic related

General

Reading

Writing

Speaking

Listening

Exam skill

Grammar

IT'S A CRIME!

Key	**146**
Record Sheet	**147**
Writing Skills Development	**148**
Tapescripts	**153**
Grammar Reference	**166**

Key

Unit 4

Quiz: *Stress and anxiety* (*page 45*)

0 – 20   You experience little or no stress and in any case cope well with it.

21 – 40   You are experiencing quite a high degree of stress and should consider how you can improve matters.

41 – 60   You are extremely stressed and should seriously consider what lifestyle changes might alleviate this tension.

Unit 5

Listening technique: *specific information* (*page 55*)

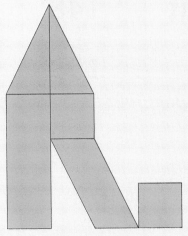

Unit 9

Questionnaire: *An ideal family* (*page 98*)

Score: 13–26
You avoid being seen as an authority figure at home and have a great deal of faith in your child's ability to cope with life's ups-and-downs independently. Are you simply easygoing, or is this a calculated policy on your part? Try not to forget those times when a little bit of leadership is called for!

27–40
You try to create a balance in your dealings with your child, erring on the side of leniency rather than authoritarianism. You probably give support when needed, but try to encourage your child to be independent and allow a little respectful criticism.

41–53
You have quite clearly defined ideas on parental responsibilities. Ask yourself whether you are not too strict with your child at times and whether you could risk allowing your child a little more freedom to make his or her own mistakes.

54–65
What is it you don't trust, life or your own children? They need to learn from mistakes – you won't always be there to protect them. And why not allow them to express themselves a little more – even if this means questioning your decisions now and again.

Exam focus (Speaking) *information gap* (*page 105*)

Student B:

Unit 11

Role play: *feedback sheet* (*page 130*)

Ideas	Strength of argument

Accuracy	Fluency
Pronunciation	Range of grammatical structure/vocabulary

Record sheet

Keep a record of formal and informal structures and vocabulary as you come across them in the coursebook.
This will then serve as a useful reference whenever you do any writing or English in Use exercises.

Formal	Informal
Emphatic structures: *Should you want to take the matter further ...*	*If you want to ...*

Writing Skills Development

Introduction

The aim of this section is to help you critically assess, and therefore improve, your written work in English, both to pass the CAE exam and for other purposes such as work or study.

Assessing your writing

Your writing will be assessed in terms of language (range of vocabulary and grammatical structure, natural and accurate use) and successful completion of the task (content, organisation, appropriate register), as well as the general impression on the target reader.

Accuracy of language
5 – very few errors
4 – errors only when attempting complex language
3 – some errors but generally satisfactory
2 – errors causing problems in communication
1 – frequent basic errors

Range of vocabulary and structure
5 – good
4 – quite good
3 – adequate
2 – elementary
1 – narrow

Completion of task
5 – very good
4 – good
3 – reasonable
2 – poor
1 – inadequate

Effect on target reader
5 – totally positive
4 – positive
3 – quite positive
2 – negative
1 – totally negative

Writing tasks

1 Look at the example on page 149 to see how to assess a composition.

2 Look at the sample compositions starting on page 150.

3 See if you can correct any of the language errors. This is good practice for proofreading skills.

4 Now try to make an overall assessment of the work. Consider the following:

Accuracy: how many errors were there in vocabulary, structures, spelling and punctuation?

Range of vocabulary and structure: is the work very simple or is it more ambitious in terms of language used? Is the language appropriate and natural?

Completion of task: have any vital pieces of information been left out? Is the register (formal, semi-formal, informal) appropriate to the task? Is the layout and organisation suitable?

Effect on target reader: was the overall effect positive or not?

5 Use the key opposite to grade the compositions, giving each piece a total mark out of 20.

6 Collect a number of compositions that you and your colleagues have written and follow the same procedure. If you achieve more than 12 marks out of 20, you're progressing well!

Task: A problem page reply (Unit 9: Family conflicts, page 102)

Writing guidelines

Content: should include an understanding of Tom and Helen's problem with at least two or three practical, well-considered solutions.

Style and register: could tend towards the informal with the advice given being direct, but not too blunt.

Target reader: should conform to the readers' expectations of a problem page reply.

Number of words: 200–250

Dear Tom and Helen,

simple past tense is better –   As I understand from your letters your problem started when Tom had retired   *or 'after Tom had retired'*

spelling –   but in my opinion the main point is that you are uncommucative!   *uncommunicative*

use reported speech –   Helen you wrote me "My job was to look after the house and children and make   *Helen, you stated that your job …*

sure Tom could relax when he came home from work" and Tom "Before I retired I   *and Tom, you admitted that before you …*

didn't really pay much attention to Helen's routine". From your sentences I could   *letters*

say that you had two different lives in a way. I mean you were so busy with your

jobs that you didn't take care of each other but you tried to let both relax after   *each other*

a work-day maybe because you wouldn't discuss or create inconveniences that   *hard day at work*

a question tag –
change punctuation –   you would have thought the day after. It's a strange way of loving! Isn't it?   *to think about*   *,isn't it?*

Now you are starting to live again together without the stress of bringing up

children in the right way, paying the mortgage and so on.

I'd like to tell Tom you are maybe too bossy and forceful for the position you filled   *that*

but remember your wife is not your secretary and you, Helen, are too exasperated   *conventional and this makes you feel exasperated*

and conventional. Try to be both patient and tender when you speak, even if you

feel angry or convinced that you are right!

Tom, I can't understand why such an active man like you doesn't look for a

word order –   part-time job. I don't suppose that you'll have any problems with your experience.

This situation is making you bored and bullying!   *and this leads to Helen feeling bullied.*

As a matter of fact you won't interfere with Helen's routine if you have a hobby

or a sport to practise, so why don't you look for somethings that you are inter-

ested in and have never done before? It would be a good idea.

Moreover, I'd like to say not to forget your love because it's for this reason that

you decided to spend a life together. Travel, discuss, go out for dinner again. It is   *This*

what love means!

Let me know how you get!   *on*

Comments: Good general content: you have completed the task quite effectively. You have created a nice tone with this letter, i.e. friendly and chatty, even though you are rather direct at times! Be more careful with checking your grammar in the final stages and also consider your use of paragraphs.

Marks: Accuracy of language – 3
Range of vocabulary and structure – 2
Completion of task – 3
Effect on target reader – 3

Sample composition 1

Task: A report for a competition entry (Unit 2: Teacher, you're the tops! page 24)

Writing guidelines for an ideal answer
Content: should include clear indication of who the nominated teacher is (name, school, etc.); description of special qualilites should be backed up with specific examples.
Register: fairly formal.
Target reader: as the target reader is a competition judge, he or she should have a favourable impression of the entry so that it is considered for the prize.
Number of words: maximum 300.

To me, teaching is quite a hard, complicated and stressful profession. But most teachers don't know it themselves. I mean I think they must reckon it's easy. However, they're good at teaching us how to cram for an exam ... what a shame!

My private English teacher wasn't only a good teacher but also a good friend to me. When I met him I was an adolescent, so I had a lot of distress and secrets which I couldn't tell my parents, brother or even friends about. Luckily for me, he was an experienced and open-minded person, so I could talk relaxed about my girlfriend, growing up, even the arguments my parents had had the previous night over the menu.

Whenever I talked about something with him, he listened seriously and carefully. And he always gave me some good, appropriate advice. He'd never abandon me and my problem. When I talked about my dream which was to be a cabin attendant for Japan Airlines, he suggested that I go to university to prepare to get a job in the airline company. Even though, I wasn't successful, I was grateful to him for having had the chance to the interview.

For three years, I enjoyed his witty lessons. Thanks to him, I'm still very much interested in English language and now I'm trying to be an English teacher like him.

Sample composition 2

Task: A travel guide for your country (Unit 3: Missing home? page 30)

Writing guidelines
Content: should cover two to three main areas as a minimum, with useful and appropriate information for travellers to the country in question.
Layout and organisation: should be written in continuous prose but could include sub-headings for each new topic.
Style and register: semi-formal.
Target reader: reader should feel well-informed after reading the guide.
Number of words: 250 words.

GRAN CANARIA: THE PARADISE OF SPAIN

Gran Canaria is often definied as a whole continent in a small island. This is because of the different features of the landscape: seaside, countryside and urban city.

As all countries it has its local customs which you will have to be aware of.

The timetable is very different from the British. The commercial areas are open from 9am to 1pm and then they are opened again at 4 until 8 or 9 in the evening.

Like in the rest of Spain, the canaries, have two big meals. The first one, around 2.30pm and the other one at 9 or 10 in the night.

The people are usualy very friendly and most of them can speak english but if you try some words in their language such as 'por favor' or 'gracias' they will be very glad.

The whole island is full of good and typical restaurants. If you want to eat very good quality seafood, you must go to the north of the island – Agaete, Banaderes – where the fishermen villages are. In these places you can eat a big amount of food for not very much money. In the capital (Las Palmas) and in the countryside – Tejeda, Santa Brigida – you would find restaurants and 'tapas bars' where you can eat wonderful meat and typical canary dishes such as 'sancocho canario' and 'papas can mojo'. However, if you are not keen on this type of food you can also find English food in the south of the island. You can also recourse to international restaurants like 'Pizza Hut' or 'McDonalds'.

Las Palmas is a big urban city, ideal for shopping. In the areas of Triana and Mesa y Lopez you can find national and international shops and beautiful sophisticated shopping centres.

Sample composition 3

Task: An article for a student magazine on giving up smoking (Unit 4: Smoking, page 44)

Writing guidelines
Content: should include a catchy title, an interesting opening paragraph and at least three methods for giving up smoking.
Layout and organisation: should be written in continuous English, but could include visual help for each tip, for example numbering points or highlighting them with an asterisk (*).
Register: could be reasonably informal.
Target reader: a light-hearted/informal approach might be most successful in keeping the reader interested; a successful article would give young smokers 'food for thought'.
Number of words: approximately 250.

Just quit smoking while you still can!

Once a close friend of mine wanted to offer me a cigarette, so he asked me, "Do you smoke?"

I said, "No".

Then he said, "Good. Don't start."

He is a serious smoker who averagely consume two to four packets per day.

So why does a smoker like him wants to give me such an advice? Does this mean that he has long been suffering the effects of smoking but just can't quit?

We all know what smoking can do to you and people around you. The effects are usually not rapid or instant but it worsen every time and trigger after a long time when the first symptom of health hazard condition shows.

So, fellow student, quit smoking while you still can!

Maybe at this point you have already thrown away the magazine, but maybe you are one of the few lucky ones who starts asking how to give up smoking and are there any means to help you give up smoking.

The answer is a positively "YES!" There are plenty of ways to help you quit, but first you've got to promise yourself that you want to do it, you will do it now and you will keep on doing it until you succeed.

*OK, let's start with this. Whenever you see people smoking, avoid staying round. Don't test your resistibility to the seduction of smoking at the beginning, you can do it when you are able to control yourself.

*When you 'accidently' bought a packet of cigarettes, tell yourself, "I don't want to smoke!" Throw them away at once!

*Whenever you feel like you want to have a cigarette, eat something else as a substitute.

*Or you can buy nicotine replacement therapies in the form of chewing gums or skin patches.

So, my dear friends, it is really up to you whether or not to quit smoking. I have made my last appeal, now it's your turn.

Sample composition 4

Task: A book review for a magazine (Unit 8: Armchair entertainment, page 89)

Writing guidelines
Content: should include title of the book and its author; a description of the characters, setting and plot (without necessarily revealing the ending); whether (and to whom) the book would be recommended.
Style and Register: semi-formal; the review should include the key features of language that are present in magazine reviews (economy of expression, use of present tense to narrate events).
Target reader: the reader should have sufficient information to decide whether he or she wants to read the book.
Number of words: approximately 250.

After having finished this book, I can say that it's a must to buy for your children. However, the book is not only for children but grown ups can also enjoy reading it. And if anyone finishes this book without tears brought to their eyes, it's time they consulted with their psychotherapist, I think.

Although, time and again, animals have been used as main characters in the story, the writer has beautifully and sentimentally described the relationship between a pig and spider, from strangers to confided friends, as well as cleverly teaching the life span of spiders to children.

The story of two animals who have different walks of life emotionally begins and ends in a shed where they first meet and start their friendship. Since the pig has been in the shed before the spider, named Charlotte, came he feels that he occupies the place and acts unfriendly to her at first. Not for long. They become friends and learn from each other. Charlotte, who is sweet and clever, teaches the pig, who was once big-headed, about life. She broadens his life and makes him realise that each people lives a different life. While he lives in a confined place and needs feeding every day by his owners, she lives freely and chooses her own way.

As the friendship is flourishing, the two friends grow up. After Charlotte has children she dies soon, by nature, and leaves her young children to fend for themselves like when she first met the pig. He's sadly left alone only to see one of her children choose to live in the shed like her.

As a child you might have thought that animals could talk. The writer has made the animals' conversations sound natural. On the contrary, the human in the story has been made to sound peculiar.

Although it ends with tears in your eyes, you'll feel happy and understand the value of friends more. This will be one of the books in your mind.

Sample composition 5

Task: A reply to a friend requesting information (Unit 10: Work values, page 111)

Writing guidelines
Content: the letter should address the questions in Debbie's letter (contact name/address for the college, details of equipment, etc.) and offer general advice on her choice of career.
Layout and organisation: should be in the form of a letter with the address, date, salutation and ending correctly laid out.
Style and register: should be informal; where possible it should repeat information in the prospectus in a less formal way; salutations and endings should be appropriate for an informal letter, i.e. use of first names rather than family names and 'with love' or 'best wishes' rather than 'yours sincerely'.
Target reader: the reader should have enough information to proceed with an application to the college.
Number of words: approximately 250.

---

218 Henley Road
Coventry
11 February, 1995

Dear Debbie,

Thank you for your letter and this time, welcome back from Spain! I'm sure you had a good time.

Now, I've got some information about a college in London which specialises in dancing. They can offer a one year course in Modern dance and drama and it'll run from 12 September, 1995 to 20 July, 1996. It costs £2,000.

According to their prospectus, you don't need any formal qualifications but you need some experience in dance or drama, and you need to be in good shape. Well, you've got some experience in dance already!

I'll give you the contact and address of the college, so if you want further details write to:

Ms Sarah Tomlinson
London College of Dance and Drama
Malborough St
London E1

Remember London's one of the most expensive cities! I think you will have to pay at least £300 per month if you live with a local family. In this case accommodation, breakfast and dinner aren't included in the fees.

Oh yes, I read an article about Danny Price the other day at the hairdresser and he gave a message to people who wish to be professional dancers. He said you need to be a good actor and have a good voice apart from being a good dancer, spend a lot of money on equipment such as clothes and shoes, exercise everyday for about 6 hours, but the good news is that you are allowed to eat lots of pasta without worrying! (Dancing helps your metabolism get faster.)

If you need any other help, just let me know. I don't know much about dancing but I know you very well.

Best wishes,
Yuko

Exam tips

The following advice was written by a group of CAE students shortly after taking the exam.

1 Read the question very carefully and underline the instructions. You must do exactly what the question tells you to do, so don't be tempted to do your own thing!

2 Make sure you know exactly who you are writing to and for what purpose. This will help you to get the right style. Try to imagine yourself in the situation so your answer will be realistic.

3 Divide your time carefully between the two answers. Section A has a lot of reading so you may have to spend slightly more time on this section.

4 Try to finish both questions with 10–15 minutes to spare so you can proofread your answers.

5 Even though it's an exam, try and enjoy yourself!

Tapescripts

Unit 1

Part 2
You the language learner

M = Maarten
R = Ruth
S = Silke

Extract 1

M: Okay, tell me, Silke, what do you think are your best things in English?
S: I think ... taking those topics, one of my best things is listening ... 'cause that depends always, of course, on who's talking to you ... his accent, his dialect, whatever, but I think it's quite ... yeah ... it's quite easy to understand, at least that's what I experienced over the past nine months.
M: And the other one?
S: And the second part would be ... I think er speaking. Speaking, let's say in terms of improvement, I'd say that speaking has got better over the time.
M: But what about speaking grammatically correctly?
S: No, that's another point. That's grammar. That's one of the weak points, I have to say. In terms of improvements, I have to stress that speaking and listening have become better, yeah, definitely. How about you?
R: I agree that you are able to express more, so you are getting more fluent in speaking, but probably...
M: But this has more to do with vocab.
R: Oh, you know, that's what I want to explain. It's not necessarily the vocabulary – you improve that but not that much. So you are able to describe things you don't have the proper words for, so you keep on describing.

Extract 2

M: I think I've improved in writing this year, actually because of the reading. So using the similar words they use in quite difficult texts you sometimes have to read – you pick up these words and start using them yourselves and that's the way, a really good way to learn a language. I also noticed this in Spanish. If you start using the words they use, it immediately ... rises your level in the language.
R: In essays you start writing more and start getting more confident in expressing things.
M: And you notice that all these teachers or lecturers use constantly like the same words like 'vis-à-vis or 'by and large' and stuff you never hear normally, at least I didn't, and now you hear these kind of words.

Extract 3

S: I recognise the improvement in reading by using the English-German dictionary in the beginning very, very often. Well, at least ...
M: The problem with the dictionary is that you don't know whether it's really the word the Englishmen would use.
S: Yes, but you could figure it out within the context.
R: Yes, you get the feeling for the word.
M: You get the feeling but it's better if you read other students' reports.
S: Where else would you look up a word that you didn't know?
M: Yeah, well, in a dictionary.
R: Don't you think you keep on looking up less words all the time because you get more confident about just feeling what those words mean? And in the beginning you didn't really know if it's an important word or not, so you just look it up.

Extract 4

R: That's right, but you only could improve slight mistakes of your grammar because considering the facts that we've been foreigners among foreigners you had no-one to correct you really properly all the time.
M: Except when somebody just knows it better than you.
R: Yes, you have to be very confident about that, you're really right. It would've been very useful to have more English people around us. The problem is that English people don't correct you because they are polite, and that would've been the biggest ... you could have made the biggest improvements if you had somebody who constantly tells you ...
M: But no-one is willing to constantly correct you anyway.
R: Not every word.
M: I asked my boys ... the boys in my corridor to correct me when I said something wrong. Sometimes, it wasn't even necessary, like, for instance, pronunciation. Well, they started laughing and I thought 'What's wrong?' And I said instead of 'bowl' I said 'bowel' which means something quite different ... at least that's what I learnt. And when you start asking for 'bowel' they start laughing, so then in this way you ...
S: You were lucky living with five English guys in one corridor.

Extract 5

S: Carl, for instance, I talked to him yesterday and he said that he didn't improve at all for his English. At least he had the feeling that he could speak better when he first came here than now.
M: Really?
S: Maybe you don't recognise your improvements.
M: I think we improved. If we lived here for a year we must have improved at least in fluency.

Extract 6

R: I don't know if our vocabulary got that much bigger because that's one part where we were probably too lazy about. Of course you could increase it more and more and you learn a lot just by listening to people and then adopting it into your own language, your own speakings, but often if you really want to learn vocabulary you really have to constantly ...
M: ... constantly register new words.
R: ... write them down.
S: I think the best way is to speak English every day, over and over.

Unit 2

Part 1
Gender in education

I = Interviewer
J = Janice

I: Today I'd like to welcome Janice Winterbottom, a teacher and educational researcher, who currently works at London University and who has just completed a study into some of the differences in the way that teachers behave towards male and female pupils. Welcome, Janice.
J: Thank you
I: First of all, why the study?
J: Well, it's rather ironic, but most teachers, I think, would say quite sincerely that they treat all pupils equally and fairly in the classroom. Indeed, this was borne out in a recent survey conducted by Manchester University last year. Virtually all of the teachers questioned felt that there was no difference in the way boys and girls were treated.
I: And yet your recent report suggests that things in the classroom are actually quite different. I mean, I can think of one example myself from when I was at school. In the old days,

boys were automatically addressed by their surnames and girls by their first names. That practice, I'm sure, is quite out-dated now.

J: On the contrary, our study shows that this is still common practice in many schools. The effect is that boys are seen as deserving less respect than girls. Fortunately, this is relative-ly easy to put right. Schools can decide immediately to intro-duce a new, more equal policy on what to call boys and girls.

I: Can you give us some more examples?

J: Yes, much of the discriminatory behaviour is less explicit, but potentially still just as harmful. For instance, in subjects such as art, cookery or science, girls are often given the responsi-bility of tidying up equipment, putting things away in cup-boards ... jobs which girls are supposedly good at. But, mm, well... this merely serves to confirm the stereotyped images our society has of men and women. And boys, by contrast, are more likely to be called upon to lift heavy objects, or move chairs and tables, thus reinforcing the view that boys are strong and girls are too weak and delicate to take part in such activities. However, teacher attitudes do not always favour the boys. Our study showed that girls are more likely to be given responsible jobs to do, like running important errands for the staff, thus implying that boys are not to be trusted.

I: But couldn't that also imply another hidden message - that girls are here to serve others?

J: Absolutely. Another example, when we examined the type of language that teachers used to control or discipline pupils ... we found remarkable differences when we observed teachers in action. Boys were frequently ordered to do things. 'Shut up!', 'Be quiet!', 'Stand over there'. Girls, on the other hand, were addressed more politely. 'Could you be quiet?', 'Would you mind moving over there?'

I: That's quite astonishing. Isn't there also a statistic, correct me if I'm wrong, on the level of oral contribution made by boys and girls in the classroom? Something like boys talk for 75% of the time, and girls only 25%. Is this really true?

J: Yes, this is an often-quoted statistic, and one which we were keen to investigate in the study. We found an exact correla-tion between this figure and the amount of teacher attention time that's given to pupils.

I: So, in other words, teachers give 75% of their time to the boys and 25% to girls?

J: That's right. And the result is, quite obviously, that girls are more reluctant to speak out in class if the class is a mixed-sex one, and that boys feel that their opinions, their contribu-tions, are valued by staff.

I: Does that mean you support the idea of single-sex schooling?

J: Well, that's a difficult one. There are occasions when girls need the support of working with other girls; however, we also believe that younger children need to get used to work-ing in mixed-sex groups from the start of their school career.

Unit 2

Part 2
Education east and west

I = Interviewer
S = Susan

I: Hello, Susan, and thank you for agreeing to talk to us.

S: My pleasure.

I: Correct me if I'm wrong, but you seem to have taught in more countries than most people have visited. What's your opinion of the British education system ... I mean, in comparison to, oh, Japan, for example? You spent a long time in Japan, didn't you?

S: Yes, I did. I've always been rather irritated by the bad press the Japanese system tends to get in the West. You know what I mean ... it's supposed to be unbearably strict and rigid,

classrooms of pupils stuck at desks, listening to the teacher all day. My own opinion, for what it's worth, is quite the reverse.

I: So, it isn't true then? I've always thought ...

S: I think it's important to look at it from a wider perspective. From my experience it seems the British ... and the American model for that matter ... has done away with intellectual ambitions. At least, that has been the case until recently. In fact I think it's true to say that education in this country is moving towards the Japanese model. It might be easier if I outline the Japanese system.

I: Yes.

S: First and foremost, it's extremely competitive. The basis of the system is a series of competitive examinations. At the end of primary school all children sit exams which determine whether the child will go to an academic school if they pass –, that is – or something like a technical school if they fail.

I: Similar to the old 11-Plus system in England?

S: Yes, that's right. Any talk of reintroducing the exam always leads to terrible controversy. It's popular in this country to give students the time to develop. The argument goes that a child's future shouldn't be decided at such an early age ...

I: And you don't agree with this?

S: Well, the fact is that yes, these exams do segregate children at an early age but they also serve as a great incentive to hard work.

I: What about the subjects they study ... is there any difference?

S: Yes, a big difference. Japanese pupils study subjects like mathematics, physics, chemistry ... languages ... they study these subjects in much greater numbers than British or American pupils. There's far more choice of subjects in these countries and children are often encouraged to take subjects that interest them. Unfortunately, children often go for the easy options ... result? A tremendous waste of potential. The whole system in Britain and America is based on the idea of making school as painless as possible. Competitiveness is a rude word. Teachers mustn't dream of creating a competitive environment. Instead, children are encouraged to help each other ... to learn cooperatively. But again ... with disappoint-ing results. So much time is wasted with children sitting round tables doing basically what they want to, while the teacher runs around trying to keep order. Children know what's expected of them in Japan. Success or failure depends on exams. Children know they have to work hard to pass them. Their aims aren't complicated by talk of course work or continuous assessment. They can focus on exams. They're the only thing that matter.

I: You said earlier the Japanese system tends to be very strict. Doesn't this only put even more pressure on these children?

S: Yes, the system is very strict. But once again, I feel with good reason. In fact it's the lack of discipline in British and American schools that puts pressure on children. I recently heard that one in six children in American schools carry guns or knives. Is that the kind of education system people want? Children benefit emotionally from a strictly enforced system of discipine. It gives them a sense of order ... of stability.

I: Yes ... that's an interesting point. Finally, what about the stan-dard of teaching? Teachers in the West always seem to be in the firing line in this country. Is that the case in Japan?

S: No, no, quite the opposite in fact. Teachers are held in great respect in Japan. Education is held very highly. Teachers gen-erally have degrees in the subject they teach, unlike in the West where more emphasis is placed on how to teach. The 'how' often means cooperative, student-centred learning methods. You see, it's a vicious circle.

Unit 2

Language awareness: questions (1)
Activity 1

Recent research into conversational analysis has shown that men and women speak different languages, especially when they live together. Women tend to make a greater effort to participate in conversations than men, responding to statements with words or expressions that show interest, concern, surprise, etc. Listen to the following example of how a man might contribute to a conversation.

Wife: Hello dear, I'm home.
Husband: Hello.
Wife: Guess who I've just seen in town? Sue!
Husband: Yes?
Wife: Yes! You remember Sue, don't you? We used to work together.
Husband: Mm.
Wife: You'll never believe it. She's left her husband! Remember Bob? Her husband? They came to our party last year.
Husband: Yeah, yeah.
Wife: Yes. She's left him! She said she couldn't stand living with him any more ... so she left him! She's bought her own house! ... Are you listening?
Husband: Yes dear.
Wife: Apparently Bob was really boring to live with ... Sue couldn't stand it any more.
Husband: Sweetheart? What's for dinner?

Activity 3

Now listen to to a similiar conversation between two women.

A: Hey, Karen, guess, who I've just seen in town?
B: Who?
A: Sue!
B: Really?
A: Yeah. Guess what? She's left her husband!
B: You're joking? Has she? I saw them the other week and they seemed, well, really happy together.
A: Did they? Well, she's left him! She moved out last week.
B: Did she? I never thought they'd ever separate.
A: Yeah ... she's buying her own house, so it must be serious.
B: Seriously? But they've been together years. In fact I was with Sue the night she met Bob.
A: Is that right? Oh, they used to make such a nice couple.
B: Didn't they? They were always buying each other little gifts and going away for romantic holidays.
A: Yeah, ... weren't they? Oh ... what a shame ... everybody seems to be splitting up these days...

Activity 6
The 'Yes-No' game

Host: And now we have Steve. OK, Steve. You know the rules, don't you ? You mustn't say 'Yes' or 'No'. Do you understand?
Contestant: OK.
Host: Don't worry, we haven't started yet ... I'll start the clock ... if you can go a minute without saying 'Yes' or 'No' you win a hundred pounds ... OK?
Contestant: Right!
Host: OK. The time starts ... now! So, Steve ... is it Steve ... or Steven?
Contestant: Steve.
Host: Where do you live, Steve?
Contestant: Birmingham.
Host: Do you?
Contestant: I do.
Host: Are you married, Steve?

Contestant: I am. I've been married ten years now.
Host: Really?
Contestant: Really!
Host: Any children, Steve?
Contestant: I have. We've got four girls.
Host: Have you?
Contestant: That's right.
Host: And what do you do for a living, Steve?
Contestant: I'm a bus driver.
Host: Are you?
Contestant: I am.
Host: Are you feeling nervous at all, Steve?
Contestant: Not at all!
Host: Seriously? Not even a little bit?
Contestant: No! Not at all ... arrggh!
Host: Sorry, Steve ... better luck next time!

Unit 3

Part 1
Missing home?

Extract 1: Gusta
I always wanted to be a vegetarian, but I never could do it. Here in England it's very easy because the meat is very horrible. They often have meat that's boiled in water and it's not chicken, but normal meat, and then it's pink and really horrible ... look terrible. I still eat fish, though, so I eat a lot of fish and chips and that's not so good for my body, yeah. Eventually I want to stop eating dead animals at all. I don't want to eat fish any more also. And what I eat a lot here is jacket potatoes with coleslaw. That's really my favourite. In my country it isn't so common to have jacket potatoes on your menu every day. And what I miss is Rochbrot, that is very brown sort of bread but it's made of very whole brown grains.

Extract 2: Petros
The educational system in Britain is really very, very different from anywhere else. Students are treated positively. They're thought to be minds to fill with education. The system tolerates everything and everything is allowed. The pedagogic idea is to treat students as to be something positive that wants to learn and always helped ... to try to help students to learn. Tutors are always trying to put themselves in students' place and they're very tolerable. It's funny with foreign students because every English people, especially tutors, don't want to be treated as racists so they are doing everything they can, sometimes they do things that are not logical, in order not to be called racist. And for foreign students that's very nice.

Extract 3: Andrea
Hello, I'm an au pair and I'm studying English here too. I've been asked to tell you something about the cultural differences, but I'm not really sure if it's the difference of living standards or culture, from the family I'm living in at the moment. And like, the children have so many toys ... they have one whole room of toys and then they always ask me what to play or what to do because their parents don't buy them things and I think 'Oh gosh, I never had something like this!' and then their parents tell me they always they are afraid because they can't buy things and so on, and other people of our level have more things and it's quite difficult to understand for me, maybe. Well, I think it's just the standard of living that's different.

Unit 3

Part 2
Getting away

I = Interviewer
H = Holly

I: So, have you done a lot of travelling, Holly?

H: No, not an exceptional amount, no, but I suppose a fair bit. I spent a lot of time travelling around Europe – as cheaply as possible I might add – hitch-hiking whenever possible, sleeping in very cheap hotels ...

I: Were these like two-week holidays or ...

H: No ... no, no, two weeks never seemed long enough. I think if I'd simply been interested in having a break – you know just getting away for a little while –, I'd have been quite happy with short holidays. In hindsight I realise now it was an excuse to run away ... not being happy with my life in England but, but not really knowing what to do. The easiest option was to go away for a few months ... or longer if possible.

I: Running away from what? Nothing serious I hope?

H: Oh no! I mean I hadn't robbed any banks ... I wasn't on the run from the police or anything like that. No ... it was just a lot of little things ... not being happy in my job ... not, not really knowing what I wanted to do ... you know, ... just feeling unsatisfied with life. It wasn't, it wasn't really anything peculiar to me, don't get me wrong – I wasn't going through an emotional crisis or anything like that. Most of my friends at the time were in a similiar situation ... bored with work, you know, doing the same thing every day. I like to think I was brave to give up my job to try and make a fresh start.

I: You gave up your job?

H: Yeah, ... on several occasions. I used to work for five or six months, save up as much money as possible, then go away until I'd spent it all.

I: Did you do this on your own?

H: Most of the time, yeah. I could never really work out if my friends were jealous or, thought I was plain crazy! I'm sure the fear of not getting another job when they got back put them off. I never really tried hard to persuade them anyway. There's a great sense of freedom about travelling on your own. It's totally up to you where you go, how long you stay anywhere. I met so many people as well. If I'd gone away with somebody, er, we would have spent all our time together and I wouldn't have made such an effort to meet new friends.

I: So, you 'ran away' as you put it, but what did you get out of travelling? That seems quite a negative reason in itself.

H: Well, this might sound a little bit over the top ... but it really did change my life. And it's not really surprising when you think about it. I'm sure it would be the same for anybody. If you're working full-time, Monday to Friday – going out every weekend with the same people to the same places – it's unlikely, that, that anything out of the ordinary is going to happen. That was certainly my experience anyway. So can you imagine what it was like travelling around for three or four months? Meeting all these interesting people, coming into contact with different cultures ... seeing things from a different perspective. I was very narrow-minded before I travelled. And I probably still would be. But meeting people from different cultures forces you, to, to re-examine all the stereotypes you have in your head ... it's a really healthy experience.

I: You're a teacher now, working full-time ... does this mean your travelling days are over?

H: I certainly hope not. I haven't explained yet, but actually the fact that I'm teaching – that's a direct result of travelling. I used to work as a shop assistant ... I didn't have any qualifications ... there's no reason on earth why I wouldn't be working in a shop now. On one trip I spent a lot of time in Spain and found myself picking up a fair bit of the language. When I got back to England I decided to study it seriously and ... well,

one thing led to another and I finally ended up at university. So ... there's a nice conditional sentence for you: if I hadn't given up my job to travel around Europe I wouldn't be teaching now!

Unit 3

Language awareness: the language of obligation
Activity 2

Tourist: Is it safe to take cash?

Agent: Well it's best if you take traveller's cheques. There's been a lot of reports of pick-pocketing recently. You should also take out some form of insurance.

Tourist: What about a visa?

Agent: No if you're there for less than a month you don't need to apply for one.

Tourist: Is it safe to take photographs?

Agent: Well, it's generally OK. But you should avoid being seen with a camera around restricted areas. And you're not allowed to take photos at the airport.

Tourist: What about vaccinations?

Agent: You don't have to be vaccinated against anything. But you ought to see your doctor for a jab against typhoid and cholera, to be on the safe side.

Tourist: How about taking money into the country? Are there any limits?

Agent: No limits exactly. But I'm afraid you have to declare all your money on entering the country, and you mustn't bring out any of the local currency.

Tourist: Are there any duty-free restrictions?

Agent: No, you needn't worry about that. You can bring back as much as you want.

Unit 3

Language awareness: reported speech.
Activity 4

Hello, it's Monsieur Laurent here ... Michel Laurent. I'm phoning about my tickets to Paris. I still haven't received them and I'm leaving tomorrow. You obviously haven't bothered to take my earlier complaint seriously.Your agency gets a lot of business from my company, but if my tickets aren't in my office by this afternoon, I'll be taking my custom elsewhere. It might be a good idea if you phone me in my office as soon as possible.

Hello, Mr Laurent, it's JJ Travel here. I got your message a few minutes ago. There really isn't anything to worry about. The tickets will be at the check-in desk for you to collect. If you'd prefer to have them today, I could get our messenger to deliver them to your office. I'm terribly sorry for causing you so much inconvenience. Our office was certainly slow in getting them to you. I do hope you'll continue to deal with us in future.

Unit 4

Part I
Alternative medicine

I = Interviewer
M = Margaret

I: Margaret, you're a trained acupuncturist and are used to giving other people treatment, but have you had any treatment yourself?

M: Yes. During recent years I've had a lot of acupuncture treatment. I've found it particularly useful for myself, not so much on the level of physical health, as on mental and spiritual health. Acupuncture has helped me to cope with stress, anxiety, worry, it's helped me sort out mental confusion, and it's helped me to become a more self-confident and assertive person.

I: Do you see this kind of medicine as more important than Western medicine?

M: Alternative medicine's particularly important for me because I believe that it works on the level of body, mind and spirit. This is very different from Western medicine which is supposed to work solely on the body and which is very powerful but which consequently can have powerful side-effects as well, unlike alternative medicine which is about treating the person as a whole. When a person's ill, there's something in their life which is putting their energy levels out of balance, and what alternative therapies try to do is help to gradually push that energy back into balance so that any disease there might be will naturally disappear, because it cannot survive when your energy is in balance.

I: What kind of people come to you for help?

M: The sort of people I've treated recently are, well, for example, people suffering from stress and anxiety. I've helped them cope with stressful situations in their lives, but also on the physical level I've treated a woman for problems with eczema, for example. Oh, another woman who suffers from arthritis of the hip and at the moment I'm treating an old lady who has several health problems, one of them being mild Parkinson's Disease. All these people have found that acupuncture has made them feel more balanced in themselves and they have certainly benefited from the treatment. Given that the treatments consist largely of balancing the energy between the different meridians of a person's body and freeing blocks of energy which may be causing ill health and which may have been there for many years.

I: How did you first get interested in alternative medicine?

M: Well throughout my adult life I've travelled a lot in Europe and especially in Asia, and that's where, when I was teaching and training teachers of English, that I became interested in acupuncture. I spent a year in China where it's common for people to have acupuncture treatment, not only if they're ill but to prevent disease. And it was after returning from China that I reached my decision to, of deciding to, become an acupuncturist myself. And I was lucky to find that the town where I live, Leamington Spa, had a very famous and very well-reputed college of traditional acupuncture.

I: Is there much training required?

M: Well so far I've followed a course which has led to the Licentiate in Acupuncture. The course lasted three years and I had to go to the college about one weekend in three. There's a lot more to it than that, though! I had a large amount of homework to do, and practice, which I did two or three evenings a week, practice where I had to locate points on different people because as you know, people have different sized and shaped bodies. Therefore the skill of locating points is not easy.

I: So, do you see your future in alternative medicine?

M: Oh, hopefully, yes. In the future I hope to set up an alternative health clinic which will involve myself as an acupuncturist but perhaps other people as well, practising alternative therapies such as homeopathy, reflexology, aromatherapy and maybe counselling. I'd like to set this up somewhere in a rural setting, where people would enjoy coming not only for the treatment but where they would be able to sit and enjoy the scenery, go for walks, have a cup of tea and basically feel free from the stresses of everyday life.

Unit 4

Part 2
Smoking

P = Paul
N = Nazir

P: So, Nazir, how are you doing with giving up smoking?

N: I'm back on them again. I'm smoking more now than I was before!

P: You were doing so well. How long did you give up for?

N: Nine weeks, well almost nine weeks.

P: What went wrong? Surely if you can go that long without a fag ...

N: That's what I would've thought before I gave up. But it's not as easy as that. The first problem was breaking the habit. I like a couple of fags with a cup of coffee before I start work. So for the first couple of days I had to, I had to force myself to keep busy first thing in the morning. I stopped drinking coffee and settled for a glass of water instead. Cigarettes don't taste so nice after water.

P: That must have been pretty difficult?

N: No. It wasn't that bad really. I was using nicotine patches so I didn't have any cravings. No, it was pretty easy. In fact after a couple of weeks I really began to think I'd cracked it. I found myself dying for a fag every so often but it didn't last long. The patches really help. You're getting a regular dose of nicotine and you find yourself thinking about smoking less and less.

P: So why are you smoking again?

N: I don't know! One day on the way to work I realised I'd not put a patch on. I couldn't find a chemist that was open, and when I finally did they didn't have any patches, and I had a really busy day ahead of me. I got into work quite early – I couldn't stop thinking about a cigarette! I was getting more and more nervous – I was literally shaking! The next thing I knew I was in the shop buying a packet of cigarettes. I only had one, then threw the packet away. Then at dinner time I bought another packet! By the end of the day I'd smoked about eight cigarettes. My will-power went after that. Within a couple of days I was back to normal.

P: So, how many are you smoking now?

N: Lots! At least two or three more than I used to smoke! I'm going to try again, though.

P: Well, good luck next time.

Unit 4

Part 3
Stress and anxiety

I = Interviewer
D = Dr David Samuels

I: And now it's time for our weekly surgery with our own resident doctor, David Samuels. Good afternoon, David.

D: Good afternoon, Jane. Good afternoon, listeners.

I: So, David, we're looking today at the problem of anxiety. How serious a problem is it?

D: Very serious indeed for people who suffer from acute anxiety problems. Most people describe many different feelings when anxious, some more unpleasant and upsetting than others. Some of the more physical signs of anxiety are hot flushes, a dry mouth, a tightness in the throat that can make you feel like you're choking. Sufferers can feel sick, have headaches or blurred vision and have numbness or pins and needles in the arms and legs.

I: That's quite a list.

D: Yes it is. And at times anxiety can reach such a peak that the person has a panic attack. The physical symptoms become so uncomfortable that the person feels something terrible is going to happen; they might believe they're going to collapse, lose control ... even go crazy. The important thing for these people to remember, however, is that these feelings are not actually dangerous and will not lead to serious illness.

I: Yes, that is an important point, isn't it?

D: Indeed it is. Anxiety develops into a problem often because of the person's reaction to these feelings. To begin with, there's the initial problem of over-reacting. People who have suffered panicky feelings tend to become very sensitive to the slightest change in their breathing or heartbeat. This makes the person feel alarmed, which in turn makes the symptoms worse. Sufferers can have the problem of association – that is, having felt anxious in one particular setting they tend to react in the same way in similar situations. People often anticipate feelings of anxiety. That means a sufferer will begin to feel anxious even before they have entered the feared situation, simply because of past experiences.

I: So it's like a vicious circle?

D: Exactly

I: What advice have you got for any of our listeners with this complaint?

D: The most important point I can make is that people shouldn't try avoiding difficult situations. It may seem a sensible precaution to avoid a situation that makes you feel anxious, but in the long run this can add to the problem. By taking such action the person is not learning how to deal with difficult situations. Avoidance can lead to the person losing more and more confidence which only adds to the problem.

I: So people need to face their fears?

D: In a way, yes. The best advice is to let the anxiety or panic attack happen and wait until it passes. The feelings will pass, believe me. A very important part of getting over such attacks is to accept them as unpleasant feelings and cope with them without running away or giving up. Never leave a situation until the fear or panic has started to go down. The following golden rules will help cope with anxiety attacks: Don't fight against or run away from the fear, just give it time to pass. Remember that the feelings are nothing more than an exaggeration of quite normal bodily reactions to stress. They're not harmful or dangerous, just very unpleasant. Try to notice what is actually happening to your body when you are panicking, not what you feel might happen. See each panic attack as an opportunity to learn how to cope with them. And finally, when the panic begins to fade, congratulate yourself for having stayed in the situation and put up with it.

Unit 5

Part 2
Sign language: Peter Llewelyn-Jones

Hello, my name is Peter Llewelyn-Jones. Perhaps I should start by telling you a little bit about myself. I originally trained as a social worker, some 20 to 25 years ago, but very quickly fell into, I suppose, working with deaf people. Now I'd never come across deaf people before, and so I didn't know quite what to expect. I think I'd assumed that most deaf people were elderly because I certainly had old deaf grannies and relatives. But I, probably to my surprise, found that the majority of people I was working with were actually quite young, in fact a whole age range from small children right through to adults.

The thing that really fascinated me about my first contacts with deaf people was their use of sign language. Now it wasn't long before I decided that social work wasn't really my cup of tea, and what instead I was more interested in was learning sign language, and learning to use it effectively. I started practising sign language just so that I could do my social work job but very soon found myself in situations where I needed to interpret for deaf people in a whole range of settings from the hospital appointments, meetings with doctors, lawyers, employment officers, right the way through to sometimes court work.

After three or four years' experience I eventually qualified as a sign language interpreter and moved up to work for one of the major voluntary organisations for deaf people in Great Britain called the British Deaf Association. There I specialised in interpreting again and was in some way instrumental in setting up a national interpreters' register in this country. Since then interpreting has been my er, the main focus of my job and now I in fact work in a university, a university department, training sign language interpreters.

One of the things that I try to do with beginners, people who've never signed before ever, is to get them to visualise how signs work. Now for a sign to be performed accurately it needs not just a certain amount of physical composure, physical accuracy, it needs a very clear mental imagery as well. Let me give you an example. I want all of you to stand up. Okay, stand up. Try and spread out a bit, make sure you've got a couple of feet around you, at least. Two or three or four feet so that you can open your arms up and not hit anybody else. Right, now I want you to imagine that in front of you is a kitchen surface, in fact it's the kitchen surface that you have at home. Okay. Now I want you to be able to see this clearly. Now think about what is on that surface. Do you have a kettle or a coffee maker, do you have any storage jars? Do you have shelves under the surface? If so where are they? I want you to see them very, very clearly in your mind's eye. Right, now this is a very simple task. All I want you to do is to make a cup of tea, okay, something you probably do every morning. You don't need me to tell you how to do it, but I want to see you do it. Now you've got to be very careful. First of all I want you to find the kettle or whatever implement it is you use to heat up water. Right, visualise it, see it on the surface. Pick it up. Now are you sure that's where the handle is on that jug or that kettle. How thick is the handle? Is there enough room inside your fist for that handle to fit. Yeah? Okay. Pick up the jug, turn around, you're now at the sink, turn the tap on and fill the kettle and, ah, what about the lid? Okay, take the lid off. Again how do you pull the lid off a kettle? Has it got a little catch mechanism? Do you have to be very careful how you pull it off? Right, put the lid down next to the sink. I want you to remember where you're putting it because you're going to have to pick it up from the same place in a minute. Fill it up. Turn the tap off. How do you hold the tap? Get your fingers into exactly the right position for holding the tap, for gripping the tap. Turn it off. Feel the force, the energy needed to actually turn the tap off fully, so it isn't dripping anymore. Right, now, you've remembered where you've put the lid. Pick the lid up again. Put it back on the kettle, turn around to the original surface, kettle down. Now plug it in. Right, how do you, can you feel, the force that is required to push the plug in the back of the kettle. I want you to actually feel it as well as show it. Switch on. Now the drawers, how do you open the drawers in your house? Pull open the drawer, you will need a spoon. What else will you need? Where do you keep the tea? Which cupboard is that in? What sort of storage jar? So come on, mime it through, work it through, using your hands, using the whole upper body in effect, but, I, I want you to build up a complete mental image of exactly what it is you're doing, exactly where everything is in your kitchen, how difficult they are to pick up, how you pick them up, how you move the muscles in your hands, how you grip things. Good ... Good.

Unit 5

Part 2
Sign language: information gap

M = Maarten
R = Ruth

M: OK, Ruth. I used six papers, six different shapes and the first one is the big one, the big square ... the, the rectangle and it's in a vertical line.

R: In a vertical line?

M: A vertical line.

R: Yes, so the ...

M: So it's standing. Yeah.

R: The column is standing in front of you ...

M: Yeah, the column, it's like a paper, like a newspaper column. OK? Then there is a small square and it's on the top right-hand corner, so on the right side and it's touching with one of its sides just, you know, lying against the column, or the ...

R: Is it laying on tops ... on top of the column or is it just touching with one ...?

M: No, it's touching on the right-hand side ... so you have the column then next to it, on the right hand side, and then on the top, just simple, just next to it.

R: So it's like a crossroads now slightly.

M: Yeah, you have a lot of imagination. OK. Then there is the rectangle ... no, what was it called, the parallelogram, and it's touching with one of its horizontal sides this small one I just described, this small square on the top right hand side.

R: What do you mean by horizontal side? The straight one ...

M: Well, because it's diagonal, two lines are diagonal, and two lines are horizontal, and it's touching with one complete horizontal line on the bottom of the small, er, square. So it's making like an 'm'.

R: With what?

M: It's the middle part of an 'm' of Maarten. OK?.

R: I don't quite get it. I have the horizontal line of this parallelogram and it is touching which side of the square?

M: The bottom side – one of the bottom lines of the ...

R: Oh yes, now I got it. So it's actually ...

M: Do you see a small 'm'?

R: Yes, I see the 'm' with a column but I don't see the square in the 'm'.

M: No, no, no, no, but an 'm' with a column – a half of the 'm' with a column, OK? Then the line between the large square and one of the small squares, so the rectangle and the small square ... yeah, so the column, let's call the column, let's call it a rectangle, OK?

R: A column and a rectangle ...

M: Yeah, the column is the rectangle.

R: The column is the rectangle.

M: And the square, the small square, so forget about the parallelogram. They are touching ... there's a line between them.

R: Where is the line?

M: If you put them together ...

R: You mean there is an extension because they're only touching in the corner anyway, don't they?

M: No.

R: Oh!

M: No, one complete side of the small square.

R: Is sitting on top of the column?

M: Not on top, on the right-hand side.

R: OK, OK, I got it ... yes, and now I, yeah, and underneath is the rectangle.

M: Yeah.

R: So I got the 'm', yeah, OK.

M: Yeah, OK. That's the way. Oh, you had it on top. OK, well now it's next to it. The way the points lying they're, they're touching each other. There I put - like the flag of a ship – the two triangles, so one is on top of the little square and the other one ...

R: Just touching with the corner?

M: No, completely touching with one side, the small sides of the triangle ...

R: The smallest?

M: Er, the two smaller sides, or the two smallest sides of the triangle are touching ... one is touching the smaller square, and the other one is touching the rectangle.

R: How can they possibly both touch it?

M: Why not?

R: The smallest side of the triangle, what is it touching?

M: It's touching the top side of the smaller square, one of the smaller squares.

R: But I only have one square, don't I?

M: Yeah, you only have one small square.

R: And it's touching the top, the whole length of the top?

M: Yeah, I think so.

R: So the whole length of the smallest side of the triangle is touching the whole length of the smallest square.

M: Yeah, at least, it's making like a hat, or like a flag of a ship, whatever you can think of. And so, one is on top of the smaller square and the other one is on the rectangle.

R: Yeah, I have like two peaks.

M: Yeah, two peaks, yeah, no, it's ending in one peak.

R: So, OK, yeah, they're opposite, they're mirroring.

M: Mirroring. Exactly!

R: So I have like a head of magic ...

M: Yeah, like a ... yeah, exactly! So now you got an 'm' with a hat. Yeah, to make it like a picture.

R: To me it looks more like an 'r' with a hat.

M: An 'r'.

R: Yeah, 'r' like Ruth.

M: I can see an 'r' in it as well. An 'r' with a hat. Fine. Then go back to the parallelogram, and if it's okay it has a line towards the right – it goes down towards the right. Furthest, on, on the furthest ...

R: Point?

M: Point of this rectangle, the right point, I have the ... I have another small smaller square, a small square, just lying there horizontally in the same line as the other two, as the...

R: As the parallelogram.

M: Parallelogram and the rectangle.

R: But the rectangle is not parallel to the parallelogram.

M: No, no, not completely, but the bottom line is.

R: The bottom line, OK, yes, so it's like an 'r' with a point, a full stop.

M: Yeah, very good.

R: And a crown on top.

M: Exactly!

R: Good. Yeah.

M: Let's have a look. Should be OK now. Yeah!

R: That was hard!

M: Yes!

Unit 6

Part 1
Garlic: five different views

Extract 1
One of my personal favourites in the book is the recipe for garlic soup. Most people, I think, are a little surprised when they discover that top of the list of ingredients is 25 cloves of garlic! That may sound quite a substantial amount but remember, when garlic's cooked, whether it's boiled or baked in the oven, then it loses much of its pungent flavour and becomes altogether much milder in taste.

Extract 2
Bram Stoker's story *Dracula* has been so appealing to filmmakers that there is hardly a decade since the film industry began that has not seen at least one film with the name Dracula

in the title. The mere mention of Count Dracula conjures up an image of the tall, pale, red-lipped monster who survives by drinking the blood of the living. He has tremendous physical power; yet at the same time he is vulnerable to such homely defences as garlic, which potential victims could put around their doorways and windows in order to have some sort of protection.

Extract 3

In the final part of this series on the British and their eating habits, we'll be looking at that most controversial of all cooking ingredients: garlic. Whether you love or hate garlic then do stay tuned for the rest of the show in which I'll be talking to chef, Anton Vaseux, about ways of incorporating garlic into your cooking. In the meantime, I had a very interesting letter from a Mr Hayes of London about how to rid one's breath of the lingering smell of garlic. He recommends chewing either a raw sprig of parsley shortly after eating a meal containing garlic or chewing a coffee bean. Both are reported to work well.

Extract 4

Today we're encouraging everybody to eat more garlic, but not many people realise that it has an extremely long history and can be used for a variety of medicinal purposes. It can be applied externally for the treatment of minor wounds – it has splendid antiseptic properties – and when taken internally there is strong evidence that garlic reduces cholesterol levels and encourages good blood circulation, thus lessening the risk of heart disease. If my patients need convincing of the benefits of eating more garlic, I merely remind them that in countries such as Egypt, Thailand and China, it has been used for centuries as a cure-all remedy.

Extract 5

Well, we tend not to use it much as a cooking ingredient in our house. Maybe that's because we're British and I think the British have always been a little afraid of garlic, particularly of the smell that stays afterwards on our breath. Having said that, one thing that my family can't get enough of is garlic bread. I buy it ready-made from the supermarket. Basically, it's just a long loaf of bread, filled with a mixture of garlic, herbs and butter. I suppose it would be easy enough to make it myself but it's a lot more convenient buying it from the shops.

Unit 6

Part 1
Garlic: growing garlic

I made three big mistakes. First of all, garlic bought from the supermarket or greengrocer is rarely suitable for British gardens. I was amazed to discover that shop garlic may come from Hungary, California, Italy, Spain, Argentina, Chile, Mexico or, of course, France. But each area has developed its own strain – by replanting the best bulbs each year, growers create a strain specially suited to their own climate. So you can hardly expect garlic to thrive here.

So it's important to start with cloves which have been specially selected for the British climate and, in practice, that usually means starting with stock from Colin Boswell of Mersley Farms on the Isle of Wight. Colin grows 30 acres of garlic and harvests about 100 tonnes a year, nearly two-thirds of the entire British garlic crop. Mind you, we import more than 4,500 tonnes so Colin's contribution to reducing the import bill is modest. But he's done us a great service. Starting off with a pink mountain garlic from France, Colin has developed a strain which thrives in Britain.

The second important factor is that you can't grow good garlic unless you plant in the autumn. Like so many plants which originate in the Mediterranean climates where the winters are cool

and damp, garlic starts to grow in late autumn and during the winter develops a vast root system which can be three to four feet deep.

Finally, harvesting. According to Colin Boswell it's best to start harvesting on 5 July, 'but in the north the end of July is better. It should be lifted from the garden when it's still green, then hung in a greenhouse or conservatory to replicate a Mediterranean summer. It needs direct sunlight and low humidity to produce a white bulb with no disease. Once picked you can keep it for a whole year before having to eat it.'

Unit 7

Part 1
A gifted child

Extract 1

Stephanie Peters: Yes ... people often remind me what a clever little girl I was ... especially my mum and dad. I sometimes get the impression they wish I'd made more of my life. I don't think they expected their daughter to be a housewife. To be fair, they never really put me under any pressure. They encouraged me ... that was all. I had my name in the papers twice; once when I was two and again at thirteen. I'd passed my exams two years earlier than anybody else in my year. I went to university at sixteen, something my parents were incredibly proud of. In fact it was then I came down to earth with a bump. I always felt very confident at school, none of the subjects were particularly difficult ... I got top marks in all the exams, I became a bit too confident really. My first year at university was a complete nightmare. I never really had to work that hard at school but being lazy didn't do me very much good at 'uni'. It was quite a shock to find myself struggling in seminars 'cos I hadn't done any reading. To be quite honest I don't think I was any more intelligent than the other students ... and with hindsight I think my talents were simply to do with being an early learner. Still, that wasn't really the problem at university; I pulled my socks up after the first year, did a lot more work and got my degree. But socially I must admit I was a bit of a misfit. I still hadn't had a boyfriend by the time I went to 'uni' ... I think my confidence left boys feeling a bit scared of me. Anyway, they weren't exactly queuing up to ask me for a date. I ended up feeling really shy around boys which was a problem at university. The first year was one round of parties and discos but I can't really say I enjoyed myself. Then Steve came along. We met in the final year and got married three years later.

I've never been particularly ambitious, so no, I'm not at all disappointed at being a housewife. Our two children keep me very busy and I'm taking a keen interest in their education. Neither of them show any particular talents yet but I'm pretty confident I'll be able to give them some useful advice if they do.

Extract 2

Everton Williams: I've been unemployed almost a year now. My trade's carpentry. My last employer closed down and I haven't been able to find anything since. Most people who knew me as a child were quite surprised when I left school at sixteen. My parents were furious, especially when they found out I'd deliberately failed my exams. They expected a lot more from me ... I used to love reading, I'd pick up anything that was lying around the house: magazines, books ... anything. I'm not sure how well I understood some of the stuff I was reading. My parents liked to give the impression I was a genius ... they were really proud of the fact I was reading all that intellectual stuff. All of a sudden I found myself hating the sight of books. I started to feel under pressure to please Mum and Dad. Maybe it was an act of rebellion, I don't know, I might've just got bored with books. I think I was quite happy around the time I appeared in the newspaper; it was a couple of years later when I went to secondary school that I started to feel unhappy. We lived in quite a small town so

I was rather a local celebrity. Unfortunately the kids at school weren't really impressed with my talents or maybe they were jealous but I ended up getting bullied quite a lot. We moved eventually but I didn't really settle into my new school and as I said, I left at sixteen. School certainly wasn't the best time of my life! I really enjoy carpentry so I don't worry about wasting my talents at all. I must admit, I do find it difficult relating to, to other people, I always have. It's nothing to do with being shy or anything like that, I just can't help finding most people boring. I'm beginning to read quite a lot again recently and very few people seem to share my interests.

Extract 3

Jamie Sutton: I've been very fortunate, I think. OK, I never did become the world-famous pianist everybody expected me to, but there again I'm not really sure that's what I wanted. I still get tremendous pleasure from playing the piano, but for me it's a hobby, not a way of earning a living. And, believe it or not, being an insurance salesman gives me plenty of opportunities to practise. A lot of my customers own pianos and I'm often asked to play for them whenever I'm in their houses on business. Whether this leaves them feeling somehow indebted to me I don't know but I seem to sell a lot of insurance to piano owners. Funnily enough, my daughter is also showing a similar talent. And I don't want to sound like I'm criticising my parents but I like to think I won't make the same mistakes as they did with me. My father was a music teacher and was keen to see me develop my talent. When I was eleven, instead of sending me to grammar school, he chose to teach me at home. Educationally I think he did a really good job: we covered all the subjects taught at school, and at sixteen I passed all my exams. But all the same, I feel I missed out on a lot of things children of my age took for granted. I was never really encouraged to take up any sports, and while other kids were out every Saturday buying the latest records, I was buying music sheets for Beethoven and Mozart. So you can imagine, whenever I mixed with people my own age I was quite disadvantaged. And that's another thing: being taught at home meant I had less time to make friends. I knew people in the area, but they were always going on about what had been happening at school, about particular teachers or classmates.

As I said earlier, I feel I've been very fortunate; I'm not a particularly shy person, I wouldn't be an insurance salesman if I was, I find it quite easy to get on with people. But I think some children with a special talent could suffer emotionally if their parents took them away from school. It's certainly something me and my wife would avoid doing with our children.

Unit 7

Part 3
Phobias

I = Interviewer
D = Dr Alan Hargreaves

I: Today is the start of national Phobia Awareness Week and to mark the occasion my guest on today's show is Dr Alan Hargreaves, a psychoanalyst who runs a private stress clinic in London. Dr Hargreaves, welcome.

D: Hello there.

I: First of all, do we take phobias seriously enough in this country?

D: Well, the whole point of this Phobia Awareness Week is to highlight the difficulties that many people are facing in everyday situations.

I: Perhaps you could start by explaining the difference between a fear and a phobia. For example, I'm not keen on snakes, but is it a phobia?

D: It's quite usual for all of us to have our own peculiar fears, but when your phobia begins to cause you embarrassment, or you feel that your phobia is disrupting your life completely, then you would be wise to seek treatment.

I: Are some phobias more common than others?

D: By far the most common fear and potentially the most disruptive is agoraphobia. The word derives from the Greek and literally means 'fear of the marketplace', but we apply it today to describe a condition in which people avoid going outside because of the awful feelings of anxiety that arise. But to go back to your previous point, like a lot of people in this country who are nervous around snakes, only a small percentage of these people have a real phobia. It's the same with aerophobia – only about five per cent of people in Britain have a truly chronic fear of air travel.

I: Now I know at the moment you're collecting stories about some of the more unusual phobias.

D: Yes, that's right. We're compiling a record of previously unheard-of phobias. For example, we had the case recently of the woman who had a phobia about buttons.

I: Buttons?

D: Yes, every time she bought an item of clothing she'd remove any buttons and replace them with zips or hooks. We used to have a sister clinic in Liverpool and our colleagues there reported on the man who used to feel highly anxious, indeed distressed, at the sight of beards. You can imagine the embarrassment this caused him at work and on the street.

I: Is there anything that would cause a phobia of facial hair?

D: Oh, that's a difficult one. He's still in therapy so we might find out one day.

I: Maybe we could move on to talk more generally about the causes and treatments of phobias.

D: Not all phobias have a specific cause but if we look at the case of claustrophobia the causes are usually of two main types. If, as a child, you were locked inside a dark cupboard as punishment for being naughty, you may re-live those feelings of distress whenever you find yourself in any enclosed space. Also, if you can remember being given an anaesthetic in hospital you may have experienced an overwhelming sense of panic and suffocation.

I: We tend to hear more about women and phobias, particulary agoraphobia. Are women more vulnerable to developing a phobia than men?

D: Absolutely not. Men are just as vulnerable as women, but what happens is that men have a tendency to keep quiet about it!

I: Is it true that gentle exposure to the object of your fear is the best way to overcome a phobia?

D: That's the principle behind behaviour therapy – the idea is that the patient gradually gets used to being with the object of dislike. There are alternatives: drugs may be used to relieve anxiety, and alternative medicine such as acupuncture, hypnosis, as well as exercise such as yoga do work for a number of people. I think that with any form of treatment the patient has got to be able to learn to trust the person helping them, whether this is a qualified professional or their best friend.

I: Well, that's about all for now. Thank you very much, and if any of our listeners need advice they can contact you ...

Unit 8

Part 1
Armchair entertainment

Extract 1

A friend of mine had been raving about this book for weeks so in the end I read it just to shut him up! I took it with me to read on the plane when I went on holiday. Anyway, I have to say that I loved it. The plot was quite complicated and every time I turned the page it seemed there was another surprise. It really kept me hooked from start to finish. I couldn't concentrate on anything else until I'd finished reading it. The ending was very chilling and really unexpected. I won't spoil it for you by telling you who the murderer was, but you'll certainly never guess until the final few pages.

Extract 2

My general feeling is that when novels are adapted for the stage or screen something tends to be lost. A really obvious point is that (of course) the actors portraying the book's characters look nothing like the pictures of them that you as the reader have created in your imagination. However, there has been one exception recently to this theory of mine. I thought the big screen version of John Grisham's book *The Firm* was far superior to the book, particularly the ending. OK, so the new version was a little far-fetched, but it's a big improvement on the original ending which I thought was rather silly and ultimately unsatisfactory.

Extract 3

I bought a copy of it as soon as it came out, even though it was in hardback, of course, and rather expensive. The whole nation was just dying to read it – the first 75,000 copies had sold out by the end of the first day of sales. It was the kind of book that people were really curious about, although a lot of my friends felt it was disgusting, exploitative and in poor taste. I suppose any 'kiss and tell' story is bound to hurt those involved, but when it's a public figure people just can't help but be curious. For every person like me who's bought the book there'll be those who disapprove and say books like this make a laughing stock of the monarchy.

Extract 4

She's one of my favourite novelists and her first novel won the Fawcett Society Book Prize in 1989. I suppose you'd characterise her as a women's writer particularly as her books are published by The Women's Press. By that I mean she writes about her experiences from a woman's point of view, but that doesn't mean that men wouldn't enjoy her work too. Her latest novel is called *Closing the Book* and describes the relationship between two female friends, one of whom is dying of cancer. It sounds as though it would be a really sad book and although it is in parts, it's generally a story about courage, hope and coming to terms with loss.

Extract 5

When I went abroad recently I thought it would be useful to read one of the 'Rough Guides' series. It was a really useful and informative introduction to the lifestyle and culture of a completely different nation. There was all the usual stuff about places to visit, but it was also packed with great tips on public transport, where to get cheap food and drink, accommodation, and so on. At the back there's a really helpful list of essential words and phrases to help you get by. Although there aren't any colour photographs, the visuals and the general layout of the book make it an appealing read.

Unit 8

Part 2
Sport

Student A: In the picture I'm looking at there are some football players sitting on the grass. Mm ... They are wearing red, it's like a uniform, an outfit. They are smiling because they've just won the game. Mm ... Some journalists or mm ... cameramen are taking photos of their smiling faces ... er ... with their trophy. Mm ... Some of the players are black and some of them are white, but anyway, they're happy to be taken photos. Mm ... Besides them there are some more players standing. I can't say anything about them because their faces are not shown on the photo but I can imagine they're also very happy about the result.

Student B: Thank you. I think you're describing Picture 5.

Student C: In this picture there's a group of footballers walking along the pitch, wearing red shirts and white shorts. Er ... There's also another player wearing a green shirt. He's blond, I think he's the goalkeeper. Let's see ... two players are wearing black tracksuits. And there's a photographer, well ... or a cameraman, pointing a camera at the players. One of the players – he's wearing a scarf round his neck, mm ... is holding a trophy or ... mm ... a medal – he's holding it up to the crowd, I suppose. I reckon they must have just won a competition.

Student D: Right, mm ... my picture shows a group of footballers too. They're also wearing white shorts and red shirts. Mm ... But the shirts have got white sleeves. One of them's got a green shirt as well, but he's ... mm ... he's dark-haired, not blond. He's holding a cup but it's ... mm ... on the ground. He's not holding it up to the crowd. These players aren't walking – some of them are ... er ... kneeling ... mm ... the one's in front – and the rest are standing. They all look really happy. Er ... Some of them are holding their hands in the air and shouting. They've just won the cup as well.

Unit 9

Part 1
An ideal family?

Okay, so '... all parents want to protect their children.' ... right, it's the end of a sentence, it must be 'from' because we've got 'protect', so it's going to be something like 'all parents want to protect their children from dangers', although 'dangers' comes up a little bit later, so, to avoid repetition, let's try 'difficulties'. 'All parents want to protect their children from difficulties. Restricting a child's freedom does not imply ...', now this is going to be a kind of ... exaggeration of 'protecting', so we need something like 'restricting the child's every movement'. So it 'does not imply restricting a child's every movement. In fact a parent's desire ...' well, it's going to be 'to' because of 'desire', it could be something like 'to protect their child from life's dangers', but we've had 'protect' before, so we need a synonym, so we'll try 'to shield'; so, 'in fact a parent's desire to shield the child from life's dangers and disappointments probably indicates a very understandable concern. It is important, however, that children should be allowed ...' Right, we need 'to' because of 'allowed', 'should be allowed to ...', now we've got a list of situations here that the child needs to cope with, that means that they should make mistakes, get into and out of difficulties, so we need something that summarises all of these, or an example in itself. Let's try ... 'to sort problems out. Children should be allowed to sort problems out, that they should make mistakes, get into and out of difficulties ...', this will be another example, so we'll try 'cope with disappointments, feel the pain of rejections, and cope ...', oh, we've got 'cope' again, we can't have a repetition so close, so we'll try 'to face disappointments, feel the pain of rejections and cope with normal human unhappiness. By allowing your child to experience ...' now this is referring back to these difficulties, these difficult situations, so it could be a word like 'such' , so 'such problems within a caring and loving family you are more likely to encourage the development of an assertive ...' it's going to be a positive word, it's about making your own decisions so we'll try 'an assertive and independent person. If your child is overprotected, he may well grow up ...', now following this we've got 'but', so there's going to be a contrast of ideas, we'll try 'he may well grow up feeling loved perhaps, but he may also be too passive.' This is a new sentence, as there's a full stop after 'passive', and after the gap there's a new sentence as well, so we need a full sentence here. Let's try 'This is not a good thing. Excessively dependent children ...'

Unit 9

Part 3
The colours of love

Dear Steven

Thanks for the letter. Sorry it's taken me such a long time to write. I only got back to England two weeks ago and I've been quite busy sorting my life out. And if that's not a good enough excuse, what about this. I'm in love! Yes, this time it's the real thing. No more of the single life for me!

I suppose you're dying to know who she is? Do you remember that night we all (a)...............(go) for that Indian meal just before I (b)...............(leave) for Greece? Do you remember Samantha? She (c)...............(sit) at the end of our table. In fact you (d)............... (see) her before that. There was that party at my house a few months earlier. She (e)...............(not be able to) find the house and (f)...............(arrive) late. Yes her! You probably remember me telling you at the time how much I liked her, but I never thought we'd get together.

Well, to cut a long story short, she (g)...............(come) out to visit me in Greece a few months ago. Maybe I should explain that since I (h)...............(leave) England we (i)...............(write) letters to each other and in one of them I (j)...............(invite) her to come out for a holiday. Anyway, she (k)...............(come) out to visit me, and we (l)...............(spend) the first couple of days being very polite and formal, I was too shy to behave in any other way! Then one morning I (m)...............(pluck) up the courage to tell her how I (n)...............(feel) about her when I (o) ....(met) her at university. Guess what? She told me she (p)...............(feel) exactly the same! We (q)...............(spend) all those months at university and her first few days in Greece not knowing that we both really liked each other!

The rest of her holiday was great. We spent the remaining days very romatically, going for nice meals and finding out all about each other. It was very sad when she had to leave, but we promised each other we'd keep in touch and see each other as soon as I got back.

That's about it really. When I (r)...............(fly) back home two weeks ago she (s)...............(met) me at the airport. The plane (t)...............(delay) in Greece, and by the time I (u)...............(arrive) she (v)...............(wait) three hours. But she was still pleased to see me so it must be love!

Anyway, now I'm back we'll have to get together so that you can meet her again. Write back soon.

All the best
Tony

Unit 10

Part 1
Work values

A professional dancer needs ... acting lessons or some drama background, needs a voice for musical theatre which means music lessons, you need your CV, you need a photo and that's just standard. Er, what you ... on top of that you need a statistics sheet, you need a jazz suit, jazz clothes, ballet shoes, tap shoes, even roller skates depending on what kind of show you're going to go for. So there's a lot more to being a dancer than you think.

Maintaining fitness? I kind of dance or move for about six hours a day. That's either creating or teaching or maintaining my stretch. Diet-wise, it's like 'Welcome to the world of pasta'. You can pig out on pasta because your metabolism usually gets faster if you're, if you're a dancer. And when it comes to coping with stress I may be different from others but I kind of ventilate my stress through dance.

What am I involved in at the moment? I'm working with Annie Lennox on a track she's just put out, choreographing *Bugsy Malone* (that's in Birmingham), I'm doing for ... an improvisation module called 'Diva' which I named for the North West Arts Board. I got a world tour happening in April, starting in Washington, that's with a group called N-Joi. I hope to be working on the next video ... choreographing the next video of *Take That*. And I suppose I'm doing little solos weekly which are in Leeds, York and London.

Long-term ... I've had to realise that I'm not chorus, I'm not a chorus dancer, I kind of stick out too much. So I wanna become like a household name ... something like ... Kellog's Bran Flakes, or something ... whatever. Really, a long-term hope of mine would be to create my own long-running West End musical ... yeah!

Background? OK, erm, I was born in Jamaica, here's a cocktail. I was born in Jamaica, I live in Oldham, Manchester. My mother's from Edinburgh. My father's from Kingston, Jamaica. I have three brothers who I love dearly. I have one sister who I adore – she's more like a princess. And I have a fish called Armani.

Training, OK. Two years in England, I trained for about six months in Paris, and about eight months in LA, but really you never stop training or learning in your art. The difficulty's when you're training is not having any money.

Problems of breaking into the arts. Well, this is where it becomes a big crock of shit, because you can't become a member of Equity, which is the actors' union or dancers' union, without good contracts and you can't get good contracts without being a member of Equity. So you kind of get into this vicious circle. My advice to people who want to get into the arts would be 'Go out into the world. Try anything else first. Everything they want to do, try and fulfil it. And if nothing they like comes out of it, then come back and be an artist or a dancer.'

Ah, personal beliefs. OK. Well, dance has allowed me to see 23 countries so far and on seeing these countries and having your eyes opened you realise that art can come from anything or anyone, so things that do become an issue in your life are things like equality and racism and if you can get ... you become peaceful with these things then it can only make you into a better person. So, I'm really happy to be a dancer.

Unit 10

Part 2
Finding the right person for the job

I = Interviewer
P = Peter

I: So Peter, you say you've had experience of these psychometric tests?
P: Well, I'm not sure what it was exactly, it was some kind of pschology test anyway.
I: What sort of job was it for?
P: Well, it's a long story. This was about twelve years ago. I'd given up my job as a heating engineer to have a nice long holiday ... about three months long actually. Not surprisingly, when I got back my job had gone. There wasn't much else around and I was feeling a bit depressed, when all of a sudden I saw an advert for a milkman's job.

I: Maybe we should explain about a milkman ... do you think?

P: Yeah ...well, basically in England, you can get your milk delivered to your house if you want to. ... like the post. A man or a woman drives around in a milk float and leaves the milk on your doorstep.

I: And it was the sort of job you fancied, was it?

P: Well, it didn't seem all that difficult ... you meet lots of people, finish quite early ... so yeah, I liked the idea. Anyway, to cut a long story short, I got the interview and went along expecting a quick chat about myself and why I'd always wanted to be a milkman ... you know the routine. But then as soon as I arrived he gave me this questionnaire and asked me to fill it in. There were about 40 questions each with three or four answers and you had to pick the one that described you best.

I: Such as? Can you remember any of them?

P: Well, there was one, 'What time do you like to get up?' About 5:00, about 7:00, about 9:00, or when you feel like it. So I thought well, obviously a milkman ... he gets up early so I ticked 'about 5:00'. Then there was another one ... 'How many weeks' holiday do you like to have each year ... four weeks, no holidays, the odd day here and there and then something stupid like six months every year. So again I thought, milkman.... a normal job, a week here and there ... so I picked four weeks.

I: That sounds sensible.

P: Yeah well, when I'd finished he took the questionnaire and started drawing this graph. When he'd finished he told me some psychologist had developed it, it was supposed to show an ideal milkman, if you can believe that. Basically, if my graph matched his one, the job was mine.

I: And did it?

P: Did it heck! When he compared the two of them, mine was completely opposite. Where his had peaks mine had troughs, and where his had troughs mine had peaks.

I: So you didn't get the job then?

P: Well actually that's not the end of the story. I told him I hadn't answered the questions honestly ... you know, that I'd filled it in like I thought a milkman would. I know it was a bit of a cheek, but I asked him if I could do it again but this time answering honestly.

I: And did he let you?

P: Yeah, he was dead good about it. So off I went again, only this time ... 'What time do you want to get up?' ... when I feel like it ... 'How many weeks holiday do you like?' ... six months ... So, I gave him the test, he did another one of his graphs and ... well, what do you think happened?

I: You got the job?

P: No I didn't, it was worse than the first time. This time me peaks and troughs were even further out. He was very apologetic but no ... I didn't get the job.

I: So I don't suppose you've got a very high opinion of these tests then?

P: You can say that again! Seriously though, what does it take to be a milkman? It's one thing to fail an interview, but to fail it without knowing why ... it doesn't seem fair. My story's probably not typical, but I'm sure most people don't answer these questions honestly ... you're always going to try and answer what you think's best. I'd be interested to know just how successful they are. I'm sure I would have made a brilliant milkman.

I: I'm sure you would. Anyway, I'm pleased to see you got over the experience.

Unit 11

Part 3
Campaign groups

Now to your letters, and as usual, much of this week's post deals with some of the many news items that made the headlines this week. First to Mrs Lovelace who writes: 'Who do they think they are at the *Evening Post*? Their latest campaign is yet more evidence that the paper's in the hands of socialists and communists. Do they really expect us to believe the whole city is phoning up to support their "Nurseries for All" campaign? Well, here's one mum who won't be signing their stupid petition: I'm too busy doing what all mums should be doing – bringing up her children!' Thanks, Mrs Lovelace. I'm sure the paper will be interested to hear your views.

However, Mr Jackson takes quite the opposite viewpoint. He writes: 'How refreshing it is to find a local newspaper that's so in touch with the pressures of parenthood. My wife and I have two young children and have spent the last six months looking for affordable chidcare facilities. We are two of those 15,000 people who felt strongly enough about the issue to put pen to paper. How many more signatures will it take before action is taken?'

John Simpson from Shildon is most concerned about the effects of the proposed Motorway on the tourist trade. He explains: 'As Managing Director of Shildon's largest hotel I am probably the last person you would expect to be involved in political protest. However, the proposal to build a motorway two miles from the beautiful village of Shildon has been badly thought out and little consultation with local residents and business people has taken place. Consequently, I am now a member of the "Save Our Village" campaign and am actively encouraging the hotel's employees to do the same. Great harm will be done to the local tourist trade if this project goes ahead. I am not prepared to see this happen.' Thank you Mr Simpson.

More criticism of local planners now, this time concerning the new office complex in the Lea Valley. Susan Seabrook writes: 'Who cares that an extremely rare species of butterfly faces extinction? Who cares that many native plants are likely to be lost forever? The property developers certainly don't seem to. What's more, the woodland has been a popular spot for families at weekends, somewhere they can escape the pressures of city life. Do we really need these offices?'

Also on this subject, Mr Gregory writes: 'I read in last week's *Evening Post* that a major campaign is needed to let everyone know how damaging the new office complex will be. What is wrong with these people? I suppose many of those complaining about butterflies and plants spend the rest of their time moaning about unemployment in the city. This new complex will create hundreds of jobs for local people. Surely that's something we should be celebrating.'

The increase in homeless figures prompted Mrs Williams to write: 'Why must we be subjected to the sight of people lying around in shop fronts in the early hours every day? Why don't these people find jobs and somewhere to live like everybody else?'

John Sinclair is of a different opinion:
'Surely the measure of a civilised society is that everybody is guaranteed a roof over their head. The growth in homelessness, which is hitting young people the hardest, is more evidence that society is failing in it's duties.'

Finally, Adam Johnson, aged fourteen, put pen to paper in support of his youth club. 'I've been attending the "New Youth Club" for the past two years. It's a great place for people of my age; we can play all kinds of sports, we hold our own weekly discos and make lots of friends. We are all very upset to hear our club might have to close. So far we have organised lots of fundraising activities but we are still a long way from the £10, 000 needed. Do any of your listeners have any ideas on how we could raise the money?' Well Adam, I'm sure our listeners will do all they can to help.

Unit 12

Part 1
Crime in society

Extract 1:
Maybe we've been lucky; by next September we'll have been living here for nine years and it hasn't happened to us yet. But it is shocking, isn't it? One of our neighbours was broken into last year, and a family at the end of the street had lots of things taken while they were on holiday. I've been feeling a lot safer since we fitted the alarm; I'm sure the sight of it outside the house acts as a deterrent.

Extract 2:
This is my second time in here. I was caught selling some designer jackets in my local pub that I'd bought cheap off a mate. He'd been pleading with me for ages to take them off his hands. No, I don't know where they came from; let's just say they fell off the back of a lorry. I wouldn't have done it if I'd've had a job, but I've got a wife and child to support.

Extract 3:
I think it's all been blown out of proportion. I've never heard of it happening in our area anyway. We've spoken about it once or twice in class. Some of the older ones have admitted to finding the idea of driving fast cars exciting, but they all seem to realise how dangerous it can be. So no, I'm not really concerned about my students getting involved in such a thing.

Extract 4:
Yeah ... I suppose it has become quite a dangerous job. I'll have retired by the summer so luckily it's not something I've got to worry about for much longer. You don't tend to hear of many assault cases round here. This is a by and large an elderly community, you haven't got to worry about being attacked. It's a different matter in the cities, though. I've lost count of the times I've heard of colleagues being assaulted whilst carrying out their duties.

Extract 5:
I've never taken anything, I wouldn't be so stupid. Some of my mates do. They never have any problems buying the stuff, you often get boys standing outside the school gates selling it. A lot of my mates say it's no different to smoking cigarettes or drinking alcohol. Maybe it isn't, but I still think they're crazy. And I don't think people should be allowed to sell things outside the school.

Unit 12

Part 3
Living in fear

Good afternoon, and thank you for inviting me to talk to your local crime prevention group. Today, in Britain, there will be more than 3000 burglaries, and we advise everyone – young and old – to take a few simple precautions to protect their homes. You can be reassured that burglars and other intruders prefer easy opportunities, like a house which looks very obviously empty, rather than a well-protected one which is too much bother.

First, let's deal with some general tips on how to avoid becoming another crime statistic. Avoid leaving signs that your house is empty. When you do have to go out, leave at least one light and the radio on, and don't leave any curtains wide open. The sight of your latest music centre or computer will tempt any burglar. Never leave a spare key in a convenient hiding place. The first place a burglar will look is under the doormat or in a flower pot! If your house is in a quiet, desolate area then this will be a prowler's dream, so deter any potential criminal from approaching your house by fitting security lights to the outside of your house.

Second, let's think about what happens if, in spite of the aforementioned precautions, a burglar or other intruder has decided to target your home. Windows are usually the point of entry for many intruders. Downstairs windows provide easy access while upstairs windows can be reached with a ladder or by climbing up the drainpipe. Incidentally, you should fix down your own ladders with a padlock and chain. Why make it easy for the criminals? Make sure that you double-check before you go to bed that all windows are locked. No matter how small your windows may be, you'd be surprised at the tiniest windows a determined burglar can manage to get through. For extra security, fit window locks to the inside of the window. You need to remember that small windows and louvre windows are a potential hazard, the latter in particular as the glass will simply slide out. As a long-term solution, I would recommend replacing louvre windows with ordinary ones.

Finally, let's consider doors. Remember that not all intruders have to break and enter. Why go to the trouble of breaking in if you can just knock and be invited in? Beware of bogus officials or workmen and, particularly if you are elderly, fit a chain and an eye hole so you can scrutinise callers at your leisure. When you do have callers never let anybody into your home unless you are absolutely sure they are genuine. Make sure that on the back door and patio doors, which can be easily forced open if you have inadequate locks, that you fit British Standard security locks.

If a burglar should manage to break into your house, install a burglar alarm if you can afford it as a final line of defence against intruders. If you are in the frightening position of waking in the middle of the night and thinking you can hear an intruder then on no account should you approach the intruder. Far better to telephone the police and wait for help. Now I'm sure there are plenty of questions ...

Grammar Reference

Unit 2: Questions (1)

1 As with question tags (see page 170), **reply questions** are formed by using the same auxiliary verb in the response as appears in the initial statement. When no auxiliary verb is used, 'do' is used. Reply questions, unlike question tags, generally conform to the following pattern: positive questions follow a positive statement, negative questions follow a negative statement.

> 'I've just come back from France.' 'Have you?'
> 'United played really well.' 'Did they?'
> 'I couldn't start the car this morning.' 'Couldn't you?'

2 Negative words like *nothing, nowhere, never,* etc., are followed by a negative reply question.

> 'I've never been to America.' 'Haven't you?'
> 'Nobody called about the advert.' 'Didn't they?'

3 Reply questions can have several functions depending on the intonation used. The following reply questions would express *surprise, interest, concern* or *indifference* respectively, in response to the following statement:

> 'I didn't get back until midnight.'

> 'Didn't you?'
> 'Didn't you?'
> 'Didn't you?'
> 'Didn't you?'

4 Reply questions can also be used to show *emphatic agreement* with an affirmative statement. In this case, however, the reply question must be a negative.

> 'What a great film!' 'Yes, wasn't it?'

This is quite logical if you view the response as a shortened question tag: 'What a great film!' 'Yes, it was, wasn't it?'

5 Reply questions and words or phrases like *really*? or *seriously*? make conversation more interactive as they invite the first speaker to elaborate.

Unit 3: Reported speech

1 **Verbs of reporting.** The following verbs are commonly used in reported speech in the following patterns:

verb + gerund	deny
	suggest
	....
	....
	....
verb + object + (that) clause	assure
	promise
	remind
	....
	....
	....
verb + (that) clause	accept
	agree
	deny
	explain
	promise
	suggest
	....
	....
verb + object + preposition	accuse sb. of
	remind sb. about
	threaten sb. with
	....
	....
	....
verb + preposition	agree with
	apologise for
	....
	....
	....
verb + infinitive	agree
	promise
	offer
	threaten
	....
	....
	....
verb + object + infinitive	encourage sb. to
	beg sb. to
	invite sb. to
	remind sb. to
	....
	....
	....

2 Rather than trying to memorise long lists of verbs and their verb patterns, complete the spaces provided with other verbs as you come across them in your reading. As you do this it might be useful to see whether the reported verb patterns you find correspond to the general functional categories below.

3 **Reported questions.** For reported questions that contain words like *where, when, who,* etc., note the following:

a 'Do' is not used in the reported question

b Reported questions use the normal word order:

He *asked me where I lived*. (not 'He asked me where do I live.')
She wanted to know where the house was. (not 'She wanted to know where was the house.')

c In questions that do not contain a question word like *where*, *when* , etc., *whether* or *if* are used:
The boss wanted to know if I'd be coming to work the next day. (Question: 'Will you...?')
He asked whether I could work a little later than usual. (Question: 'Can you...?')

4 Reported suggestions, advice, orders and requests.
When reporting *suggestions*, *advice*, *orders* or *requests*, the infinitive construction is often used:

My neighbour told me to turn the music down.
The doctor advised me to give up smoking.

Suggest is not used with an infinitive construction but is either followed by a *that* or an *...ing* clause:

The doctor suggested that I take up some form of exercise.
She suggested taking up some form of exercise.

5 Reported hopes and intentions. When reporting *hopes* and *intentions* a 'that' clause or an infinitive is generally used, depending on the reporting verb:

She felt (that) she could have done better.
He hoped to arrive by about 9.00.

Unit 3: The language of obligation and permission

1 Modal verbs are often used when stating obligation or giving permission. The following structural points should be remembered whenever modal verbs are used:

a These verbs do not change their form: there is no -s, -ing, -ed or infinitive form.

b Because they have such limited forms it is sometimes necessary to use other verbs:
You won't be able to enter the country without a passport. (not 'can')
I had to go to the dentist yesterday. (not 'must')

c Most modal verbs are followed by the infinitive of a verb without *to* with the exception of *ought to* and *need to* (+ verb)
I must go now. (Not 'must to go')
You can leave when you're ready.
You ought to see a doctor.

2 Must/have to

a *Must* is used when the obligation comes from the speaker, *have to* when the obligation is external to the speaker or imposed by an outside body:
Keys must be left at reception. (on the authority of the hotel manager)
You have to leave your keys at reception. (one guest to another)

b *Mustn't* is used to show negative obligation, *don't have to*, *haven't got to* (informal) or *don't need to*, to show there is no obligation:
Tourists mustn't enter the country without a valid visa.
We haven't got to /don't have to/don't need to make a reservation.

c *Have to* is used to express past obligation (see 1b). To express a future obligation *must* is used when the obligation also exists in the present, *will have to* when it is clearly a future obligation:
We had to pay a deposit before they let us take the TV away.
You must let us know if you're going to be late.
You'll have to get your suit cleaned when you go for your interview.

3 Needn't have/didn't need to. *Didn't need to* is used to show that something wasn't necessary and so wasn't done, *needn't have* to show that something was done unnecessarily:

We didn't need to make a reservation ... we knew it would be empty.
Look! The train's empty! We needn't have made a reservation.

4 Should/ought to. *Should* and *ought to* express obligation in the sense of communicating strong advice. Note the difference in meaning between the following:

You should take these tablets before every meal. (strong advice)
You should have taken the medicine. (It wasn't taken and the patient is still ill)

5 Can/may/could. *Can, may* and *could* are all used to give and ask for permission. (For an explanation of formality see below.) *Could* and *to be allowed to* are used to express general permission in the past. However, *to be allowed to* must be used when referring to a particular occasion in the past or the future.

I couldn't/wasn't allowed to stay up late when I was younger.
I was allowed to re-take the exam after they discovered I was ill.
You won't be allowed to get in wearing jeans.

6 Levels of formality. There are many other words and phrases that express obligation and permission in addition to modal verbs. However, it is important to use them appropriately. Keep a record of formal and informal structures on page 147.

Formal	Informal	Both
must not	mustn't	must
to be obliged to	don't have to	have to
it is advisable	It's best if	can
to be permitted	let	mustn't
to be required	Is it all right if ...?	ought to
to be recommended	don't need to	to be allowed to
It is not necessary to	needn't	should
It is the responsibility of		
May (I possibly) ....?		
(I wonder if I) Could ...?		
Might (I possibly) ...?		

Unit 4: Active and passive

1 Passives are generally formed with the verb *to be* in the appropriate tense and the past participle:

present simple	*The finished product is distributed to retail outlets.*
present continuous	*Repairs are being carried out following the explosion.*
past simple	*War and Peace was written by Tolstoi.*
past continuous	*Drinks were being served when the alarm went off.*
present perfect	*A pay increase has been awarded to all staff.*
past perfect	*The damage had been done by the time I arrived.*
future simple	*Dinner will be served at 8.00.*
future perfect	*The repairs will have been carried out by next week.*
infinitive	*He hopes to be promoted.*

2 You will, however, often come across passive forms with the verb *to be* omitted, particularly in newspaper headlines or signs:

Liverpool beaten by underdogs
Shoes repaired while you wait

3 The passive is often used for the following reasons:

a to create formality. Compare the following:
It is hoped that efficiency will improve with the new working practices.
We hope the new working practices will improve efficiency.
Your overdraft has been extended.
I've extended your overdraft.

b when the agent is obvious:
Building work being carried out.

c when the agent is not known:
Mr Smith was attacked on his way home from work.

d when the agent is people in general:
This product should not be re-frozen.

e when the thing or person affected by the action is more important than the agent. Compare the following:
Prime Minister sacked.
British Gas are to lay off 500 workers over the next year.

f when the agent is unimportant, such as when describing a process:
The components are manufactured in Germany and assembled in Coventry.

g when the agent wishes to avoid being seen as responsible for an action. Compare the following:
The company will be signing a multi-million-pound contract next year.
Unfortunately, wages will be frozen.

Remember to keep a note of formal and informal structures on page 147.

Unit 4: Defining and non-defining relative clauses

1 Defining relative clauses are essential to the meaning of a sentence and consequently cannot be omitted. **Non-defining relative clauses** give extra information and are therefore not essential to meaning. Compare the following:

English students, who do their homework regularly, deserve a lot of praise.
English students who do their homework regularly deserve a lot of praise.

In the first sentence, all English students deserve praise. The fact that they all do their homework regularly is interesting but not essential information. In the second sentence, it is only those students who do regular homework who deserve praise.

2 In defining relative clauses *that* or *who* is used after people, *that* or *which* after things. *That* tends to be used more in spoken English. It is also common for the pronoun to be omitted when it defines the object of the clause, particularly in spoken English:

He's the man (who/that) I was telling you about.
It's a tool (that/which) you use for getting stones out of horses' hooves.

Note that it is not possible to omit the relative pronoun when it is the subject of the sentence:
*That's the woman won the lottery. (incorrect)

3 In non-defining relative clauses *who* is used after people, *which* after things. It is not possible to use *that* in non-defining relative clauses and the relative pronoun cannot be omitted. Commas are used to show that the information is extra and not essential.

The Prime Minister, who is on an official visit to the USA, fell ill today.
British Telecom, which is now a private company, made huge profits last year.

4 Non-defining relative clauses are commonly employed in written English but rarely used in conversation.

5 In both defining and non-defining relative clauses, *when* is used after times, *where* after places:

It was a period when people tended to live in extended families.
That's the hotel where we had our honeymoon.

6 In both defining and non-defining relative clauses, prepositions can either go before the relative pronoun or at the end of the relative clause. The latter is common in spoken English, the former in formal writing.

That's the man (who) I was telling you about.
This is the man about whom much has been written.

7 *Whose* is used in both defining and non-defining relative clauses to show possession:

Where's the man whose car was stolen?
The director, whose first film broke box office records, has now retired.

8 Expressions of quantity like *much, many, some, a few, all,* etc. can be followed by *of whom* or *of which* in non-defining relative clauses:

The judge dismissed the evidence, much of which was totally irrelevant.
The refugees, many of whom were malnourished, arrived in their thousands.

Remember to keep a record of formal and informal structures on page 147.

Unit 5: Time conjunctions

1 Time conjunctions are not generally followed by *will*:

I'll give you a ring when I get home. (not 'I'll give you a ring when I will get home.')
It'll be 10.00 before I have finished this job. (Not 'It'll be 10.00 before I will have finished this job.')

2 When describing past actions, if it is important to show that one action is the result of another or happened immediately after another, the past tense should be used in both clauses:

When he stood up he hit his head on the shelf.
The car started as soon as she turned the key.

3 To show that one action was obviously completed before another began, the past perfect should be used in the first action:

When the children had eaten their breakfast they went to school.
I went home as soon as I had spent all my money.

4 When describing a future action the present perfect should be used in the first action:

Once Jane has washed the car we'll go into town.

Unit 6: Expressing possibility

For general rules governing the form of modal verbs, see The Language of Obligation and Permission, page 167.

1 The following **modal verbs** are used to express varying degrees of likelihood ranging from certain to possible:

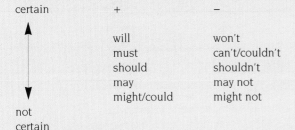

certain   +   −

will   won't
must   can't/couldn't
should   shouldn't
may   may not
might/could might not

not
certain

2 These verbs can be used to express degrees of likelihood in the past with the addition of the perfect infinitive ('have' + past participle):

It can't have been Tom who called. He's away on business.
We must have missed the last train. The ticket office is closed.

3 These modal verbs can also be used to express likelihood in the present and future with the exception of *could not* which is only used for the present and past.

She can't be 35! She doesn't look a day over 25.
There's the phone. That'll be John.
I might not be home till late. The traffic's terrible. (Not 'could not')
He should pass if he works hard.

4 The following words or phrases are also used to express likelihood informally:

There's <u>no way</u> United can win now. There's only ten minutes left. (certain)
I'm <u>certain/sure</u> I left it here. (certain)
It's <u>odds on</u> the plane will be delayed. (probable)
I <u>bet</u> he'll be late. (probable in the opinion of the speaker)
He's <u>bound to</u> pass the exam. (probable)
I'm <u>fairly certain/sure</u> he didn't phone. (possible)
<u>Perhaps/Maybe/It's likely</u> she'll be on the next bus. (possible)

Remember to keep a record of formal and informal structures on page 147.

Unit 7: Verb forms (1)

1 The **present participle** (*..ing*) form of the verb can be used as the subject of a sentence:

Smoking is bad for your health.
Receiving letters is much nicer than getting a telephone call.
Learning English is great fun!

2 There are certain verbs after which the *...ing* form of the verb must be used:

I really enjoy playing tennis.
He denied being anywhere near the bank on the day of the robbery.
He won't mind missing the film. He's seen it before.

3 You will see below some of the main verbs that are followed by the *...ing* form of the verb. Complete the spaces with other verbs which follow the same pattern as you come across them.

admit	escape	....	....
avoid	finish	....	....
consider	imagine	....	....
deny	mind	....	....
enjoy	practise	....	....

4 The *...ing* form of the verb is used after all prepositions:

I'm so nervous about meeting him.
I'm looking forward to seeing you in the summer.
They're thinking of going to Greece.

For more verb patterns see page 172.

Unit 7: Will, would and used to

1 Will and *would* have several functions:

a as a request, *would* being generally more polite:
Will you answer that, I'm busy.
Would you mind passing the sugar?

b to show willingness, or to make an offer
My lighter won't work.
I called him again and again but he wouldn't get out of bed this morning.
OK. I'll answer it.

c to express criticism. Will and would are stressed:
She <u>will</u> insist on interrupting people all the time.
She <u>would</u> do that. That's just like her.

d to make a prediction:
Do you think she'll come?
There's the phone. That'll be Steven. (a certain deduction about the present)

e to express the future in the past:
Little did he know that he would be elected President the following year.

f to give advice:
If I were you I'd go and see a doctor.

g to hypothesise about the past, the present or the future:
We would have arrived earlier if we hadn't got lost.
What would you say if I told you I loved you?
What will they do if we arrive late?

For more information about conditionals see page 171.

h to describe a past habit:
He would sit in his chair by the fire reading the newspaper.

2 Compare the uses of *would* and *used to* in the following sentences:

My grandfather used to/would bring me chocolate every time he came to visit.
I used to live in London. (Not 'would live')
As kids we used to/would rush home from school and change for a game of football.
She used to drive a Ford Fiesta. (Not 'would drive')

Both would and used to describe past habits, would being rather more nostalgic. However, would can only be used to describe repeated actions in the past, whereas used to can also express past states and situations.

Unit 8: Questions (2)

1 **Question tags:**

a contain the same (modal) auxiliary verb as appears in the main sentence + pronoun (but see exceptions below):
You haven't seen my keys, have you?
He should have arrived by now, shouldn't he?

b use the verb 'to be' if this is the main verb in the sentence:
You're not tired, are you?
She's not angry again, is she?

c use *do* in the tag, when the sentence does not contain an auxiliary verb or *to be*.
They went to Spain last year, didn't they?
You take sugar, don't you?

d have *aren't I* or *am I* in the tag:
I know, I'm an idiot, aren't I? ('am I not' would be extremely formal and ironic and 'amn't I' is rarely used)

e usually have a positive tag with a negative sentence, or a negative tag with a positive sentence:
You haven't got the time, have you?
He'll be home by now, won't he?

f after imperatives use the verbs *will, won't, can, can't, would* or *could* in the tag:
Phone me when you arrive, won't you?
Turn the TV down, could you?

g use *will you* after a negative imperative:
Don't forget to pay the gas bill, will you?

h can sometimes have a positive tag with a positive sentence, mainly where ellipsis (omission of words) takes place:
Lend me a pound, will you?
Turn the TV down, could you?

2 Intonation is extremely important in question tags. It is this that gives the meaning to the question tag. Consider the following:

a tags that act as genuine questions will normally have a rising intonation:
You're not married, are you?
He hasn't phoned, has he?

b tags that are asking for confirmation usually have a falling intonation:
OK. We've finished, haven't we?
We met at last year's conference, didn't we?

c when making informal requests, tags normally have a rising intonation:
Make me a cup of tea, will you?
Do me a favour, could you?

d a question tag used in an order will often have a falling intonation:
You won't forget, will you?
Don't be late, will you?

Unit 8: Future forms

1 Will is used:

a to make a simple prediction:
Do you think he'll come?
I'll probably see you next week.

b to describe a future fact:
I'll be 21 next birthday.
The Queen will be opening the new leisure centre.

c to describe a spontaneous decision about the future:
I think I'll go to see a film this evening.
I'll just phone Sue to see if she's coming.

For further uses of *will* see page 170.

2 Going to is used:

a to make a prediction based on present evidence:
Look at those clouds. It's going to rain.
I feel terrible ... I think I'm going to be sick.

b to describe future plans or intentions that have already been decided:
I'm going to the cinema this evening. (a decision made earlier)
I'm going to stay in this evening. There's something on TV I want to watch.

3 Present continuous is used to describe a future arrangement:

I'm seeing the dentist at 3.00. (an appointment has been made)
We're flying to Madrid this weekend. (the tickets have been booked and confirmed)

Note that, in comparison to *going to*, the present continuous implies that somebody has agreed to your plans and therefore allowed you to make an arrangement.

4 Present simple is used to describe future schedules, timetables or calendar events:

Lessons start at 9.00.
The train leaves from platform 3 at 2.30.
The Christmas holiday runs from December 20th to January 3rd.

5 The **future continuous** (will be ... ing) is used:

a to describe an activity that will be in progress at a particular time in the future:
This time next year I'll be living in Greece.
Don't phone her at 9.00. She'll be eating her dinner.

Note that this structure is also used to express a certain deduction about the present:

Don't phone her now. She'll be eating her dinner.

b to ask politely about somebodys plans and often preceding a request:
Will you be doing anything this Saturday? ... I was wondering if you wanted to come round for dinner.
Will you be using the car tonight? ... I was hoping I could use it.

c to describe a future activity that will take place in the normal course of events:
We will be flying at an altitude of 20,000 feet.
I'll be arriving at platform 4.

6 The **future perfect** (continuous) is used to describe an action that will be finished or will have been completed by a particular time in the future:

I'll have taken the exam by the time I see you next.
We'll have been living in London for three years by this time next month.

Unit 9: Conditionals

1 Tenses are often used to express varying degrees of 'distance', in terms of time, to show social distance, or in terms of what we perceive to be fact (real or possible) and non-fact (unreal or unlikely/impossible). **Conditional sentences** refer to factual or non-factual hypothetical situations and can be in any of the following forms:

a zero conditionals to describe a general truth or fact. (no tense shift)
I get a terrible hangover if I drink too much red wine.
Provided he's eaten some breakfast, he's not so short-tempered.

b first conditionals to describe a probable future result given a certain situation. (no tense shift)
If you don't take your medicine you won't get better.
Provided she comes soon, we should get there on time.

c second conditionals to describe the possible result of a hypothetical situation. Because the situation is seen as less likely or improbable, a shift in tense takes place:
If you won the lottery what would you do?
What job would you do if you could do anything you liked?

d third conditionals to describe a hypothesis about the past. As it describes a situation in the past, the hypothesis is impossible and therefore a further shift in tense takes place:
I might never have met you if we hadn't been introduced.
They wouldn't have scored if the goalkeeper had seen the ball.

e mixed conditionals to describe an impossible situation based on past and present time references. As with second and third conditionals, the past perfect is used when describing the past situation, the past tense to describe the present:
If she had stayed on at school, she'd be at university now.
I wouldn't be living here now if I hadn't changed jobs last year.

2 Note that:

a *if* is not always essential in zero or first conditional sentences

b *will* can often be replaced by another modal verb in conditionals generally

3 Further points about the use of conditional sentences:

a there are several alternatives to *if* depending on the context:
I'll meet you outside the cinema, <u>unless</u> you have a better idea.
You can stay up to watch the film <u>provided/providing</u> you do your homework first.
<u>Were</u> I to be President, I would increase taxes substantially. (formal)
<u>Supposing</u> he doesn't come, what shall we do?

b in formal contexts (as in 3a above) and when giving advice, *were* can replace *was*:
What would the consequences be if I were to break the contract?
If I were you I'd see somebody about that cough.

c when making a request, a second conditional is often more polite than a first conditional construction.
Would it be all right if I had tomorrow off?

See Past Forms below, for a more detailed explanation of creating 'distance'.

Unit 9: Past forms

1 Past simple. This is used to describe situations, events or actions that happened in the past:

I spent my childhood in London.
The opening of Parliament took place this morning.
I went to bed early last night.

The past simple is used to describe a sequence of actions in narrative:

I got up, had a shower and then ate breakfast.

2 Past continuous. This is used:

a to describe temporary situations. Compare the following:
I was living with some friends over the summer.
I lived with my parents until I was 25.

b in narratives for descriptions and particularly for setting the scene:
It was a beautiful summer's morning. The sun was shining, the birds were singing and I was feeling full of optimism.

c with the past simple. The progressive describes a longer action, the simple refers to a shorter action that takes place mid-way through the longer action:
I was driving along the road when the accident happened.

d to make a request or suggestion more polite:
I was wondering if I could have next week off.
I was hoping you could come round tonight .

3 Past perfect simple and continuous.

a The past perfect is used to show that one action happened before another in the past:
I woke up at 7.00. I'd had a terrible nights sleep.
I left before the end of the film as I'd seen it before.

b You should not overuse the past perfect. Once past in the past has been made clear, the past simple can be used:
I got home from work feeling utterly exhausted. I'd spent the whole day in various meetings, argued with several unhappy customers and got held up in traffic on the way home.

c The past perfect should be used to show that one action was completed before the next one began. Compare the following:
When they had dinner they talked about their holiday.
When they had had dinner they talked about their holiday.

d The past perfect continuous is used to emphasis duration or a repeated activity:
I'd been smoking for ten years when I finally decided to give up.
He'd been thinking about her on and off all week.

4 Future in the past. The following past forms can all express the future as seen from the past:

His contemporaries were unaware that he <u>would become</u> a leading politician. (found more often in literary rather than spoken English)
I couldn't phone. I <u>was seeing</u> John at 6.00 and so I had to rush. (as with present continuous for arrangements)
We <u>were going</u> for a meal that evening so I put on my best suit. (as with 'going to' for an intention)
I <u>was to</u> start work later that year in the company's London head-quarters. (a planned arrangement, found mainly in literature)

Unit 10: Verb forms (2)

1 The **infinitive** can be used:

a as the subject of a sentence introduced by *it* when describing a particular action:
It was nice to hear from you.
It is easy to understand why he got so annoyed.

Compare this to the *...ing* form as the subject, which is usually used to describe a more general activity:
Learning a foreign language isn't easy.
Smoking is bad for your health.

b after many adjectives:
I was surprised to hear from you so soon.
She'll be happy to help you.
I was so pleased to be invited.

c to show purpose:

I went to the shop to buy some matches.
He phoned Helen to find out about the party.
I started learning French to impress a girl I'd met.

d after the object of certain verbs:

I told him to meet me at 6.00.
He wouldn't allow me to go early.
I couldn't persuade him to take the exam.

e after certain verbs:

I can't afford to have a holiday this year.
He pretended to be a policeman.

Here are some of the more common verbs that are followed by an infinitive. Add any more verbs as you come across them:

afford	decide	promise	....
agree	expect	refuse	....
appear	forget	seem	....
ask	hope	start	....
begin	manage	try	....
choose	pretend	want	....

2 Certain verbs can be followed by either an infinitive or an '*...ing*' form but with different meanings:

Did you remember to bring the cheese? (I hope you didn't forget)
I remember being very quiet as a child. (a memory)

I stopped to have a drink. (I stopped what I was doing in order to have a drink.)
I stopped having a drink with my lunch. (I stopped drinking at lunchtimes.)

She went on to be a famous politician. (later in her life)
He went on being an idiot. (he continued being an idiot)

I'll never forget feeling nervous on my first day at school. (memory)
I forgot to post the letter. (I didn't post it)

For further verb forms see page 169.

Unit 10: Participles (2)

1 Adjectival participles can be used like reduced relative clauses:

Merchandise (which is) sold through our company carries a two-year guarantee.

2 Past participles have a passive meaning, present participles have an active meaning:

Photographs taken in restricted areas will be confiscated.
Tourists taking photographs in restricted areas will be prosecuted.

3 Participles with an adverbial function can also have particular meanings:

Taken daily, vitamin C can help you fight off colds. (If you take vitamin C ...)

Turning off the light, I went to sleep.
(After I turned off the light ...)
Feeling tired, I went to bed. (Because I felt tired ...)
We painted the living room red, creating a very warm atmosphere.
(As a result ...)
Putting my hand in my pocket, I realised I'd forgotten my keys.
(When ...)

4 Adverbial and adjectival participles are generally used in written rather than spoken English and are useful in creating a formal style.

Remember to keep a record of formal and informal structures on page 147.

Unit 11: Multi-word verbs

1 A **multi-word verb** is a general term for all of the following:

a phrasal verbs
b prepositional verbs
c phrasal-prepositional verb

The difference depends on whether the word that follows the verb is a preposition (prepositional verb) or an adverbial particle (phrasal verb), or both (phrasal-prepositional verb). This distinction is important as a preposition takes an object, whilst an averbial particle does not, although the verb it accompanies may do. Consequently, multi-word verbs can be categorised into four types:

Type 1 – verb + adverb (phrasal verb):

My car broke down this morning.
Company profits have fallen off this year.
The thieves got away.
Can I break in for a moment?

Type 2 – verb + adverb + object (phrasal verb). The object can come before or after the adverb so long as the object is not a pronoun:

I spent the afternoon handing out leaflets in town. (Or 'handing leaflets out')
I spent the afternoon handing them out. (Not 'handing out them')
I couldn't pass up the opportunity of a free holiday. (Or 'pass the opportunity up')
I couldn't pass it up. (Not 'pass up it')

Type 3 – verb + preposition + object (prepositional verb). The preposition must follow the verb:

I'm staying in tonight to look after the children.
I won't stand for this behaviour any longer.
I couldn't get over the news.
We decided to pass over his stupid remark.

Type 4 – verb + adverb + preposition + object (phrasal-prepositional verbs):

I'm not going to put up with your attitude any longer.
They couldn't come up with any new ideas.
You should try to cut down on the number of cigarettes you smoke.
Right. Let's get down to business.

2 Many multi-word verbs can fit into more than one category depending on their structure:

I couldn't get my feelings over to my colleagues. (Or 'get over my feelings' – phrasal)
I couldn't get over the shock. (Not 'get the shock over' – prepositional)

3 Multi-word verbs often have more than one meaning:

What time do you get off work? (finish)
I must get these letters off this evening. (post)
I cant get this stain off my shirt. (remove)

4 Multi-word verbs are extremely common in spoken English. However, they are often avoided in formal English when Latinate or more general formal equivalents are used. Compare:

How on earth do you put up with him?
This school will not tolerate bad behaviour.

Shall we get down to work?
The meeting commenced with a speech from the Managing Director.

Remember to keep a record of formal and informal structures on page 147.

Unit 11: Emphatic structures

Inversion, putting the verb before the subject, is commonly used in literature, formal writing and speeches to create emphasis.

1 After negative adverbial expressions:

<u>Scarcely</u> *had I arrived home* <u>when</u> *the phone started ringing.*
<u>No sooner</u> *had I gone to bed* <u>than</u> *the phone rang.*
<u>Under no circumstances</u> *should visitors bring guests back to their rooms.*
<u>Not until</u> *inflation has been reduced will the country's economy prosper.*
<u>Rarely</u> *have economists offered such an optimistic forecast.*

Note the tense change from past simple to past perfect after *scarcely* and *no sooner.*

2 In sentences replacing *if*:

Had we realised the seriousness of the situation, we could have acted sooner.
Should you have cause for complaint, please contact the company immediately.
Were we to enter negotiations our position could be compromised.

3 After *only* or *so*:

Only after years of painstaking research did scientists find a cure for the disease.
So serious is the situation that the Prime Minister is expected to return today.

Remember to keep a record of formal and informal structures on page 147.

Unit 12: Articles

1 The **definite article** is often used when talking about particular rather than general nouns. This may be because of any of the following reasons:

a the noun has already been referred to or is understood:
A man and a woman were walking along a country lane. The man was listening attentively as the woman told him a little of her background.
That's the car I was telling you about.
I'm just going to the bank.

Note: the definite article is often used in this way when referring to something shared by the community and therefore known to all (*In the high street, It's next to the post office*).

b when making reference to something unique:
The Queen is opening a new motorway today.
He's the tallest man I've ever seen.

2 The definite article is also generally used:

a with adjectives that are used like nouns:
The rich are getting richer, the poor are getting poorer.

b when talking generally about an object in the context of science or technology:
The telescope is commonly thought to have been invented by Galileo.
The car is one of the major causes of pollution in modern society.

3 The **indefinite article** is generally used:

a with a countable singular noun when referred to for the first time: see 1a above.

b to refer to jobs:
I want to be a teacher.
She is working in Spain as a translator.

4 Articles are often omitted:

a when referring to plural countable and uncountable nouns generally:
Children grow up so quickly these days, don't they?
Traffic was brought to a halt due to the demonstration.

b after many expressions containing a preposition:
on foot, at night, for breakfast, by car, at home, etc.

5 Note the difference in meaning in the following:

John's in hospital. (hospital seen as a social institution, therefore he is a patient)
John's in the hospital. (hospital seen as a building, therefore he is a visitor)

Sam now goes to secondary school (school as a social institution)
He went to the school to collect his children. (his children's school)

When we are referring to attendance at an institution, e.g. hospital, school or prison, we omit the article. When making reference to a particular hospital, school, prison, etc., we use the definite article.

Unit 12: Perfect tenses

1 Perfect tenses are formed with the auxiliary verb *have* and a past participle:

I've seen this film before.
She'd never been to London before.
I'll have finished by the time you arrive.

2 Continuous forms contain *have been* and the past participle:

We've been living here for six years now.
She'd been thinking about him all afternoon.
I'll have been working here for ten years by September.

3 The **present perfect** (simple and continuous) is generally used when there is some connection between the past and the present and often refers to experience, news or something of present importance. If the action or state is situated firmly in the past and has no connection with the present, a past tense is used:

I've never been to America. (during my lifetime, which is not yet over)
He never went to America. (he is dead and therefore focus is on the past)

I've lost my keys. (so I can't start my car)
I lost my keys. (but I found them this morning)

The Prime Minister has resigned. (News. He isn't Prime Minister any more)

4 The **present perfect continuous** is generally used to convey temporary situations or to emphasise duration or continuation. Compare this to permanent or finished activities or states expressed by the present perfect simple:

I've been living in my friend's house. (temporarily)
I've lived in Birmingham for three years.

He's been cooking all afternoon. (we don't know if he has finished)
I've cooked the meat. (I've finished)

5 The **past perfect** is used to refer to the 'past in the past', the continuous form to describe actions or situations that continued up to the more recent past reference:

I wasn't hungry as I'd eaten earlier that evening.
He'd never been abroad before and so he couldn't get used to foreign currency.
I'd been watching TV all afternoon when I finally decided to go out for a walk.
The company had been trading for 50 years before it finally went bankrupt.

Note: native speakers tend to use the continuous form when this is possible.

6 The **past perfect** should be used if it is important to stress the sequence of events, but need not be used if the order of events is self-evident:

When I'd read the newspaper I went to bed.
After I arrived at work I made myself a nice cup of coffee.
He went to University at the age of twenty-one. He (had) left school at sixteen and started an apprenticeship in the building industry, where he stayed until finally deciding to return to full-time education.

7 The **future perfect** is used to say that an action or event will have been finished or completed by a specified time in the future, the continuous form being used to emphasise continuation or duration:

I'll have eaten dinner by the time you arrive.
They'll have opened the new hospital by next year.
We'll have been living here for six years soon.

For the use of time conjunctions with perfect forms see page 169.

The authors would like to thank the following: all the students at Henley College and the University of Wolverhampton who helped with the tapescripts and the trialling of this book; Margaret Quirk, Peter Llewelyn-Jones and Danny Price who kindly agreed to be interviewed; Karen Jamieson and Andrew Jurascheck for their editorial assistance, continued support and good humour. And finally, a general thank you to EFL practitioners for the inspiration provided by their thoughts and ideas.

To our families

The authors and publishers would like to thank the following for permission to reproduce copyright material:

She Magazine for 'Teacher you're the tops', © National Magazine Company; Hamish Hamilton for *The Happy Isles Of Oceania* by Paul Theroux, © Cape Cod Scriveners Co.1992; Penguin Books Canada for *Talk, Talk, Talk* by Jay Ingram, © Jay Ingram; *The Observer* for 'Garlic Bred' by Graham Rice, 'Easy living at Japan's colleges' by Ken Sullivan, and 'Where women rule', © The Observer; *The Guardian* for 'Home Alone' by Jean Ross, 'In the final analysis' by Katharine Viner, 'Mine's a pint of wine, thanks' by Ben Laurance, and 'When fanatics opt for murder', © The Guardian ; *The Times* for 'Write on but is it science' by David Guest, © Times Newspapers 1994; *New Woman* for extracts from book and film reviews (*Lovers and Liars*, *The Joy Luck Club* and *Century*); *Marie Claire* for extract from book review by Carolyn Hart issue No. 68, April 1994 p.104; Trades Union Congress for 'A new deal for youth'; *The Independent* for 'Right to smack ruling triggers furore' by Nicholas Timmins, 'The making of little monsters' by Peter Thomas and '£100,000 for boss, £5 each for staff'; *The Daily Telegraph* for 'Aaaaaargh ... I'm with Diana on this one!' by Mick Brown, © The Telegraph plc, London, 1994; Virgin Publishing for *The Y-Plan* by Lesley Mobray and Jill Gaskell, © 1990 Lifetime Vision and Central London YMCA, published in 1995 by Virgin Books; Jenny Glew for 'Acupuncture gets to the point' by Jenny Glew; Sterling Inc. for *Great Lateral Thinking Puzzles* by Paul Sloane and Des MacHale; Penelope Leach for 'The no smacking guide to good behaviour' by Penelope Leach; Carfax Publishing Company for 'McDonald's abroad' by James R Curtis published in *The Journal of Geography* 1982; Ann Kent for 'Quit while you're ahead' by Ann Kent; BAA plc for 'Mind your language'; A.M. Heath for *1984* by George Orwell, © the estate of the late Sonia Brownell Orwell and Martin Secker and Warburg Ltd; Oxford University Press for the phonetic chart and verb definitions from *The Oxford Advanced Learner's Dictionary* by A.S. Hornby, published 1994; BBC Worldwide Limited for *The Unforgettable Memory Book* by Nick Mirsky; Longman Group Limited for timelines from *The Anti-Grammar Grammar Book* by Nick Hall and John Shepheard; University of Cambridge Local Examinations Syndicate for OMR Candidate Answer Sheets; Jill Hartley for 'Hands-on Holidays' by Jill Hartley.

While every effort has been made to trace the owners of copyright material in this book, there have been cases where the publishers have been unable to locate the sources. We would be grateful to hear from anyone who recognises their copyright material and is unacknowledged.

The publishers are grateful to the following for permission to reproduce photographs and other material: Allsport: p. 91; Barnaby's Picture Library: p. 7(TM, BL, BR); Bubbles: pp. 136(BR), 137(MR), 138; The Bridgeman Art Library: p. 31; Collections / Anthea Sieveking: pp. 79, 137(B); Comstock Photo Library: p. 81(M, B); Sally & Richard Greenhill: pp. 7(TL, TR, BM), 44, 114; Hulton Deutsch Collection Ltd: pp. 109(montage), 134(montage); The Hutchinson Library: p. 34(TL); Images Colour Library: p. 45; The Kobal Collection: p. 64(TL); Lupe Cunha: p. 22(BL, BR); Performing Arts Library: p. 110; Popperfoto: pp. 6(montage), 17(montage), 90, 115, 121(montage); Range Pictures: pp. 6(montage), 121(montage); Reed Consumer Books: p. 64(MR); Rex Features: pp. 72, 129; Robert Harding Picture Library: pp. 64(TR), 71, 136(MR); Ronald Grant Archive: p. 87(montage); Science Photo Library: pp. 40(montage), 64(TM), 76(montage); Telegraph Colour Library: pp. 9, 59, 87(montage), 98(montage), 105, 109(montage), 134(montage), 137(ML); Tony Stone Picture Library: pp. 17(montage), 34(TM, M, BL, BM, BR), 43, 51(montage), 58, 87(montage), 92, 94, 98(montage), 100, 127, 134(montage)

The publishers would like to thank the following for their co-operation in the piloting of this book: the University of Wales (ELSIS), Exeter Academy, EF Cambridge and UTS Oxford Centre.

First published in 1996 by
Phoenix ELT
A division of Prentice Hall International (UK) Ltd
Campus 400, Maylands Avenue
Hemel Hempstead
Hertfordshire, HP2 7EZ

© International Book Distributors Ltd 1996

Designed by Robert Wheeler

Illustrations by Archer/Quinnell, Kathy Baxendale, Peter Bull, Roy Choules, Joan Corlass, Gillian Martin, Jenny Searle, Joseph Silcott, Martin Shovel.

Studio photography by Sue Baker and Steve Richards

Cassettes produced by Anne Rosenfeld at Air-Edel

Printed and bound in Hong Kong by Wing King Tong Co. Ltd

Library of Congress Cataloging-in-Publication Data

Joseph, Fiona.
    Candidate for CAE / Fiona Joseph & Peter Travis.
        p. cm.
    ISBN 0-13-305616-3 (alk. paper)
    1. English language—Textbooks for foreign speakers. 2. English language—Examinations—Study guides. I. Travis, Peter.
II. Title.
PE1128.J67 1995
428'.0076—dc20   95-41319
                                                                                        CIP

British Library Cataloguing-in-Publication Data

A catalogue record for this book is available from the British Library

ISBN 0-13-305616-3

5 4 3 2 1
1999 98 97 96